TEACHING CHILDREN WITH AUTISM IN THE GENERAL CLASSROOM

TEACHING CHILDREN WITH AUTISM IN THE GENERAL CLASSROOM

STRATEGIES FOR EFFECTIVE INCLUSION AND INSTRUCTION
IN THE GENERAL EDUCATION CLASSROOM

EDITED BY
VICKY G. SPENCER, PH.D.
CYNTHIA G. SIMPSON, PH.D.

PRUFROCK PRESS INC.
WACO, TEXAS

Library of Congress Cataloging-in-Publication Data

Teaching children with autism in the general classroom : strategies for effective inclusion and instruction in the general education classroom / [edited by] Vicky G. Spencer, Cynthia G. Simpson.
    p. cm.
  Includes bibliographical references.
  ISBN-13: 978-1-59363-364-6 (pbk.)
  ISBN-10: 1-59363-364-5 (pbk.)
  1. Autistic children--Education--United States. 2. Asperger's syndrome--Education--United States. 3. Inclusive education--United States. 4. Behavioral assessment. I. Spencer, Vicky G. II. Simpson, Cynthia G.
  LC4718.T42 2009
  371.94--dc22
                              2009005233

At the time of this book's publication, all facts and figures cited are the most current available. All telephone numbers, addresses, and Web site URLs are accurate and active. All publications, organizations, Web sites, and other resources exist as described in the book, and all have been verified. The authors and Prufrock Press Inc. make no warranty or guarantee concerning the information and materials given out by organizations or content found at Web sites, and we are not responsible for any changes that occur after this book's publication. If you find an error, please contact Prufrock Press Inc.

Prufrock Press Inc.
P.O. Box 8813
Waco, TX 76714-8813
Phone: (800) 998-2208
Fax: (800) 240-0333
http://www.prufrock.com

Dedication

We would like to dedicate this book to those educators who have chosen to devote their lives to advocating for and teaching children with special needs in their classrooms. Every child who enters your classroom will leave with the knowledge that someone believed in him or her. Your actions in the classroom today will impact the future of your students.

CONTENTS

ACKNOWLEDGMENTS

We are very fortunate to have had many people support us through the production of this book. First and foremost, we would like to thank the authors who have contributed each of the chapters in this book. Their knowledge and expertise combined have created a well-rounded handbook for general and special education teachers who teach children with autism in their classrooms. The time commitment each of the authors has dedicated to writing is truly appreciated. Your shared wisdom will support the successful inclusion of children on the autism spectrum in the general education classroom.

We also would like to thank our colleagues who have supported us through the writing process and encouraged us to move forward with our own dreams. A special thank you to Lonna Beers, the librarian at the Lone Star College University Center, for the endless hours of research and numerous reference materials you gathered for us. In addition, we want to thank those teachers who read each of the chapters in this book and willingly integrated new teaching strategies into their classrooms.

Lastly, and most importantly, we would like to thank our spouses for their love, support, and encouragement during the writing process. Your patience and understanding of our late night writing and long distance phone calls is truly appreciated. We could not have finished this book without your support!

INTRODUCTION

VICKY G. SPENCER & CYNTHIA G. SIMPSON

I F you are reading this book, you are probably a general education teacher or in a field that relates to the lives of students with autism as they proceed through the educational system. The motivation behind this book stemmed from the need so frequently expressed by general education teachers who were working with students with autism in their classrooms. In addition, many parents of children with autism expressed concerns about the minimal services or lack of services that were provided in the general education classroom. Unfortunately, their concerns were validated as many general education teachers stated that they had little or no training in the area of autism. At the same time, these teachers wanted to know and understand best teaching practices for this population, but they wanted the information presented in a format that was specifically written for the general educator.

In response to this information, we contacted experts in the field who bring years of experience in working with students with autism in both the general and special education classroom setting. The information these individuals presented within this text provides preservice teachers, general and special education teachers, parents, and administrators with an understanding of the diagnosis of autism and how that diagnosis plays out in the general education classroom.

Although the term *inclusion* does not appear in the federal legislation governing the education of students with disabilities, the Individuals with Disabilities Education Improvement Act (IDEA; 2004) does require that students with disabilities participate in all assessments or alternate assessments with necessary accommodations. This accountability aligns with the premise that if students with disabilities are taking the same assessments as their typical peers, then they have to be ensured access to the same general education curriculum. If the goal of education is for students to be successful adults who can be contributing members of our society, then they must be provided with the same opportunities to learn. The overall result of this movement has been an increase in inclusive practices.

The concept of inclusion has been a point of controversy over the last two decades with its numerous definitions and philosophies and often can have negative connotations to some educators and parents. Unfortunately, this has been a response to situations where students with disabilities have been placed in general education classrooms with minimal supports and an untrained teacher. Although there is variation among the way inclusion is defined, most focus on the settings where students with disabilities receive their education, be it the general education classroom, special education classroom, or even a separate school. Because of the discrepancies in the way inclusion is viewed, this book refers to a belief system that focuses on the responsibility of educating all students so that they can reach their potential. Thus, the principles of the book can be applied across settings: general and special education classrooms, private and public school systems.

The book is divided into eight chapters with each focusing on a specific area of need for students with autism. Chapter 1: Understanding Recommendations for Identification and Programming begins with an overview of autism and addresses the issues involved with identification and programming for these students. Chapter 2: Setting Up the Classroom provides information on setting up the classroom and developing and using routines and visual schedules. This type of information will be the foundation for Chapter 3: Effective Academic Instruction for Students With High Functioning Autism or Asperger's Syndrome, which focuses on academic instruction including the most effective teaching strategies, assessment issues, and using accommodations and modifications to enhance academic performance. Because of the social skill deficits and behavioral problems that often accompany many students with autism, Chapter 4: Socialization and Children With Autism Spectrum Disorders will examine the characteristics of socialization and provide interventions for teaching appropriate social skills while Chapter 5: Behavioral Interventions for Children and Youth With Autism Spectrum Disorders teaches the process of performing a functional behavior assessment and developing behavior support plans.

One area that is frequently overlooked, or at least downplayed, is the importance of instructional technology in the classroom. Because many educators, parents, and students often have limited information on this area of support, Chapter 6: Using Instructional Technology in the Classroom will focus on basic information regarding technology and practical ways to use these tools in the general education classroom. The final two chapters provide information often omitted in the educational literature. It is for that reason we specifically included information that will address the needs of parents who have a child with autism in Chapter 7: Supporting Parents of Children Diagnosed With Autism: An Acceptance and Commitment Therapy Approach. Parents are faced with understanding the diagnosis, choosing the best treatment for their child, learning how to work collaboratively with all of the different professionals who may be involved in the child's educational program, navigating issues of quality care, and handling the emotional impact of the situation faced by these children and their families. Because part of the general education teacher's responsibility is to work collaboratively with the parents of the students in the classroom, Chapter 8: Building Learner-Focused Collaborative Relationships addresses these collaborative roles as well as the additional factors that parents of students with autism often are faced with as they strive to make sure that their child has the best educational plan available.

One additional part of each chapter is the inclusion of case studies. Application can be key to understanding, so the authors have provided case studies specific to the information in their chapter. Moreover, it is the intent of the authors that teachers can take this information and use it as a tool in working more effectively with students with autism in the general education classroom.

Reference

Individuals with Disabilities Education Improvement Act, PL 108-446, 118 Stat. 2647 (2004).

CHAPTER 1

UNDERSTANDING RECOMMENDATIONS FOR IDENTIFICATION AND PROGRAMMING

SHARON A. LYNCH

AUTISM is a common developmental disability that usually is diagnosed in young children during the first 3 years of life. Although it once was considered a rare disorder, the Center for Disease Control's Autism and Developmental Disabilities Monitoring Network estimates that 1 in 150 children in the U.S. is now diagnosed with autism (Centers for Disease Control and Prevention, n.d.). Autism is four times as common in boys as in girls (American Psychiatric Association [APA], 2000). Worldwide there is an increase in the number of children diagnosed with autism, although the statistics vary due to differences in how autism is diagnosed in other countries.

There is considerable variation in the severity of autism and its impact on development, and it is considered a spectrum of disorders, or autism spectrum disorder (ASD). The term *spectrum* is used because children with autism differ widely from one another. Some children with autism may be able to read and perform academic skills close to grade level, while others will have considerably more severe cognitive problems. Some children with autism are fluent speakers, while others may be nonverbal.

Families of children with autism generally notice problems during infancy and the preschool years (Robins, Fein, Barton, & Green, 2001). Preschoolers with autism typically show little interest in other people, do not point to items of interest in the environment, and may not respond to their names. Toddlers with autism usually do not engage in the "give and take" game of handing toys or items of interest to others in order to interact with them. Parents of children with autism often describe the child as "aloof" or having "a mind of his own." The hallmarks of autism include impairments in social interaction, lack of verbal and nonverbal communication, repetitive actions such as flapping one's hands or rocking, lack of interactive play, unusual responses to sensory stimulation, and insistence on routines.

CAUSES OF AUTISM

There is not a single definitive cause of ASD, although most authorities agree that it has a neurological basis. Brain structures have been found to differ in individuals with ASD, specifically smaller size of the cerebellum (Egaas, Courchesne, & Saitoh, 1995); abnormalities in the limbic system with decreased Purkinje neurons (Bailey, Luthert, Dean, Harding, & Janota, 1998); and a smaller facial nucleus, which controls facial expression (Rodier, 2000). Research also indicates a genetic component in 5% to 10% of the cases of autism (Muhle, Trentacoste, & Rapin, 2004). In twin studies, Bailey et al. (1995) found that the identical twin of a child with autism has a 60% chance of having autism and an 86% chance of having some autistic characteristics. When a family has one child with autism, there is an increased chance of having an additional child with autism (Ritvo et al., 1989).

There are other factors that are speculated to be the source of autism. Some believe that viruses and toxins are causal agents, but there is no evidence of their causing autism specifically, although they can lead to brain damage (Prelock, 2006). Parents often report the beginning of symptoms of autism following immunizations, but research has not substantiated the measles, mumps, and rubella (MMR) or other vaccines as presenting a risk factor for autism (Kaye, Maria Del Mar, & Jick, 2001; Madsen et al., 2002). Other factors that have been purported to cause autism include allergies, gastrointestinal abnormalities, thyroid deficiencies, and vitamin deficiencies. Results of scientific studies at this time do not support any of these as explaining autism (Filipek et al., 2000; Prelock, 2006). Commercial vendors of special diets or supplements often claim to have research evidence for their treatments, but this support typically is based on parent reports and testimonials of individuals who have purchased the product rather than research with controlled, scientific studies.

In summary, there is a biological basis for autism, with evidence of brain differences in individuals with ASD. The brain structures found to be involved include the cerebellum, cerebrum, limbic system, and brain stem (Prelock, 2006). Genetic studies with twins and siblings of individuals with autism support a genetic link for autism, although the exact nature is not clear. Other suggested causes such as dietary deficiencies, digestive problems, allergies, viruses, and environmental toxins have not been substantiated scientifically.

DIAGNOSIS OF AUTISM

The text revision of the *Diagnostic and Statistical Manual* of the American Psychiatric Association (*DSM-IV-TR*; APA, 2000) establishes the diagnostic criteria for autism. The first diagnostic category is qualitative impairment in social interaction based on problems with nonverbal behaviors such as eye contact, facial expression, body postures, and gestures; lack of peer relationships at the child's developmental level; lack of spontaneous sharing of enjoyment or achievement with others; and lack of social reciprocity or "give and take." What teachers may see in the classroom is a child who does not look at peers or smile at them, seemingly a loner who does not play with other children or initiate contact with classmates.

The second category that the *DSM-IV-TR* addresses in the diagnosis of autism is qualitative impairment in communication. This communication problem includes delayed or absent language, accompanied by lack of gestures and nonverbal communication; inability to sustain a conversation; and lack of social and imaginative play. Those children who cannot speak will need specific training in using gestures and nonverbal means of interacting or some type of assistive technology to help them communicate. Many children with autism who can speak lack the ability to start conversations or keep them going. In the classroom they typically answer questions with a short response, often a single word. When other children engage in pretend or creative play in centers or on the playground, the child with autism usually does not participate unless taught how to interact.

The third category for an autism diagnosis in the *DSM-IV-TR* involves restricted and repetitive patterns of interest and behavior. Included within this area are exceedingly restricted patterns of interest; insistence on sameness within the environment; preoccupation with parts of objects; and repetitive, stimulatory movements often referred to as "stims." Children with autism may be interested in only a few topics in the classroom such as dinosaurs, plumbing, tornadoes, or Disney characters. Some children may carry around odd objects such as the cap to a detergent bottle or a strainer. When routines or class schedules are disrupted on early dismissal days or picture day, it can be traumatic for the child with ASD. The child may demonstrate repetitive movements or stims when bored, stressed, or upset. Examples of these repetitive actions include rocking, flapping, jumping, hand flicking, staring at lights, fanning the pages of books, and eye poking. When the repetitive movements are mild and do not interfere with learning or socialization, they often can be ignored in the classroom. However, when these movements interfere with socialization or with the learning of the child or others, an intervention is needed.

Finally, a delay or deviation from typical development in the areas of communication, socialization, and imaginative play needs to be noted before age 3 for autism to be diagnosed. The family usually notices these differences at an early age. As a result, most children with ASD are enrolled in either early childhood intervention programs with special education services or in private therapeutic programs. Because of the success of early intense behavioral intervention using applied behavior analysis (ABA; Lovaas, 1987), many families invest considerable time and resources in ABA programs during the preschool years.

On the other hand, a sizeable number of children with ASD have unusually strong areas of ability. Verbal children with ASD may be able to tell you virtually everything written about their area of interest. For example, a 7-year-old who is interested in buses may be able to tell you where buses are manufactured, the different models of buses, the number of passengers they carry, and how the motor works. Other children with autism may be able to tell the day of the week a particular date occurred or the batting averages of all of the players in the National League. Even children who cannot speak may have remarkable memories for where to find their favorite toys or where to locate a food that they like at the grocery store. Parents may report that they knew that their child was not unintelligent, because of the child's particular strength or talent.

In addition to the diagnostic criteria for autism, the *DSM-IV-TR* specifies the criteria needed for the different forms of ASD: autism, Pervasive Developmental Disorder-Not Otherwise Specified (PDD-NOS), Asperger's syndrome, Rett's syndrome, and Childhood Disintegrative Disorder. PDD-NOS is a form of autism where the symptoms are either not present by age 3, or where there is a severe and pervasive impairment in the development of reciprocal social interaction or verbal and nonverbal communication skills, but not all of the criteria are met for the autism diagnosis. However, the treatment for a child with PDD-NOS will not differ from that of a child with the autism diagnosis. In Asperger's syndrome, the *DSM-IV-TR* criteria are met for qualitative impairment in social interaction, and children present a substantial problem with social, occupational, or other areas of functioning. However, there is no communication or cognitive delay in development. Rett's syndrome is a nonhereditary progressive neurological disorder predominantly in females caused by a genetic mutation. Children begin life as typically developing babies and lose skills throughout their lifetime beginning around the age of 18 months. Girls with Rett's syndrome display characteristic hand movements such as wringing, clapping, tapping, and putting their hands in their mouths. Although this disorder differs significantly from other ASDs, it has been included in the *DSM-IV-TR* with autism. Finally, the *DSM-IV-TR* includes Childhood Disintegrative Disorder with other ASDs. In Childhood Disintegrative Disorder, children develop normally, and then begin demonstrating autistic behaviors after age 3 or 4. They also begin to lose language, social, cognitive, and motor skills. This diagnosis is considered rare, with only 1 to 6 children diagnosed per 100,000. In summary, the autism spectrum is composed of these five disorders: autism, PDD-NOS, Asperger's syndrome, Rett's syndrome, and Childhood Disintegrative Disorder. All of these children should be evaluated for special education services in public schools.

THE EVALUATION PROCESS

The Individuals with Disabilities Education Improvement Act (IDEA) of 2004 requires a full individual evaluation to establish that the child meets the criteria for 1 of the 13 types of disabilities that are addressed by this federal statute. The definition of autism according to IDEA is listed below:

- Autism means a developmental disability significantly affecting verbal and nonverbal communication and social interaction, generally evident before age 3, that adversely affects a child's educational performance. Other characteristics often associated with autism are engagement in repetitive activities and stereotyped movements, resistance to environmental change or change in daily routines, and unusual responses to sensory experiences.

- Autism does not apply if a child's educational performance is adversely affected primarily because the child has an emotional disturbance.

- A child who manifests the characteristics of autism after age 3 could be identified as having autism if the criteria above are satisfied.

The full individual evaluation required by IDEA mandates that the educational team evaluate the child in all areas of suspected disability. This evaluation must be conducted by individuals who have been appropriately trained using nondiscriminatory procedures. The areas that must be addressed include language dominance and proficiency, sociological factors, physical factors, mental factors, emotional/behavioral factors, and academic and developmental achievement. IDEA (2004) requires the team to

use a variety of assessment tools and strategies to gather relevant functional, developmental, and academic information about the child, including information provided by the parent, that may assist in determining

(i) Whether the child is a child with a disability

(ii) The content of the child's IEP, including information related to enabling the child to be involved in and progress in the general education curriculum (or for a preschool child, to participate in appropriate activities). (CFR § 300.8 b)

The most effective approach to an evaluation for children with autism is an interdisciplinary team whose members are familiar with children with autism (Prelock, 2006). This team typically includes a psychologist, an education specialist such as an educational diagnostician or developmental specialist, a speech-language pathologist, and an occupational therapist. For an initial evaluation there usually will be some type of screening procedure before the child is referred to the team. The autism screening process will determine if the child is likely to have this disorder and will filter out those children who are not likely to have some type of ASD. Screening is brief, and may involve a parent interview, child observation, and tasks for the child to complete. Some of the screening instruments used in diagnosis of autism include the Autism Screening Instrument for Educational Planning-3 (Krug, Arick, & Almond, 2009), the Gilliam Autism Rating Scale-2 (Gilliam, 2008), and the Modified Checklist for Autism in Toddlers (Robins et al., 2001). Most of these tests have a cut-off score where scores above a specified level indicate a significant probability of autism.

The special education teacher typically will have observations, data, and classroom testing that provides information about the child's learning style, academic performance in the classroom, and developmental level. The general education teacher is a good source of information regarding the student's socialization with peers, adaptation to change, ability to transition between classes and activities, and independent work habits. Parents are the experts in knowing their children: their strengths and weaknesses, their likes and dislikes, and their past learning experiences. Because parents provide the ongoing support system for their children throughout the school years, it is critical that educators honor their preferences and aspirations for their children.

Related service personnel (e.g., speech-language pathologists, occupational therapists, physical therapists) are valuable contributions to the team. Because of the sensory differences of students with autism, the occupational therapist provides critical information for the evaluation. Often sensory processing deficits are overlooked in the evaluation process (Lynch, 2000); these sensory processing issues contribute to the behavioral difficulties of children with autism. Understanding the child's sensory preferences is important in designing the behavior intervention plan. Because children with autism have problems with verbal and nonverbal communication, the speech-language pathologist (SLP) is an important member of the team. The SLP will have vital information gained from working with the child in therapy sessions, as well as data collection, developmental information, and standardized testing information.

Communication Evaluation

The full individual evaluation of a child with disabilities includes information about the child's language dominance and proficiency. Dominance refers to the language that the child uses best to express himself (expressive language), as well as understand spoken communication (receptive language). After determining language dominance, the team establishes language proficiency (i.e., how well the child understands and communicates). The SLP typically takes the lead role in evaluating language in children with disabilities. Standardized tests often are used, including various editions of the Clinical Evaluation of Language Functions (CELF), the Preschool Language Scale (PLS), or the Peabody Picture Vocabulary Test (PPVT). Some children with ASD do not respond well to standardized tests that must be given under strict conditions with specific wording. Criterion-referenced tests lend themselves to more flexible administration and, as a result, may yield more meaningful results. This type of test provides information about what the child was able to do on the test, as well as those skills that will require instruction for mastery. Some criterion-referenced tests include the Brigance Inventories (Brigance, 1998) and the Assessment of Basic Language and Learning Skills (Partington, 2007). Additionally, the child's ability to use sign language or gestures should be addressed if this is his or her primary mode of communication.

Physical Factors

Children with autism often demonstrate sensory processing differences that should be noted and considered in programming. These children may be overly sensitive to textures, sounds, or visual stimuli. On the other hand, some children with autism may not consistently respond to sound, and parents may suspect a hearing loss. In fact, unusual responses to sensory stimuli are one of the hallmarks of autism and are listed in the diagnostic criteria of autism in the *DSM-IV-TR*. Prior to administering any type of tests, the child's vision and hearing abilities must be determined.

The school nurse usually will screen hearing using pure tone audiometry at a loudness of 15–20 decibels in the frequencies of 1000, 2000, and 4000 Hz. When a child passes this screening, it establishes that he or she can hear faint tones across a variety of pitches. In order to respond appropriately, children must understand that they need to raise their hand when they hear the tone. With demonstration and practice, many children, including those with autism, can learn to respond appropriately. However, this requires that the adults involved in the screening take the time to work with those children who may not understand the directions or what they are supposed to do when they hear the tone. The school nurse also may screen for middle ear functioning using immittance measures. The nurse places a probe in the outer ear that makes a seal and measures the compliance of the middle ear. The readings from this test indicate if there is a problem in the middle ear, such as fluid or serous otitis media. Children who suffer from allergies often have middle ear problems, and if this condition is left untreated it can have a negative effect on hearing, speech, and possibly reading. The child may be referred to an audiologist if the team is unsure of the child's ability to hear. The audiologist may use behavioral audiometry to see if the child will look at a toy or puppet when a sound is presented, or may use speech audiometry to determine the child's ability to respond to speech. Physiological measures such as auditory brainstem responses can be used, but this requires hospitalization and sedation.

Typically, the school nurse will screen vision by having the child name letters or point in the direction of the "floating E." For children with significant disabilities and young children, there are other tests that require the child to point to the picture shown on the screen in order to determine visual ability. Children with autism, particularly those who are young, may not able to respond to these screening measures. The team may rely on parent and teacher reports and observations. If the team is unsure of the child's vision, he or she may be referred to an optometrist or ophthalmologist. The optometrist or ophthalmologist should be one who is accustomed to working with young children or persons with disabilities in order to effectively evaluate the child's vision. There are physiological measures of vision that examine the brain's ability to detect visual stimuli, but again, these tests require hospitalization and sedation.

A school health questionnaire usually is completed by the parent. There may be specific nutritional concerns, such as special casein/gluten free diets or allergies. In this case, families will provide information to the school regarding special foods or medications for allergies. Because autism is a neurological disorder, seizures may be present. Information from the family, the child's physician, and the school nurse is important in this case. If the child takes medication, this should be noted in the evaluation. The teacher also needs to be informed of any side effects of the anticonvulsant medication such as irritability, drowsiness, or other characteristics. School health records and the school nurse are a good source of information to be considered in the evaluation.

Emotional/Behavioral Factors

The full individual evaluation also will address emotional and behavioral factors. Although autism is no longer considered an emotional disorder, behavioral factors that are specific to the child should be addressed in the evaluation. Examples of the type of information include the problem behaviors the child displays, what triggers the behaviors, and the pay-off of the behavior for the child. Pay-offs, often called *consequences*, of the behavior may result in the child gaining something he or she desires such as attention, sensory stimulation, or items like food, activities, or toys. For example, the child may learn that flapping his hands gets the teacher's attention. When the child desires this type of attention, the behavior is reinforced even when the teacher reprimands the child. On the other hand, behaviors may result in the child avoiding an undesired event. For example, a child may bite his hand or hit his face repeatedly when presented with a difficult task. When teachers remove the task, the child's challenging behavior is reinforced. The behavioral section of the evaluation also may include information on the preferences and types of reinforcers that are effective.

Another item in the behavioral section concerns the child's ability to follow the regular code of conduct. When the child is not able to follow the school code of conduct, the Individualized Education Program (IEP) committee will develop a behavior intervention plan (BIP). This plan specifies the types of problem behaviors, strategies to prevent them from occurring, and steps that should be taken if they do occur. When the child demonstrates serious ongoing behavior problems, then a Functional Behavioral Assessment (FBA) also will be part of the IEP for the child. This assessment will determine the function of the challenging behavior, followed by a BIP to teach alternative ways for the child to get his or her needs met. For example, if the child hits others to avoid a difficult task, then strategies will be implemented to decrease task demands, as well as teach the child to ask for help or ask for a break.

Cognitive Factors

Many times there is an abundance of information in the student's legal folder, particularly if the individual has been in special education for several years. Previous reports, particularly narrative reports from psychologists and speech pathologists, provide a picture of the child's development over time. Developmental, intellectual, and academic achievement scores sometimes document the child's progress. Previous IEPs contain important information about the student's past educational experiences and progress. IEPs with individualized, behaviorally stated objectives that the student has mastered provide insights into program quality, as do computer-generated IEP objectives that are repeated year after year and are marked "continue" at each annual review. It is always a good idea to read the student's legal folder to gain a better understanding of the child, the background, and previous educational experience. Sociological factors such as family background, history of schooling, and significant environmental factors are addressed in the evaluation.

Because of language factors, attention problems, and interfering behaviors, it can be difficult to administer a standardized test to a child with autism. Many standardized tests require verbal comprehension levels that are too abstract for students with autism. Others change tasks radically with each subtest, bringing the student to the point of difficulty and then transitioning to the next activity. Such an experience may be very disturbing for the child with autism and the test score may not be a valid indicator of the child's abilities. Also, standardized tests may not have enough easy items to allow the child to experience early success, and the child may become quickly frustrated.

The standardized tests of intelligence that are most commonly used with children with autism include the Stanford-Binet Intelligence Scales-Fifth Edition

(SB-V), Leiter International Performance Scale-Revised (LIPS-R), the Universal Nonverbal Intelligence Test (UNIT), and the Test of Nonverbal Intelligence-Third Edition (TONI-III). The SB-V uses manipulatives and has an adequate number of easy items, but the fact that it changes tasks frequently may frustrate some children. This test also requires the child to respond to verbal instructions, even for nonverbal portions of the test. However, the SB-V provides Change Sensitive Scores in addition to standard IQ scores, so that progress can be tracked over time. The LIPS-R is completely nonverbal and the initial training items can be demonstrated with hand-over-hand assistance. Items follow a similar format, and manipulatives are used in the early tests. However, subtests on the LIPS-R that are normed for children above the age of 5 do not provide manipulatives or demonstration, so older children with autism may not respond to task requests. The UNIT also is completely nonverbal, but the items are fairly abstract and the test is not normed on children under 5 years of age. The TONI-III tends to be somewhat abstract for many students with autism because it is an "easel-type" test with only line drawing designs. Due to these limitations of standardized IQ tests with children with autism, the scores from these tests may not be an accurate reflection of their abilities.

With younger children, developmental scales are appropriate indicators of cognitive and developmental abilities. However, these tests should never be used on older children who were not included in the normative group. Not only does this practice violate the test norms, but it also leads to decreased expectations and recommendations for more restrictive settings (Lynch-Linehan & Brady, 1995).

Adaptive Behavior

Adaptive behaviors are the personal and social skills that enable an individual to adjust to the demands of the environment. Included in this area are self-help skills, social skills, communication skills, and for older individuals, vocational and independent living skills. Adaptive behaviors consist of real-life skills such as grooming, dressing, safety, following school rules, the ability to work, money management, cleaning, and personal responsibility. To evaluate adaptive behavior, a standardized interview such as the Vineland Adaptive Behavior Scale is administered to the parent or caregiver. A standard score is derived, which is used to diagnose mental retardation or cognitive disabilities, but the information about the child's self-help skills and ability to negotiate the environment are important for the teacher. This information also should be considered by the IEP team in determining the amount of assistance the child may need in the general education classroom. For example, the child who needs help in the cafeteria and restroom will need more help in the inclusive classroom than the child who is independent in eating and toileting.

Academic and Developmental Skills

Standardized academic tests sample core academic skills and are administered using explicit instructions and scoring guidelines. Generally there is minimal explanation or demonstration of expected responses. These tests usually begin around the kindergarten level and contain only a few easy items. Standard scores, including age or grade equivalents, typically are reported. Some standardized academic tests include the Woodcock-Johnson-III Tests of Achievement (WJ-III), the Wechsler Individual Achievement Test-III (WIA T-III), and the Kaufman Test of Educational Achievement-II (KTEA-II).

For young children with disabilities, it generally is preferable to give more credence to criterion-referenced tests to determine the child's ability to perform academic and developmental skills. In addition to the problems discussed earlier with standardized tests for young children, there are other difficulties when testing young children. These difficulties include inconsistency of responses, lack of a standard preschool curriculum for young children, short attention spans, lack of uniform access to instruction, reliance on language, and expected compliance with instructions (Willis & Dumont, 2005). Young children vary greatly in their ability to attend and comply with instructions, and test results may be more related to the child's physical state (hunger, need for sleep, mood) than on the ability being assessed.

Standardized testing generally is reported in units that are related to the normal curve. The mean or average score is set at the middle of the normal curve, and other scores are reported in terms of their difference from the mean. Although descriptive categories may vary slightly, Table 1.1 will aid in understanding a test score.

When reading a report on a child with autism, one should remember that how the child scores will depend on a number of factors: the child's interest in the task, the effort the child gave, the rapport with the examiner, the attention and language requirements of the task, and whether or not the child understood what was expected. Also, the testing process usually interrupts the child's routine and removes the child from the familiar environment. Both of these conditions are difficult for children with autism. However, teachers can gain valuable understanding when they read reports with a focus on what the child is able to do and where the child will need assistance.

On the other hand, criterion-referenced tests sample a larger number of specific skills than standardized academic tests, and items can be administered over a period of days. Some criterion-referenced tests that are commonly used are the Brigance Inventories and the Assessment of Basic Language and Learning Skills-Revised (ABLLS-R). There are several different Brigance Inventories for children of various ages and ability levels. The ABLLS-R consists of 25 different academic and developmental skills areas that are broken down into small incremental steps for evaluation and training. This criterion-referenced test was developed for use with applied behavior analysis programs for young children, and is appropriate for young children with autism and individuals with significant disabilities. The

TABLE 1.1

WHAT STANDARDIZED TEST SCORES MEAN

Score Range	Interpretive Description	Percent Included
Above 130	Superior	Top 2% of those tested
116–130	Above Average	About 14% of those tested
85–115	Average	Middle 68% of those tested
70–84	Below Average	About 14% of those tested
Below 70	Lower extreme	Lower 2% of those tested

Brigance Inventories and ABLLS-R both are used to document the child's current skill level, and the results also can be incorporated into the goals and objectives in the student's IEP. Additionally, the tests can be administered to document progress on the skill objectives. Many of the objectives that are included in the IEP also can be incorporated in instruction in the general education classroom.

INFORMAL EVALUATION PROCEDURES

Two types of informal evaluation procedures also may be used in the evaluation: play-based assessment and contextual assessment. The play-based assessment process was developed by Toni Linder (2008) to evaluate young children with suspected disabilities. In play-based assessment, the play facilitator interacts with the child in a well-equipped playroom while the parent and parent facilitator observe and talk informally. Other members of the assessment team such as the school psychologist or educational diagnostician, special education teacher, and therapists observe the process and note which skills the child is able to perform from their individual assessment protocols. First, the team notes skills that are demonstrated spontaneously, and then the play facilitator tries to elicit skills that were not demonstrated. The process also involves a peer play partner, a snack, and a parent time for instruction. After the evaluation is completed, the team views the videotape of the assessment, discusses findings, and writes the assessment report as a group.

The contextual assessment process is designed for school-age children with significant disabilities who may not respond well to standardized tests, and for whom play-based assessment would not be developmentally appropriate. This type of evaluation involves familiar caregivers and an assessment specialist who observe the student in the typical environment. Some of the areas examined include the opportunities to interact with others, opportunities for choice-making and self-direction, communication skills, social interaction, self-help skills, motor abilities, academic performance, preferences and reinforcers, and relationships in the home, school, and community. This goal of this process is to provide a picture of the child's current abilities within the context of the daily environment so that programming can address vital skills and opportunities for the individual.

IMPLICATIONS FOR INSTRUCTION

The purpose of assessment is to diagnose the problem, develop interventions to assist the child in becoming more capable and independent, evaluate progress, and determine program effectiveness. Standardized testing and informal assessment both yield information that will help the teacher in developing an instructional program and making accommodations in the general education classroom. Standardized testing provides some indicator of where the child stands in relation to peers. Informal assessment information enables instructors to have an idea of what the child is able to do and what he or she needs to learn.

The diagnostic criteria for ASD also have important instructional implications. Table 1.2 lists some behaviors that the teacher may observe in a child with autism in the classroom. It also lists what the teacher's natural reaction might be, and what the teacher can do instead. Finally, it lists the *DSM-IV-TR* characteristic that the behavior typifies. When the teacher understands the nature of autism it promotes a better understanding of the child's behavior and how to react in a more supportive way.

IMPLEMENTING THE IEP

The Individualized Education Program (IEP) is the heart of instruction for students with disabilities. This document sets forth the goals, objectives, and services that the child will receive. It also determines the setting where the child will be educated, as well as the accommodations and modifications to be used in the classroom. Because the general education teacher is involved in implementing the IEP in the inclusive classroom, it is critical that the teacher be involved in the IEP process. Research indicates that the IEP process is more effective when general education teachers are involved in meaningful collaboration as part of the educational team (Shick, 2007). However, teachers also need training in order to be effective participants in the planning process (Avramidis, Bayliss, & Burden, 2000). This training can be provided through university preparation programs, conferences, and teacher in-service programs. Research conducted by McLean (2001) found that most teachers believed that they had received adequate in-service training and materials for implementing student IEPs, although some of the teachers surveyed had not been trained at all. When teachers are involved in

TABLE 1.2

BEHAVIORS OBSERVED IN CHILDREN WITH AUTISM

What the Child Does	One's Natural Reaction	What the Teacher Should Do	DSM-IV-TR Characteristic of Autism
"Refuses" to answer questions	Go on to the next person and assume the child does not know the answer	Use simple language for questions; provide pictures and visual cues	Qualitative impairment in communication
Does not follow instructions	Consider the child noncompliant	Use gestures or sign language; pair the child with a peer	Qualitative impairment in communication
Does not look at teacher when being spoken to	Consider the child disrespectful	Make sure that you have the child's attention before speaking; establish a signal like raising the index finger before speaking	Lack of eye contact
Often has a blank look on his or her face during instruction	Assume the child is not learning	Assess learning using pictures, visual cues, choice making	Difficulty with nonverbal behaviors such as facial expression
Lacks friends	Assume that the child does not value others and does not want friends	Provide opportunities for positive peer interaction; peer learning activities	Lack of peer relationships at the child's developmental level
Is a loner on the playground and in the cafeteria	Assume the child prefers to be alone	Provide a lunch buddy for the cafeteria; promote interaction with socially adept peers	Lack of social reciprocity
Always talks about the same thing (e.g., dinosaurs or plumbing)	Remind the child that we are not talking about dinosaurs	Use the child's area of interest in instruction; pair the area of interest with other areas to expand repertoire of conversation	Restricted and repetitive patterns of interest and behavior
Flicking hands while looking at ceiling lights	Tell the child to stop or ask him why he is shaking his hands	Redirect the child and provide an activity involving hand movements	Repetitive movements
Cries or is aggressive when the routine changes	Tell the child to be quiet or send him to the office	Use a picture or visual schedule and warn of changes in routine	Adherence to routines

the IEP process there is a better connection between the goals and objectives and the curriculum (Fisher & Frey, 2001), and IEP objectives are of higher quality (Hunt & Farron-Davis, 1992).

General education teachers do not necessarily need to design special activities to address IEP objectives. In fact, research supports the method of integrating target skills from the IEP into the typical classroom activities (Cheney & Demchak, 1996). Activity-based objectives that are set within the context of typically occurring *classroom events* can be used to teach both academic and social skills. An inclusion matrix can be developed for planned integration of accommodations, modifications, and IEP objectives into the typical classroom activities. To develop an inclusion matrix, the instructor develops a chart with the target IEP objectives listed at the top and the classroom schedule listed on the lefthand side of the chart. The modifications, accommodations, or activities for the child with autism are listed in the appropriate box within the chart. The case study at the end of this chapter demonstrates how an inclusion matrix was developed for Carlos, a 10-year-old boy with autism in a fourth-grade classroom.

Instructional Strategies

Some key principles in teaching children with autism in the regular classroom include setting high expectations, providing a predictable and organized classroom, promoting peer understanding, developing social skills, adapting academic subjects, and modifying conversational language (Humphrey, 2008). Although classroom situations can arise that interfere with the typical routine, a classroom that has a predictable schedule and place for materials is very important for the child with autism. The teacher also needs to keep explanations and directions short and simple, with the use of pictures, objects, and other visual cues. Students with autism have improved social outcomes when they are educated in inclusive settings where they are accepted, visible, and valued members of peer groups (Boutot & Bryant, 2005).

Managing transitions is a key strategy in the general education classroom (Goodman & Williams, 2007). Visual schedules that provide pictures of daily or weekly activities are helpful so that the child understands the routine and what is expected. With young children, songs that are associated with cleaning up, lining up, and finishing play time can help the child to move more easily from one activity to the next. Choice-making is another strategy that can facilitate transitions by providing the child with some options of how the next activity will take place. For example, if it is time to begin work on a math activity that requires the children to be seated, the child with autism can be given the option of working with cubes or chips for counting.

Because children with autism vary greatly in their academic abilities, the teacher should pay close attention to the results of assessment in designing instruction and

Modality/Output	Oral	Written
Expressive	Speaking	Writing
Receptive	Listening	Reading

FIGURE 1.1. The relationship between written and oral language.

making adaptations. As stated earlier in the chapter, assessment results also should be combined with observations of teachers and caregivers because the child may not necessarily demonstrate all of his or her skills on a standardized test. The teacher needs to begin instruction at a level that is moderately difficult. If the instruction is too difficult, the child is likely to become frustrated and demonstrate negative behavior; if instruction is too easy or boring, the child will quickly lose interest.

Some children with autism have excellent decoding skills and can correctly read virtually any word they see. It is not uncommon for the child to have such strengths without direct reading instruction. Although this is an area of strength, the teacher should not assume that the child understands all that he or she reads. The teacher will be more accurate when considering the child's oral language and language comprehension relative to reading comprehension. Because children with autism may have significant difficulty with oral language and language understanding, these are limiting factors for reading comprehension.

Figure 1.1 provides a framework for the relationship between reading and oral language. Expressive oral language consists of speaking, while receptive oral language consists of listening; expressive written language consists of writing and word processing, while receptive written language consists of reading. The implications of this relationship are wide-ranging for children with language disorders, particularly children with autism. The teacher cannot assume that the child comprehends what her or she reads orally, and will need to support reading with pictures or video instruction, and provide scaffolded explanations of the material as well. In many reading curricula there are extensive assumptions of background knowledge and the ability to make inferences. Children with autism typically have difficulty with inferences, so the teacher will need to preteach concepts that will be needed to comprehend the reading selection.

For example, a basal reading text in first grade presents a story about Nan and Sam, riding in a van, who are moving their furniture to a new house. The child with autism may easily read the story orally, but has no concept of moving from one house to another. The child can easily answer the "who" and "what" questions based on the selection, but when asked, "Why do you think Nan and Sam are moving?" the child may not respond. When examining the situation more closely, it becomes apparent that the story never states that Nan and Sam are moving, and the child with autism has no concept that a family can move from one house to another. Also, the "why" question is a high-inference question without a specific answer that can be found in the text. In this situation, the teacher should preview the reading selection and preteach the concept of moving with concrete examples using props or a short video. Then the teacher might talk with the class about why people move or change houses. This provides some of the background information for understanding the story and will help the child with autism, as well as others in the classroom who may lack prior experience.

Many children with autism also learn rote mathematical information quickly, and can count and memorize math facts with ease. They often can see patterns and determine what comes next based on the sequence. However, application and word problems typically are much more difficult. With word problems, there is a large language factor, so the child may need help in understanding the problem. In the primary grades, role-play is a useful method for teaching beginning addition and subtraction. For example, the word problem states, "Bobby has 6 cars. He gives 2 cars to Josh. How many cars are left?" With children in pairs, the teacher can have the children role-play with car counters to answer the question. As children become more familiar with concepts, simple manipulatives such as blocks or poker chips can be used as counters. Later, the child can be taught to make tally marks or circles to solve problems more independently.

Physical education instruction should target age-appropriate motor skills, using appropriate teaching strategies while managing challenging behaviors. Unique and novel equipment also is helpful in engaging children with autism in physical education activities (Zhang & Griffin, 2007). If physical education instruction takes place in a large group of multiple classes, then an instructional assistant may be helpful, particularly at the beginning of the school year when the student is not familiar with the routine. The physical education teacher also should recognize that proximity is a key factor for children with autism. If the child does not follow instructions it may be that he or she did not attend to directions that were given at a distance or that the child did not understand what was expected.

CASE STUDY

Carlos is a 10-year-old boy in the fourth grade. He was diagnosed with a language delay at the age of 2 and with autism at the age of 3. Beginning at age 3, his parents enrolled him in an intensive early intervention program where he made significant gains. He began speaking in sentences at age 4, and was toilet trained at age 5. He also began reading at the age of 4 without formal instruction. Carlos is extremely interested in the computer, and his parents think that he learned to read from the computer software that they had purchased for his older sister. Carlos

	TABLE 1.3		
	THE RESULTS OF CARLOS' EVALUATION		
Test	**Area**	**Score**	**Interpretation**
Stanford-Binet Intelligence Scales, Fifth Edition	Verbal IQ	55	Very Low
Stanford-Binet Intelligence Scales, Fifth Edition	Nonverbal IQ	75	Low
Stanford-Binet Intelligence Scales, Fifth Edition	Full Scale IQ	63	Very Low
Woodcock-Johnson III Tests of Achievement	Basic Reading Skills	99	Average
Woodcock-Johnson III Tests of Achievement	Reading Comprehension	73	Low
Woodcock-Johnson III Tests of Achievement	Math Calculation Skills	101	Average
Woodcock-Johnson III Tests of Achievement	Math Reasoning	74	Low
Woodcock-Johnson III Tests of Achievement	Written Expression	81	Low Average
Woodcock-Johnson III Tests of Achievement	Oral Expression	75	Low
Woodcock-Johnson III Tests of Achievement	Listening Comprehension	71	Low
Vineland Adaptive Behavior Scale-II	Adaptive Behavior Composite	81	Moderately Low

lives with both parents, who are college graduates, and his older sister. English is the dominant language and the only language spoken in the home. The maternal grandparents live nearby and assist with afterschool care.

Currently Carlos is in a fourth-grade classroom with a coteaching arrangement with his special education teacher, Mr. Wills, and his general education teacher, Ms. Hauser. Mr. Wills is scheduled in this classroom for all classes in the afternoon, and Ms. Banks, a teaching assistant, supports Carlos in his classroom in the morning. He receives speech therapy twice weekly with conversational language goals, and occupational therapy once weekly with goals to improve handwriting.

Carlos was evaluated by the school evaluation team with the test results listed in Table 1.3. The licensed specialist in school psychology on the autism team recommended a diagnosis of autism based on the following characteristics and observations:

- *Qualitative Impairment in Social Interaction*: lack of eye contact; lack of gestures and pointing to make needs known; lack of social interaction at home (as reported by parents) and school (as observed on the playground and in the cafeteria); lack of friendships (as reported by teachers and parents); lack of spontaneous seeking to share enjoyment or achievements (without being asked, must be initiated by others);

♦ *Qualitative Impairments in Communication*: a significant language delay (as reported by the speech-language pathologist and test scores in the Comprehensive Evaluation of Language Function and Woodcock-Johnson III Tests of Achievement); lack of conversational speech unless taught a specific script of responses; repetitive use of language such as reciting commercials heard on TV when walking in line; lack of imaginative play when presented with toys and during observation on the playground; and

♦ *Restricted Repetitive and Stereotyped Patterns of Behavior*: repetitive motor mannerisms of flapping hands, humming, and rocking during seatwork.

A sample list of Carlos' academic skills and needs in the areas of reading and communication is presented below.

Reading
Carlos can:
♦ decode words at a seventh-grade level,
♦ answer comprehension questions involving factual information regarding material read at second-grade level,
♦ read at a rate of 92 correct words per minute in grade-level material, and
♦ self-select reading material from the school library.

Carlos cannot:
♦ answer comprehension questions involving "why" questions, predicting outcome, or telling main idea, sequencing of events, or drawing conclusions;
♦ identify synonyms and antonyms of vocabulary words;
♦ identify similarities and differences across text such as topics, characters, or themes; and
♦ summarize text selections.

Communication
Carlos can:
♦ formulate 5–6 word sentences;
♦ describe items by function, feature, and class; and
♦ answer who, what, when, and where questions.

Carlos cannot:

- tell how two items are the same and different,
- answer why questions,
- answer and ask questions reciprocally in a conversation, and
- describe prior events (e.g., What did you do last night?).

Because there are a number of skill areas where Carlos needs work, these typically would be addressed on his IEP. The IEP also would address skill objectives in those areas that the teachers and family consider important, even though they may not be addressed in the individual evaluation. Because teachers and families are firsthand observers of the child's needs in the daily environment, they have insights on direct needs that may not be a part of the evaluation. A sample activity matrix for Carlos' communication objectives is developed in Figure 1.2.

The material from Carlos' diagnostic report provides information about where he functions in comparison to peers, but it can underestimate his ability to progress in the general education curriculum. Because his teachers are aware of the characteristics of autism that he demonstrates they are better able to understand his need for support in the general education classroom. The evaluation provides more than test scores; the strengths and needs provide a starting point for Carlos' learning objectives when considered together with parent information, teacher information, and state standards.

For Carlos and other children with autism, it is important for teachers not just to be aware of the child's strengths and needs, but also to be able to incorporate instruction on objectives into the daily routine. When the general education teacher, special education teacher, teaching assistant, therapists, and family all work toward these same goals, it improves the child's ability to learn and generalize important skills throughout the environment.

Activity/ Objective	Tell How Items Are Same/ Different	Answer *Why* Questions	Reciprocal Conversation	Describe Prior Events
Arrival	—	One targeted *why* question with assistant	On arrival, en route to cafeteria	What did you do last night?
Breakfast	—	One targeted *why* question with assistant after eating	Conversation opportunities with peers at breakfast	What did you watch on TV last night?
Classroom Entry/ Restroom	—	One targeted *why* question with teacher	Brief conversation with assistant or teacher	What did you eat for breakfast?
Reading/ Language Arts	Work on same-different in context of reading stories, help from assistant	Work on *why* questions from reading selections with teacher	—	What story did we read today?
Learning Centers	Work on same-different in context of activity folder games	—	Work on conversation with skilled peer during center games	What game did you play with at centers?
Math	Work on same-different in context of money, measurement	Work on *why* questions in context of money, measurement	—	What did you work on during math?
Lunch	—	One targeted *why* question with assistant after eating	Conversation opportunities with peers at lunch	What did you eat for lunch?

FIGURE 1.2. Morning activity matrix for Carlos' communication objectives.

References

American Psychiatric Association. (2000). *Diagnostic and statistical manual of mental disorders-text revision* (4th ed., Text rev.). Washington, DC: Author.

Avramidis, E., Bayliss, P., & Burden, R. (2000). A survey into mainstream teachers' attitudes towards the inclusion of children with special educational needs in the ordinary school in one local education authority. *Educational Psychology, 201*, 191–211.

Bailey, A., LeCouteur, A., Gottesman, I., Bolton, P., Siminoff, E., Yuzda, E., et al. (1995). Autism as a strongly genetic disorder: Evidence from a British twin study. *Psychological Medicine, 25*, 63–78.

Bailey, A., Luthert, P., Dean, A., Harding, B., & Janota, I. (1998). A clinical pathological study of autism. *Brain, 121*, 889–905.

Boutot, E., & Bryant, D. (2005). Social integration of students with autism in inclusive settings. *Education & Training in Developmental Disabilities, 40*, 14–23.

Brigance, A. (1998). *Brigance Inventory of Academic Skills*. North Billerica, MA: Curriculum Associates.

Centers for Disease Control and Prevention. (n.d.). *Prevalence of autism spectrum disorders*. Retrieved December 23, 2008, from http://www.cdc.gov/ncbddd/autism/faq_prevalence.htm#whatisprevalence

Cheney, C., & Demchak, M. (1996). *Providing appropriate education in inclusive settings: A rural case study.* (ERIC Document Reproduction Services No. ED394761)

Egaas, B., Courchesne, E., & Saitoh, O. (1995). Reduced size of corpus callosum in autism. *Archives of Neurology, 52*, 794–801.

Filipek, P. A., Accardo, P. J., Ashwal, S., Baranak, G. T., Cook, E. H., Dawson, G., et al. (2000). Practice parameter: Screening and diagnosis of autism. *Neurology, 55*, 468–479.

Fisher, D., & Frey, N. (2001). Access to the core curriculum. *Remedial & Special Education, 22*, 148–158.

Gilliam, J. E. (2008). *Gilliam Autism Rating Scale* (2nd ed.). Austin, TX: Pro-Ed.

Goodman, G., & Williams, C. M. (2007). Interventions for increasing the academic engagement of students with autism spectrum disorders in inclusive settings. *Teaching Exceptional Children, 39*(6), 53–61.

Humphrey, N. (2008). Autistic spectrum and inclusion: Including pupils with autism spectrum disorders in mainstream schools. *Support for Learning, 23*, 41–47.

Hunt, P., & Farron-Davis, F. (1992). A preliminary investigation of IEP quality and content associated with placement in general education versus special education classes. *Journal of the Association for Persons With Severe Handicaps, 17*, 247–253.

Individuals with Disabilities Education Improvement Act, PL 108-446, 118 Stat. 2647 (2004).

Kaye, J. A., Maria Del Mar, M. M., & Jick, H. (2001). Measles, mumps, and rubella vaccine and the incidence of autism recorded by general practitioners: A time-trend analysis. *Western Journal of Medicine, 174*, 387–390.

Krug, D., Arick, J., & Almond, P. (2009). *Autism Screening Instrument for Educational Planning-3.* Austin, TX: Pro-Ed, Inc.

Linder, T. (2008). *Transdisciplinary Play-Based Assessment-2.* Baltimore: Paul H. Brookes.

Lovaas, I. (1987). Behavioral treatment and normal educational and intellectual functioning in young autistic children. *Journal of Consulting and Clinical Psychology, 55*, 3–9.

Lynch, S. A. (2000). Sensory processing: Overlooked in assessment. *The DiaLog, 31*, 7–10.

Lynch-Linehan, S., & Brady, M. P. (1995). Functional versus developmental assessment: Influences on instructional planning decisions. *Journal of Special Education, 29*, 295–309.

Madsen, K. M., Hviid, A., Vesteraard, M., Schendel, D., Wohlfahrt, J., Thorsen, P., et al., (2002). A population-based study of measles, mumps, and rubella vaccination and autism. *New England Journal of Medicine, 347*(19), 1477–1482.

McLean, S. (2001). A survey of middle level teachers' perceptions of inclusion (Doctoral dissertation, University of Manitoba, 2001). *Dissertation Abstracts International, 61*(7-A), 2596.

Muhle, R., Trentacoste, S. V., & Rapin, I. (2004). The genetics of autism. *Pediatrics, 113*, 472–486.

Partington, J. W. (2007). *The Assessment of Basic Language and Learning Skills-Revised.* Pleasant Hill, CA: Behavior Analysts.

Prelock, P. A. (2006). *Autism spectrum disorders: Issues in assessment and intervention.* Austin, TX: Pro-Ed.

Ritvo, E. R., Jorde, L. B., Mason-Brothers, A., Freeman, B. J., Pingree, C., Jones, M. B., et al. (1989). The UCLA-University of Utah epidemiologic survey of autism: Recurrence risk estimates and genetic counseling. *American Journal of Psychiatry, 146*, 1032–1036.

Robins, D., Fein, D., Barton, M., & Green, J. (2001). The modified checklist for autism in toddlers: An initial study investigating the early detection of autism and pervasive developmental disorders. *Journal of Autism and Developmental Disorders, 31*, 131–144.

Rodier, P. M. (2000). The early origins of autism: *Scientific American, 282*, 56–63.

Schick, A. L. (2007). Changing the IEP development process: Impact on collaboration and teachers' perceptions of IEP usefulness (Doctoral dissertation, University of Denver, 2007). *Dissertation Abstracts International, 68*(3-A), 830.

Willis, J., & Dumont, R. (2005). *Ten top problems with norm-referenced achievement tests for young children.* Retrieved December 23, 2008, from http://alpha.edu.edu/psychology

Zhang, J., & Griffin, A. (2007). Including children with autism in general physical education: Eight possible solutions. *Journal of Physical Education, Recreation & Dance, 78*, 33.

CHAPTER 2

SETTING UP THE CLASSROOM

SUE PALKO & CHRIS FRAWLEY

I N 1943, Leo Kanner first documented autism as a disorder through his observation of 11 children with similar characteristics including impairments in social interaction, deficits in communication, and restricted and repetitive patterns of behavior, which has been expanded to include autism spectrum disorders (ASD), Asperger's syndrome, and Pervasive Developmental Disorder-Not Otherwise Specified (PDD-NOS; American Psychiatric Association, 2000). Since that time the number of students being identified with this diagnosis has continued to increase with the Centers for Disease Control and Prevention (n.d.) estimating that in 2007, one in 150 eight-year-old children in different areas of the United States had a diagnosis of ASD.

Not only has the prevalence of ASD changed the face of general education classrooms but legal mandates such as No Child Left Behind (NCLB; 2002) and the Individuals with Disabilities Education Act of 2004 have led to the placement of more students with ASD in general education classrooms. This legislation holds school divisions accountable for every child's progress and ensures that students with disabilities have access to the general education curriculum. Although both of these laws help ensure individuals with disabilities have access to the general education setting and curriculum and that schools use teaching methods that are scientifically based, "few models and procedures have been advanced to facilitate the successful placement and maintenance of learners with ASD in the general education classroom" (Simpson, de Boer-Ott, & Smith-Myles, 2003, p. 117). Further, these laws do not address the physical structure of the general education classroom and how that structure may impact the success of students with ASD. This chapter will address the issues that need to be considered regarding the physical arrangement of the classroom, developing functional schedules and teaching routines, and procedures that can help meet the needs of students with ASD as they participate in these inclusive school environments.

ARRANGING THE PHYSICAL ENVIRONMENT

Students with ASD have varying needs that should be considered when structuring the general education classroom. Students with ASD are visual learners who function best when auditory input is supplemented with visual or written information and external organizational support (Handleman & Harris, 2006). Taking the time to plan and prepare the environment of the classroom is a key component in preparing students with autism for school success.

When creating an optimal learning environment for students, teachers first should consider the organization of the physical environment. Physical structure is the way in which teachers and parents set up and organize a person with autism's physical environment (Stokes, 2008). By providing structure to the physical environment, students with autism learn that the world is an organized and predictable place instead of one filled with random events and disconnected objects that can overwhelm and confuse them (Mesibov, Shea, & Schopler, 2005).

There are many ways to create an organized physical environment. The physical arrangement of the classroom, where and how furniture and classroom materials are placed, is a good place to begin. When thinking about the furniture, it is important to create clear visual boundaries for different areas of the classroom. These boundaries can be established through the careful placement of tables, bookshelves, chairs, and other furniture. As Stokes (2008) explains, typically developing children automatically segment their environments, which can be a difficult task for children with autism. By creating these boundaries to segment different work areas in the classroom, it helps students with autism understand what happens in each area and to establish a path of travel to each one.

In an elementary classroom, for example, two adjacent bookshelves forming an L and a desk and chair (inside the L shape) can create an independent work area. A large piece of carpet with colored stickers to designate seating space(s) placed in the front of the room can designate a whole-group learning space (Mesibov & Howley, 2003). Screens also can be used to identify work and play areas and colored tape placed on a tile floor near a table and chairs can designate a small-group learning area or quiet area. Students can familiarize themselves with the room setup and become more confident in functioning in the physical layout of the classroom.

In both elementary and secondary classrooms, consideration should be given to where the student with autism will sit. There are some questions the student and the teacher can consider when making seating arrangements in middle or high school settings. For example, is it better for the student to be placed near the front of the room in order to hear the instruction, and will it be less distracting near the front of the room? Should the student be placed on the side of the room furthest from the doorway to limit distractions in the halls? Is it better if the student has an empty desk next to his desk because he has sensory issues and needs the space? Would it be helpful if the student had the same seat assignment in every classroom throughout the day? Taking the time to find the right seat assignment is especially important because of the larger class size and linear seating arrangements found in most secondary classrooms. Also, some teachers might find study carrels a welcome addition to their classroom. They can be placed in a quiet area of the room to be used as an independent work area or a quiet workspace for any student who may need to limit his or her distractions.

Classroom Materials

The organization of classroom materials is another area to consider when planning the classroom environment. Students with ASD benefit from visual organization of materials as well as the physical organization of the furniture. By organizing classroom materials, the teacher creates an orderly environment that supports students by illustrating how their classroom can be neat and organized. Visual clutter can be distracting for many students. Materials need to be organized in a way that will benefit both the students and teacher. Separate containers such as baskets, plastic tubs, shelves, and trays can be used to store materials. The containers can be labeled with a word and a picture to explain the contents. Letter trays can be placed in specific areas to indicate where to place completed homework and classwork. Students can be taught how to store their own materials in a desk or locker. A map of the contents of the desk or locker can be created to help students with storing their materials in an orderly manner (Kluth, 2003).

Another aspect of the physical structure that teachers can address is the type of furniture to include in their classroom. Comfortable classroom furniture for student use creates a more relaxed environment for all students and helps create a sense of community and belonging. A variety of seating options can be placed in different areas of the classroom. Rocking chairs, seat cushions, floor mats, lounge chairs, couches, armchairs, and bean bag chairs can be used in a classroom library area, a quiet spot, or writing area.

By planning the placement and organization of the materials and furniture, teachers help students with autism to define the basic organization of the classroom and decrease visual and auditory distractions, reduce anxiety and promote independence, as well as more effective and consistent work (Mesibov et al., 2005).

Lighting

Although sensory differences are not currently included as core symptoms of ASD, they can be problematic for some students with ASD. For example, the lighting in the classroom is another area teachers may consider as they work to create classroom environments conducive to learning for all students, but particularly students with autism. Individuals with autism have reported that fluorescent lighting can affect their behavior, their comfort level, and their ability to concentrate. The right lighting can calm and soothe students, as well as energize and inspire them (Kluth, 2003).

Teachers can adjust the lighting in their classrooms in a number of ways. First, they can try to reduce the amount of fluorescent lighting. Teachers can experiment by using natural lighting in place of fluorescent lighting, such as raising the blinds to illuminate the classroom. Other lights, such as floor lamps and table lamps, can be used to supplement the natural lighting. If reducing the fluorescent lighting is not an option, then consider moving the seats of students with autism to different areas in the room in order to increase their exposure to natural lighting and reduce their exposure to fluorescent lighting. Additionally, some students may benefit from using colored overlays or transparencies on their classwork to help reduce the amount of glare from the lights (Kluth, 2003).

Sound

Students with autism also might have sensitivity to sounds found in the school environment, such as the pencil sharpener, voices in the hallway, bells, and noises in the cafeteria, to name a few (Aspy & Grossman, 2007). Sounds in the classroom environment can affect a student's ability to concentrate and learn. If classroom noises are distracting for students, the teacher might consider placing carpet in certain areas of the classroom to reduce noise or place adhesive felt pads or tennis balls on the bottoms of chair legs to reduce the noise caused by chair legs scraping on a tile floor.

Some students are even distracted by the "hum" of fluorescent lighting fixtures, so the teacher may need to rely on the natural light or consider bringing in lamps in order to reduce the extraneous noise. Physical education teachers also should be aware that the echoes produced in a gymnasium or in small rooms such as locker rooms or bathrooms can be problem areas (Moyes, 2001). It is important for all teachers to remember that if the classroom is structured for the student who needs the most structure, whether it is a student with autism or a student with a different disability, all of the other students will adjust and benefit.

Case Study: Setting Up the Classroom

It is the week before school starts and Mrs. Tobin, a second-grade teacher, is preparing for the upcoming year. She is thinking about how to arrange her classroom to meet the needs of her students. Mrs. Tobin and Ms. Connelly, a special education teacher, met earlier in the week to discuss Derrick and Patrick, two students with ASD who will be included in Mrs. Tobin's classroom this year. Mrs. Tobin has taught students with disabilities in her classroom in previous years, but this is the first time she will teach students with ASD.

To help Mrs. Tobin prepare for the upcoming year, Ms. Connelly shared information about individuals with ASD, and more specifically, the instructional needs of Derrick and Patrick. As she sat in her classroom thinking about how to create an optimal learning environment for this year's class of second graders, Mrs. Tobin reflected upon the information Ms. Connelly shared with her. Ms. Connelly explained that it would be important to consider the classroom environment for Derrick and Patrick. There were some things Mrs. Tobin could do to help create a successful learning experience this year for Derrick and Patrick, as well as her other students.

Mrs. Tobin remembered that Ms. Connelly shared information about creating visual boundaries for the different areas in her room. She decided it would be helpful to move her furniture to create areas the students would use. A corner of the room, along with two bookshelves set perpendicular to the walls, created a quiet library area. Books were placed in baskets on the shelves. Her old rocking chair and a couple of beanbags were put on the floor inside the space for students to sit upon as they read. A library sign with a picture of a child reading on the sign helped to label the area and its purpose.

The computers were instructional supports Mrs. Tobin knew her students would often use. She moved the two computer desks against the wall, next to each other, and placed a sign above them on the wall labeled "Computer Area" with a picture of a student working on the computer on the sign. Ms. Connelly also said that it would be helpful for students to have a quiet area in the room to complete work or to spend a few minutes away from the rest of the class. Mrs. Tobin looked around her room and determined that a small table and two chairs would serve this purpose well. She placed them in the back of the room, against a wall, with the chairs facing each other across the table. Mrs. Tobin created a sign for the area that said "Quiet Area" and added a picture of a person with an index finger to his mouth saying "Shhh."

Because the students often come to the front of the room for whole-group instruction, Mrs. Tobin placed a large piece of carpet and her easel and chair in the front of the room to designate this space as the whole-group learning area. She placed a few carpet squares (stacked under the easel) for students (e.g., Derrick, Patrick) who would benefit from having their own "space" or carpet square when sitting in the front of the room with the whole class.

After looking around her room, Mrs. Tobin identified other areas that needed to be designated for a particular purpose. She made a large "Homework" sign, with a student writing in a notebook and placed it next to the space on her board where she posts homework assignments each day. Mrs. Tobin made similar signs for the math, science, and social studies work areas. Each area consisted of a couple of student desks placed together and a couple of chairs seated at the desks. Students could see the books and materials for each area on top of the desks. After creating these signs, Mrs. Tobin looked around her room and reflected that Derrick and Patrick, as well as all of her students, would benefit from the visual boundaries that had been created in the classroom and the labels for each area.

Next, Mrs. Tobin considered ways to better organize the classroom materials. She liked Ms. Connelly's idea about labeling containers with words and pictures to reflect their contents. She used a picture communication software program suggested by Ms. Connelly to create labels for the shelves of math games, the baskets of books in the library, the containers of art supplies, and the doors of cabinets that held various classroom supplies. Mrs. Tobin also labeled the trays on her desk for student classwork and homework. In addition, Ms. Tobin created desk maps for Derrick and Patrick to help them organize the contents in their own desks.

After organizing the classroom materials, Mrs. Tobin examined the lighting in her classroom. Ms. Connelly had mentioned that lighting could be an area of concern for students with ASD because of their sensory differences. Mrs. Tobin decided to keep the blinds on the windows raised at all times to increase the amount of natural light in the room because florescent lighting can be distracting. She also decided to consult the custodian about reducing the number of fluorescent bulbs in the classroom or replacing them with an alternative bulb. If she is unable to do anything with the fluorescent lights, Mrs. Tobin decided she would consider moving Derrick's and Patrick's desks closer to the windows in order to increase their exposure to the natural lighting.

During their initial meeting, Mrs. Tobin and Ms. Connelly discussed Derrick's and Patrick's sensitivity to different sounds. Ms. Connelly explained Derrick's sensitivity to loud noises, particularly the fire drill. She also suggested that they talk with Derrick's and Patrick's parents to learn if there were other specific sensitivities to sound. In the classroom, Mrs. Tobin considered the different sounds in her room to make sure the students were not seated near sounds that may bother them (e.g., the bell, the clock, the exterior hallway). Ms. Connelly also suggested providing Derrick and Patrick with earplugs/headphones for certain times of the day or in specific areas of the building (e.g., when changing classes, eating lunch in the cafeteria; Kluth, 2003) to help minimize the impact of different sounds.

Last of all, Mrs. Tobin scheduled a meeting with Ms. Connelly and Derrick's and Patrick's parents to discuss sensitivities to sound and any other issues that might still need to be addressed. She would know more about how to successfully meet the students' needs after talking with their parents and meeting the students. Mrs. Tobin was excited about the start of this school year. She felt more prepared after talking with Ms. Connelly and arranging the physical structure of her classroom.

Developing Functional Schedules

Schools and classrooms need schedules and routines in order to function smoothly, but this may be even more necessary for students with ASD. Because one of the defining characteristics of ASD is an insistence on sameness (Prelock, 2006), the slightest change in a schedule may be problematic. One method that has been successful for some students with ASD has been the use of visual supports (Johnston, Nelson, Evans, & Palazolo, 2003). Visual supports are used to prompt joint attention, encourage conversation, promote recall, enhance attention, increase comprehension of language concepts, and facilitate communicative intent and social initiation (Johnston et al., 2003)

The research around the use of visual supports with individuals with ASD suggests that they are able to process two- or three-dimensional visual supports better than transient information (Quill, 1995). In other words, individuals with ASD often are able to process visuals such as pictures or objects better than they can process the spoken word or sign language symbols. The sign language symbol, like the spoken word, disappears once it is stated. Visuals have been found to assist students in making sense of their environment, predicting scheduled events, and anticipating changes throughout the day (Dettmer, Simpson, Myles & Ganz, 2000).

In a recent research study, Mesibov et al. (2005) stated three reasons to use visual schedules. First, visual schedules can help students with language. A visual support, along with auditory input, helps a student to comprehend what he is supposed to do next and/or the expectations for a task or portion of the day. Another reason to use a visual schedule is that it can help students with transitions. Transitions during the school day can be difficult for students with autism. Visual schedules provide a routine for the students. They can refer to the schedule during a transition, which can help to reduce inappropriate behaviors. The third reason for using visual schedules is that they may assist the student in developing independence. The student can read the schedule to know what to do next instead of relying on verbal prompts from the adults in the classroom. Students with ASD have been described as being manipulative, inconsistent, distractible, lacking focus, and dependent on those around them. The use of visual schedules dispels these myths and helps to promote their independence.

Determining the Hierarchy of Visual Schedules

The first thing to consider when creating a visual schedule is which type of schedule can provide the most meaning to the student. There are three specific levels or hierarchy of schedules that will be discussed. These include object schedules, picture schedules, and written schedules. The Treatment and Education of Autistic and Related Communication-Handicapped Children (TEACCH; 2006) model suggests using the following hierarchy when determining what will work best for a student. If the teacher is unsure of the student's level of functioning, then it is best to begin with an object schedule, which is the easiest for a student to understand. An object schedule is a schedule that uses objects that will be used in the activity. For example, the schedule may read "seat work" and have a pencil taped next to the word.

The next level is a picture schedule. A picture schedule uses photographs of the activities to communicate to the student what he will be doing. Other options for visuals in the picture schedule are colored-line drawings or black and white drawings (Mesibov, Browder, & Kirklan, 2002). Teachers want to choose whatever has the most meaning to the student. It also is important to pair the written word with the object, picture, or line drawing to assist the student with moving up the schedule hierarchy to the highest level, a written schedule.

Determining the Appropriate Visual Schedule

The first step in determining which type of visual schedule to use is to consider the purpose of the schedule. Although schedules are necessary to serve a variety of purposes, presented below are three forms of schedules that correlate to the specific needs of the student: "first-then board," part-day schedule, and full-day schedule. When considering the types of schedules, teachers should ask themselves the following questions: Does the student need the schedule to help him or her know what will happen during a particular class period? Does the student need the schedule to make the transition from one activity to the next one? Does the student need the schedule to see the flow of the entire day? Whatever the purpose, one of the first things a teacher needs to consider is whether or not the student will benefit from a first-then board, a part-day schedule, or a full-day schedule. The most basic type of a schedule is one in which the student only has to attend to one visual cue at a time to determine what is next. An example of this is what is known as a first-then board (see Figure 2.1).

Younger students and students with more significant ASD may need to start with a first-then board. A first-then board tells the student which activity to engage in first and which activity to engage in second using the word *then*. The board includes pictures with words describing the activities. The activity in the then position on the board needs to be highly reinforcing for the student. The first-then board is based on the principle that if a student wants to perform a certain activity,

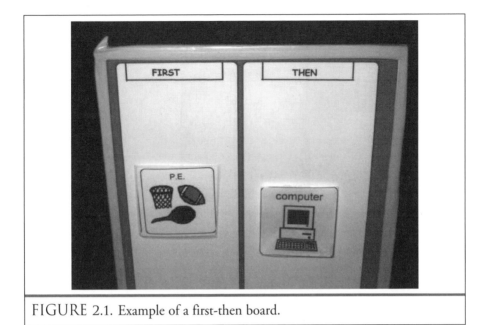

FIGURE 2.1. Example of a first-then board.

he or she will perform a less desirable activity in order to gain access to the more desired activity (Neisworth & Wolfe, 2005).

Another type of visual schedule that meets the needs of students who may need additional information about the specific activities they will be involved in is a part-day schedule. A part-day schedule is a schedule with a portion of the student's day laid out in the visual schedule format. This may be the first 2 hours of the student's day or it could be the morning and the afternoon. Although some students only need the schedule to show an outline of their day, other students may need information about the specific activities they will be involved in during the class. Remember that when designing a part-day schedule, the hierarchy of object, picture, or written must be considered.

Some students with ASD need to know the specific order in which things will occur in their classroom. They may not have the ability to read the environmental cues or the ability to process the auditory information provided in the classroom. A part-day schedule may keep students from becoming overwhelmed and anxious about what activities will be taking place within a particular class period or portion of the day. Thus, having a visual schedule may help to reduce the challenging behaviors the student with ASD can sometimes exhibit (Bopp, Brown, & Mirenda, 2004; see Figures 2.2 and 2.3).

The last type of visual schedule presented is the full-day schedule. This schedule describes the student's entire day. The schedule can be included in a personal digital assistant (PDA), notebook, binder, or some other organizational tool. Figure 2.4 is an example of a full-day schedule written on a piece of notebook paper. The

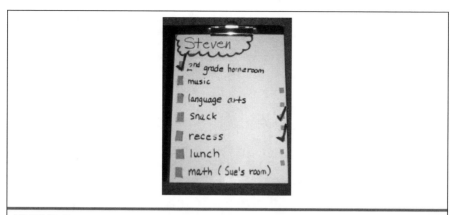

FIGURE 2.2. Example of an elementary part-day schedule.

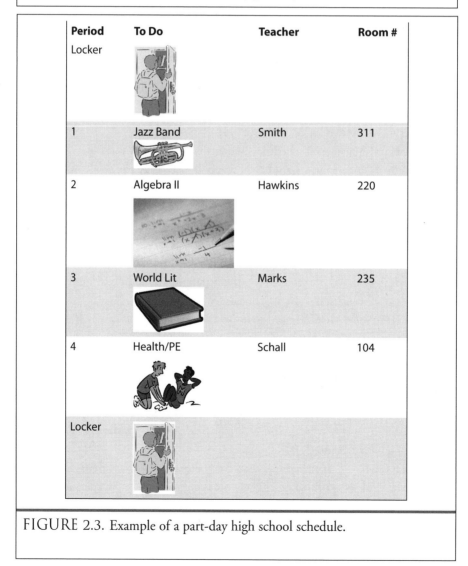

Period	To Do	Teacher	Room #
Locker			
1	Jazz Band	Smith	311
2	Algebra II	Hawkins	220
3	World Lit	Marks	235
4	Health/PE	Schall	104
Locker			

FIGURE 2.3. Example of a part-day high school schedule.

```
┌─────────────────────────────────────────────────────────────┐
│   ┌─────────────────────────────────────────────────────┐   │
│   │              My Weekly Schedule                      │   │
│   │                                                      │   │
│   │   ❏   Put things in my locker                        │   │
│   │   ❏   Go to homeroom                                 │   │
│   │   ❏   Go to math in room 203                         │   │
│   │   ❏   Go to earth science in room 210                │   │
│   │   ❏   Go to computer lab in room 103                 │   │
│   │   ❏   Eat lunch                                      │   │
│   │   ❏   Go to workshop in room 201                     │   │
│   │   ❏   Choice: Study hall in room 208                 │   │
│   │        or                                            │   │
│   │   ❏   Break in Mr. Ladd's room                       │   │
│   │   ❏   Guidance office                                │   │
│   │   ❏   Go to English in room 230                      │   │
│   │   ❏   Go to locker and get books for homework        │   │
│   │   ❏   Go home: Monday, Wednesday, Friday             │   │
│   │   ❏   Computer Club: Tuesday, Thursday               │   │
│   └─────────────────────────────────────────────────────┘   │
│                                                               │
│   FIGURE 2.4. Example of a written schedule.                  │
└─────────────────────────────────────────────────────────────┘
```

FIGURE 2.4. Example of a written schedule.

student checks off each activity as it is completed. It is important for teachers to remember to incorporate choices into the schedule when teaching a student to use one. The student needs to be taught that sometimes the schedule changes, which is OK. This can be done by using a visual representation of "Oops" or "Surprise." Whatever is used, the teacher wants the experience to be positive for the student so he does not associate change as a negative experience.

Teaching Students to Use a Schedule

The key to using a visual schedule with any student with ASD is to teach the student how to use the schedule by breaking it down into manageable parts and teaching a portion at a time. Next, consideration has to be given as to how the student will indicate that he has completed an activity. Some students, like some adults, find it very gratifying to cross off activities on their schedules after they have been completed. For example, the teacher may say, "First, you are going to go to English, and then you will go to Algebra I." The student would cross off English when he leaves the room, so that he could see that he would be going to Algebra I next.

Case Study: Creating Student Schedules

Mr. Baker teaches U.S. history at the secondary level. The school year is underway and everything seems to be going well. He has several students with disabilities included in different classes throughout the day. Mr. Baker works collaboratively with Ms. Draper, one of the special education teachers, to ensure that the students' instructional needs are being met. Ms. Draper attends a meeting with Mr. Baker and shares that she is receiving a new student. The student, Roger, has the label of Asperger's syndrome. He is coming from another state and has been fully included in all general education classes. Mr. Baker has heard other teachers talk about having students with ASD in their classes. Some of the teachers have had a successful experience in teaching a student with ASD in their classroom, while some teachers have described it as the most difficult challenge of their teaching career. Ms. Draper explains to Mr. Baker that based on Roger's Individualized Education Program (IEP), he can exhibit some challenging behaviors. However, if he uses his visual schedule, these behaviors are much more manageable. Mr. Baker is not sure what all of this means but it sounds time-consuming to him. After processing the information, Mr. Baker asks Ms. Draper these questions:

- What will the visual schedule look like?
- Does Roger have to have an individual schedule for each class or does the schedule cover the entire day?
- Will I have to write the schedule out for Roger each day?
- Where will we keep the schedule?
- Would any of my other students benefit from using the visual schedule?

These are just a few of the questions that the general education teacher may need to discuss with the special education teacher and the student. There also will be additional questions that arise based on the needs of the individual student.

ESTABLISHING ROUTINES AND PROCEDURES

Routines and procedures are important to all aspects of life and bring a sense of organization to the world around us. Most people are able to adapt to the changes that occur as a normal process of the daily routine, but students with ASD may find changes to their routine very difficult (Bruey, 2004). By establishing routines and procedures, teachers are not only helping the students in their classes who have ASD but they also are creating a sense of community in their classroom.

Most classrooms have a morning routine that may go something like this: get off of the bus, walk to the classroom, hang up your coat and backpack, sit down at your desk, and begin writing in your literature journal. This type of routine brings order to the beginning of the day, and teachers can make the day more predictable for all students when a framework for the day is provided. This framework also assists students with ASD to make sense of their environment and may reduce the anxiety that can come from unexpected changes (Mesibov et al., 2005). Research also has shown that providing predictable routines can reduce or eliminate challenging behaviors for some students with ASD (Mesibov et al., 2002).

- Arrival
- Roll call/Lunch count
- Tardies
- Assignments
- Absences/Make-up procedures
- Getting supplies
- Collection and distribution of papers
- Going to the restroom
- Teacher's attention signal
- Collection of assignments
- Working in groups
- Independent seat work
- Working at a center
- Lining up to leave the room
- Going to the clinic, office, media center, or elsewhere
- Asking questions
- Getting help from the teacher
- Responding to fire drills, "codes," or other alerts
- Packing up at the end of the day
- Organizing materials

FIGURE 2.5. Possible activities/times for writing procedures and routines for students.

By establishing routines and procedures in the classroom, teachers are setting the student up for success (see Figure 2.5).

Teaching Routines and Procedures

After establishing the routines and procedures for the classroom and other locations within the school, teachers need to teach them to the students. When teaching routines and procedures, it is important for students to understand the purpose of the routine. Let students know how the use of a specific routine will help them in their daily activities. For instance, if a routine involves placing a folder in a designated spot, the student should be aware that by putting the folder in this location the teacher will be able to access it quickly and provide the student the feedback on the submitted assignment. In addition, teaching routines and procedures at the beginning of the school year may decrease anxiety for some students by reducing a possible stressful transition into a new classroom.

There are a couple of strategies that can be used to teach procedures. Two of those involve modeling and role-playing. For example, the student may need to be shown appropriate behavior for walking in the hall or how to go through the morning arrival routines. Students may act out the correct way and the incorrect way of completing these processes. The student also may be paired with a peer buddy who can model the appropriate procedures.

Another possible strategy is using a checklist that will provide a visual representation of the procedures. This may involve placing an index card on the student's desk as he enters the classroom or having it written in a spiral notebook. Then, the student can check off each completed step. Just like the visual schedule, the student will need to be taught how to use the checklist.

Another strategy is the use of a large visual that can be placed in the classroom and used by all of the students. For example, the procedures for the morning routine could be written on the chalkboard. Another example may involve making sure the student with ASD is prepared for class. Some students with ASD may have a difficult time remembering which supplies they need for each class. A designated supplies area in the room can be helpful for these students. Instead of having to provide materials each day for the students or engaging in a discussion with the student about being prepared for class, the designated supplies area, which may be a shelf or bin, can be provided that includes a list of the supplies he will need for class. Again, checklists could be used to show completion.

After the procedures have been taught, it will be necessary to allow students an opportunity to practice the routine. Many students with ASD have difficulty processing auditory information, therefore, by practicing and modeling routines with the students, they are more likely to learn the routines and respond with some automaticity when given a direction in class (e.g., turn in their homework, leave class when the bell rings; Hodgdon, 1995).

The beginning of school is an exciting and sometimes overwhelming time for everyone. Teachers want to be sure not to overwhelm their students by teaching too many routines or procedures at one time. Teach the most important ones first and build on those. Teachers also will need to revisit some of these procedures after holiday breaks, student absences, or when there are changes with the schoolwide schedule (e.g., during statewide testing).

Case Study: Establishing Routine

Mr. Lopez is a high school biology teacher. He has three students with ASD included in his classes throughout the day. In the teachers' lounge one day he talked with Mr. Green, one of the other science teachers, about his classes and made some comparisons between their classes. Mr. Lopez commented that three periods during the day seem to run more smoothly than the other class periods. Mr. Green inquired as to which periods they were and why he thought they were running more smoothly. After giving it some thought Mr. Lopez said, "I can only hypothesize that it is because I have taken more time to teach the students in those classes the routines and procedures that I expect. He added that they also were the classes that included the students with ASD. "Because of the characteristics that can accompany students with ASD, I have been more structured and consistent with my class procedures, routines, and expectations." The two teachers continued their conversation and brainstormed ideas for the changes Mr. Lopez could make to streamline the other classes. The following is a list of questions that Mr. Lopez considered when structuring his classrooms.

- What do I want students to do when they enter my class?
- What do I want them to do during transition periods?
- How can I teach the students these procedures and routines?
- How do I write them so that they are positive and observable?

CONCLUSION

With the growing number of students who are being identified with ASD and receiving much of their instruction in the general education classroom, teachers are faced with the challenge of knowing how to provide a strong academic environment for all of their students. Often, the physical structure of the classroom is not given a great deal of consideration in preparing for the needs of the students. However, knowing and understanding the characteristics that accompany a diagnosis of ASD, much more is required to ensure an appropriate learning environment.

Consideration also may have to be given to the lighting used in the classroom and the classroom noises and the effects they may have on students with ASD. Again, the more knowledge the teacher has regarding the characteristics that accompany a diagnosis of ASD, the easier it will be for the teacher to address the physical aspects of the classroom.

Last of all, providing students with ASD with visual supports, such as visual schedules, can reduce their anxiety by predicting scheduled activities and anticipating change. Visual schedules also can promote smooth transitions throughout the school day. In order to structure the classroom for students with ASD so that they can understand and comply with the expectations, teachers will need to provide clear and predictable routines and procedures. Typically, these routines and procedures will benefit all of the students in the classroom and promote an environment that contributes to a successful learning experience for everyone.

REFERENCES

American Psychiatric Association. (2000). *Diagnostic and statistical manual of mental disorders* (4th ed., Text rev.). Washington, DC: Author.

Aspy, R., & Grossman, B. G. (2007). *The Ziggurat Model: A framework for designing comprehensive interventions for individuals with high-functioning autism and Asperger syndrome.* Shawnee Mission, KS: Autism Asperger Publishing.

Bopp, K. D., Brown, K. E., & Mirenda, P. (2004). Speech-language pathologists' role in the delivery of positive behavior support of individuals with developmental disabilities. *American Journal of Speech-Language Pathology, 13*, 5–19.

Bruey, C. T. (2004). *Demystifying autism spectrum disorders: A guide to diagnosis for parents and professionals.* Bethesda, MD: Woodbine House.

Centers for Disease Control and Prevention (n.d.). *What is the prevalence of autism?* Retrieved September 29, 2008, from http://www.cdc.gov/ncbddd/autism/faq_prevalence.htm#whatisprevalence

Dettmer, S., Simpson, R. L., Myles, B. S., & Ganz, J. B. (2000). The use of visual supports to facilitate transitions of students with autism. *Focus on Autism and Other Developmental Disabilities, 15*, 163–169.

Handleman, J. S., & Harris, S. L. (Eds.). (2006). *School-age education programs for children with autism.* Austin, TX: Pro-Ed.

Hodgdon, L. (1995). *Visual strategies for improving communication: Practical supports for school and home.* Troy, MI: QuirkRoberts.

Individuals with Disabilities Education Improvement Act, PL 108-446, 118 Stat. 2647 (2004).

Johnston, S., Nelson, C., Evans, J., & Palazolo, K. (2003). The use of visual supports in teaching young children with autism spectrum disorder to initiate interactions. *Augmentative and Alternative Communication, 19*, 86–103.

Kanner, L. (1943). Autistic disturbances of affective contact. *Nervous Child, 2*, 217–250.

Kluth, P. (2003). *"You're going to love this kid!" Teaching students with autism in the inclusive classroom.* Baltimore: Paul H. Brookes.

Mesibov, G. B., Browder, D. M., & Kirklan, C. (2002). Using individualized schedules as a component of positive behavioral support for students with developmental disabilities. *Journal of Positive Behavior Interventions, 4*, 73–79.

Mesibov, G. B., & Howley, M. (2003). *Accessing the curriculum for pupils with autism spectrum disorders: Using the TEACCH programme to help inclusion.* London: David Fulton.

Mesibov, G. B., Shea, V., & Schopler, E. (2005). *The TEACCH approach to autism spectrum disorders.* New York: Kluwer Academic/Plenum.

Moyes, R. (2001). *Incorporating social goals in the classroom: A guide for teachers and parents of children with high-functioning autism and Asperger syndrome.* London: Jessica Kingsley.

Neisworth, J. T., & Wolfe, P. S. (2005). *The autism encyclopedia.* Baltimore: Paul H. Brookes.

No Child Left Behind Act, 20 U.S.C. §6301 (2001).

Prelock, P. A. (2006). *Autism spectrum disorders: Issues in assessment and intervention.* Austin, TX: Pro-Ed.

Quill, K. A. (1995). Introduction. In K. A. Quill (Ed.), *Teaching children with autism: Strategies to enhance communication and socialization* (pp. 1–32). New York: Delmar.

Simpson, R. L., de Boer-Ott, S. R., & Smith-Myles, B. (2003). Inclusion of learners with autism spectrum disorders in general education settings. *Topics in Language Disorders, 23*, 116–133.

Stokes, S. (2008). *Structured teaching: Strategies for supporting students with autism.* Retrieved from http://www.specialed.us/autism/structure/str10.htm

TEACCH. (2006). *Information on autism: Educational approaches: Structured teaching.* Retrieved from http://www.teacch.com/structureteach.html

Effective Academic Instruction for Students With High Functioning Autism or Asperger's Syndrome

Janet Graetz

Characteristics and Classroom Implications

Today a growing number of parents and educators realize that students with high functioning autism (HFA) and Asperger's syndrome (AS) are best educated in the general education classroom. The general education curriculum is central to educational programming as communicated by the No Child Left Behind (NCLB) Act (2001) and the Individuals with Disabilities Education Act (IDEA; 2004). The question of where programming will take place has shifted from more restrictive settings (e.g., resource room, self-contained classroom) to inclusive environments. The inclusive environment is appropriate when the student can "participate in academic activities at increasingly independent levels with or without modifications, demonstrates acquisition of new skills, demonstrates generalization of acquired skills and attends to group instructions" (Simpson, de Boer-Ott, & Smith-Myles, 2003, p. 127). Although students with HFA/AS are afforded equal opportunity, they face increased challenges in the general education classroom that are a result of increased academic requirements and their unique learning style.

For many students with disabilities, particularly those with an autism spectrum disorder, few studies address their involvement with the general education curriculum. Most studies describe instructional methods and accommodations that are successful for students with learning disabilities that include the use of mnemonics, graphic organizers, visualizing strategies, and self-regulation strategies (Graham & Harris, 2005; Mastropieri & Scruggs, 2007; Pressley, 2005).

During the last 10 years, there has been an increase in education-related publications that focus on best educational practices for students with autism spectrum disorders. Some of these publications include packaged curricula that mainly address social needs (Bellini, 2008; Gutstein & Sheely, 2002; Schmidt & Heybyrne, 2004; Wagner, 2002), while others address therapeutic approaches (Dunlap, Kern, & Worcester, 2001). To date, no single curriculum has been identified that meets the unique learning styles of individuals with HFA or AS in the general education classroom (Arick, Krug, Fullerton, Loos, & Falco, 2005).

Although the No Child Left Behind Act (2001) requires that educators base their practices on scientifically based research, because of the limited numbers of students with autism spectrum disorders and the heterogeneity of students, few documented studies explore curricular approaches with this population. Most research on effective curriculum for students with autism spectrum disorders (ASD) highlight programs for preschool and early childhood classrooms. The Committee on Educational Interventions for Children with Autism (National Research Council, 2001) outlined the outcomes and interventions for children with ASD and noted that outcomes should stress personal independence and social responsibility. This report focused on young children with ASD and did not delineate possible different interventions or classroom strategies for children with high functioning autism or Asperger's syndrome.

Although researchers may be uncertain as to what comprises the best curriculum for students with HFA/AS, the curriculum is a blueprint for learning. The curriculum provides the answer to the question "What should students know and be able to do as they progress through school?" Many students with HFA/AS will progress through school and be exposed to the same educational information as their peers. Unfortunately, for students with HFA/AS, specific deficits, especially in the area of executive function, may affect their success in the general education classroom.

Executive Function (EF) and Executive Dysfunction (EDF)

Executive function is the "cognitive process that serves ongoing, goal-directed behaviors" (Meltzer, Pollica, & Barzillai, 2007, p. 1). These processes include planning, attention, flexibility of thought, and self-regulatory processes such as working memory and self-monitoring (Hill, 2004; Reed, 2002; Schetter, 2004). Executive function is a multidimensional construct that appears to emerge with age and may not be evident in preschool children (Griffith, Pennington, Wehner, & Rogers, 1999). At this time, more research is needed to better understand the development of executive function in children with autism and its relationship to academic and social success (Prior & Ozonoff, 2007).

The skills related to executive function, such as goal-setting, flexibility of thought, planning, inhibition, organization, and self-regulation, can affect a student's success in accessing the curriculum. How does a general education teacher know if this is an issue for a student with HFA/AS? Special educators may have the student take specific assessments that reveal issues of executive functioning. For example, the Wisconsin Card Sorting test (WCST) examines flexibility of thought as individuals are asked to shift from one concept to another (Heaton, Chelune, Talley, Kay, & Curtis, 1993). The WCST can be administered to students in elementary and high school. Another more comprehensive instrument of executive functioning, the Delis-Kaplan Executive Function System (D-KEFS), provides a battery of tests to examine planning, inhibition, flexibility of thought, and concept formation (Delis, Kaplan, & Kramer, 2001). Both of these tests should be administered by the school psychologist or other trained professional.

What does this mean for the general education teacher? Although you may not give or have access to the results of these formal tests, if you are working with a child on the spectrum, you can informally assess the skills of executive function by direct observation of the student. You may create a checklist of questions that examine the following:

- Does the student have difficulty moving from one task/activity to another?
- Is the student able to plan ahead and make goals?
- Does the student discuss the future?
- Is the student able to use a planner?

These questions may give you informal information about the student's executive functioning but do not overestimate executive impairments. Kids will be kids and a child who refuses to listen one day may be having a bad day; his behavior does not necessarily reflect executive dysfunction. It is more important to ask, "Do I see these behaviors in multiple environments and have I seen them over time?"

GETTING TO KNOW YOUR STUDENT

Many students with HFA/AS are verbal and are able to share their thoughts about their school, classroom, interests, hopes, and fears. Although characteristics of individuals with Asperger's syndrome may include rigidity of thought, unusual interests, poor impulse control, and desire for sameness, these characteristics do not describe who the student is nor recognize his or her gifts (Attwood, 2007). In addition to reading the student's file, the teacher should sit down and talk in depth with the student. Kluth (2003) suggested that teachers create a survey that asks students about their learning styles, strengths, classroom rules, needs, and best moments. Survey questions and prompts can be adapted for specific ages and may include the following:

- How do you learn best?
- Tell me about a time when you felt really happy in school.
- Tell me about a time when you felt really happy away from school.
- Think about your favorite teacher. What did you like about his or her teaching?
- What do you like to read?
- Describe the perfect school day.
- Tell me about you as an expert.
- When you get anxious, how do you relax?
- What else do you want me to know about you?

If the student has strengths in the arts, he may draw pictures that indicate his likes and dislikes that then can be discussed. If the student had a portfolio of academic work from the previous year, you may discuss this with him as well and ask the following:

- Of which pieces of work are you most proud?
- Which work was the most difficult for you?
- Why do you think this was difficult?
- As your new teacher, how can I help you with this?

ASSESSING ACADEMIC PERFORMANCE

Multiple assessments are required to gather information that reflects the student's achievement. Both general and special education teachers can work together to gather information and record a child's progress. The information gathered ultimately will help improve learning for the student. If the assessment and instruction are aligned, students will gain information about particular qualities of their work and their learning style.

In many instances, students with HFA/AS will be evaluated using the same assessments as other students with appropriate accommodations. Large-scale assessments that report on student achievement and academic competencies are viewed as important by our schools and society. Although valid and useful, large-scale assessments frequently are more removed from instruction and may not give the general education teacher a concise picture of what the student with HFA/AS actually knows. To derive information that is useful, it is necessary to have a combination of assessment measures that give a comprehensive view of student achievement.

Although these assessment instruments will vary depending on grade level, most include standardized tests, classroom assessments, and portfolios.

Standardized Tests

Students with HFA/AS may not understand the reasoning behind standardized tests that disrupt their day and require an inordinate amount of their time and attention. The classroom teacher should discuss testing with the student so that he or she better understands the goal. For instance, teachers may say that the school needs a "snapshot" of the student's academic achievement and that the standardized test will provide that "snapshot."

Standardized assessments may present difficulties when testing students with HFA/AS. If the tests are highly dependent on language, and require lengthy verbal directions and responses, students may do poorly (Watson & Marcus, 1999). In addition to language skill deficits, difficulties with inattention, inability to progress rapidly and shift their focus, and inability to remain focused for long periods of time may further complicate the testing situation.

Standardized testing frequently may cause a disruption to the student's regularly scheduled day that will be difficult for a student on the autism spectrum. To minimize the anxiety of testing day, the student should become familiar with the room in which he will be tested (if different from his regular room) and be introduced to the person who may monitor the test. Students may not understand how much time will be allowed for the test. A statement such as "you have a few more minutes" is too abstract for the student. Use a visual to display time, such as the Visual Red Timer, which shows time elapsing. In addition, be aware that sensory issues may affect testing, such as noisy fans or blowers in the room, visual distractions through doorways and windows, heat, and overhead lighting.

Classroom Assessments

Assessments prepared by the teacher may better assess student knowledge. Although testing may be required, talk to the student about his preference for test questions. Teachers may consider the type of question that best assesses student knowledge: multiple choice, short answer, true and false, or essay. Students who enjoy technology may use the computer for testing.

When possible, utilize the student's strengths and interests to assess knowledge. If the test involves word problems for math, incorporate the student's interests into the math problems. For example, if the student has an interest in cement mixers, work this item into the classroom test. Students do need to learn that not all topics are going to involve their special interest but, when possible, their use may better indicate student knowledge.

Some students with HFA/AS may not understand how (or why) projects and assignments may be graded. When possible, use specific, concrete grading formats such as rubrics. Rubrics present information concretely, and using rubrics, students know the criteria for excellent, fair, or poor work. Do not make the written criteria within each area too wordy.

In addition to standardized testing and classroom assessments, the general education teacher may wish to administer an informal criterion-referenced test, such as the Brigance® Comprehensive Inventory of Basic Skills-Revised (CIBS-R). The CIBS-R is an informal assessment that can be given by the teacher and identifies present levels of performance, connects assessment with instruction, includes pretests and posttests for many academic areas, and is appropriate for students in pre-K to grade 9.

Portfolios of Academic Work

The portfolio can document a student's progress and may be more informative than documentation of a series of quizzes or tests. The student can become part of the decision process in choosing pieces of work that he wants to submit to the portfolio. Some students with AS are perfectionists who may not want imperfect work added to their portfolio. You can discuss this with the student and perhaps decide on two portfolios: "My Best Work" and "Work in Progress," for example. Items should be dated and labeled. Again, incorporate rubrics or scaled sets of criteria that concretely demonstrated to the student what was expected and how the assignment was graded.

Some students with HFA/AS may have poor handwriting abilities or dysgraphia. Students with dysgraphia appear to have perceptual problems (reversing letters/numbers, writing words backwards, writing letters out of order, and very sloppy handwriting) that appear to be directly related to sequential information processing. As a result, the student may need to slow down in order to write accurately. Unfortunately, by slowing down, students can become "stuck" on concentrating so greatly on the mechanics of writing that they lose their train of thought. If handwriting continues to be laborious for specific students, their work could be completed on a computer and they could include recorded messages of oral projects in their portfolios.

Portfolios also should include photographs and video of the students as they work independently and with their peers. For example, if a student is hesitant to talk in front of the class, he or she may be given the opportunity to videotape himself and show this tape to the class. As the year progresses, he may feel more comfortable with standing and talking before his peers. Either way, there should be visual documentation of this progress in the portfolio.

Determining Academic Objectives

Several questions should be addressed when addressing academic objectives: (a) What is the student's current level of performance (in specific areas)? (b) What

Program-at-a-Glance	
Student: *Adam*	**Date**: *September 2008*

IEP Objectives	**IEP Accommodations**

Social/communication
   • *Takes turns in conversations*
   • *Uses gestures*
 	
Language Arts
   • *Answers comprehension questions*
   • *Computer journal writing*
	• *Receives special education support for communication support with peers*
	• *Permitted walking breaks*
	• *Home/school communication book*
	• *Designated location in classroom for breaks*

Academic/social management needs
   • *Peer planning and training*
   • *Reduced information per page*
   • *Graphic organizers*
   • *Use of visual red timer*
	• *Core team meetings weekly*
	   • *Whole team meetings monthly*
	   • *Share information on AS to all staff*

FIGURE 3.1. Program-at-a-Glance guide.

Note. Adapted from Janney and Snell (2000).

are typically developing students asked to do in this course/within this timeframe? (c) What aspects of the student's disability (HFA or AS) may interfere with the successful completion of these goals? (d) Is the student making progress in the general education curriculum? (e) What is the history of the student's progress in academic areas? and (f) What is the expected postsecondary setting for this student?

These questions may be reviewed when the student's Individualized Education Program (IEP) is developed by the team. The IEP is a legal document that will drive the child's education program and will include the strengths of the student, areas of need, and educational objectives. The IEP does not substitute for the general education program; instead, it enhances it and enables it to be realized. The general education teacher will be informed about the student's IEP and should have access to it. Because IEPs can tend to be bulky and cumbersome, Janney and Snell (2000) suggest that the special education teacher develop a Program-at-a-Glance guide for the general education teacher that provides a quick overview of the student's educational program, including a brief list of IEP objectives, accommodations, and behavioral guidelines. Figure 3.1 presents an example of a Program-at-a-Glance guide.

The IEP should always remain focused on the future goals of the student. The future goal for many students with HFA/AS will include postsecondary settings that include community colleges and 4-year universities. Do not assume that the presence of autism will negate the student's seeking of higher education.

Academic Issues: Elementary School

Young students with HFA/AS may appear academically ahead of their peers. Their vocabularies may rival that of their teachers and yet difficulties in executive function may hinder an easy assimilation of academic content. Although these students' vocabularies may be expansive, difficulties frequently are noted in the area of comprehension and concept formation. In early elementary grades this lack of concept formation may be difficult to recognize. After third grade, as the curriculum becomes more integrated, teachers may begin to notice problems as the student falters and is unable to grasp concepts.

Academic Issues: Middle School and High School

Many of the academic objectives in middle and high school will revolve around social competence. By now, the student is achieving some academic success, yet his or her social success may suffer. During the middle school years, academic objectives remain important but will be overshadowed by the student's difficulties in making friends, understanding the conversation of fellow teens, and the challenge of middle school life. Students may appear to be resistant, egocentric, and adhere to routines and rituals more than in elementary grades. This intense behavior may result from the increased social and academic demands of middle school and high school. Teachers should always be alert to behaviors that affect classroom success and seek support from the special education teacher and other related professionals involved with the student's programming.

STRATEGIES AND INTERVENTIONS

Characteristics of HFA/AS, including a narrow band of attention and difficulties with abstract thinking, organization, and the pragmatics of language, may necessitate that the curriculum be altered to ensure that it is understood (Moore, 2002). Teachers should examine how instructional practices, the use of visuals, student strengths and gifts, peer supports, transitions, independence, and collaboration can optimize success in the general education classroom. A summary of possible problem areas and strategies for solutions is presented in Figure 3.2 and discussed in more detail below.

Optimizing Success: Instructional Practices

The teacher is, as Haim Ginott once said, "the decisive element in the classroom." If the teacher adopts an attitude of one-size-fits-all, students with HFA/AS are likely to fail. Teachers who develop an accommodating classroom that conveys a climate of warmth and acceptance will promote success for all students. Accommodating classrooms enable students to make choices, become engaged in active

Potential Difficulties	Possible Strategies
Student becomes overly agitated when testing or when other new situations are present	Identify a safe haven or relaxation area within the room or in another room, such as the library
Student feels overwhelmed by verbal interactions	Experiment more with written words, signing, or gestures
Processing and following instructions	Write instructions on board or have them written on the student's desk Use few words ("Sit at your desk") Repeat instructions one-on-one Allow extra time for processing Include pictures to accompany oral information
Student is unable to remain seated during instruction	Allow for frequent breaks but make sure the student know what he is to be doing during the break and where it will occur
Student does not understand how long each activity requires	Set specific time limits for activities and use a Red Visual Timer to help the student understand the concept of time
Answering open-ended questions	Structure the question to reduce confusion and choices
Reluctant to ask the teacher for help	Establish a special signal that indicates the student needs help. The teacher may learn the sign for the letter "H" and teach it to the student. When the student requires "help" he signs the letter "H"
Student does not have materials/ books for class	Use transparent zip folders for pens and pencils Use color-coded folders for each academic/subject area
Refusal to enter specific rooms that may have sensory challenges: unusual smells or lighting (chemistry room, cafeteria)	Allow the student to take more frequent breaks
Unable to get started on work	Break the work into parts and use visuals to designate the work assignment
Difficulty starting/ completing homework	The student has spent a lot of energy making it through the day. How important is homework to this student? What are some different homework assignments that could be given that may address the student's interests?
Unable to complete work/projects that develop over time	Use a written/visual planner that specifically lists the activity and date for completion of smaller assignments

FIGURE 3.2. Summary of areas of difficulty and possible strategies.

Note. Adapted from Kluth (2003), Ozonoff and Schetter (2007), and Simpson et al. (2003).

learning, and encourage student interaction. In addition, teachers in accommodating classrooms adapt their teaching strategies for the entire class, thereby requiring fewer individual accommodations.

Mastropieri and Scruggs (2007) suggested that teachers implement the PASS variables to promote learning in inclusive settings. PASS includes the following: (1) **P**rioritize objectives, (2) **A**dapt instruction or the environment, (3) Use **S**ystematic instruction (SCREAM) variables during instruction, and (4) Implement **S**ystematic evaluation procedures. Objectives are *prioritized* that align with the needs of the individual student. Once the objectives are identified, the teacher decides what materials, instruction, or environmental components may need to be *adapted* for learning to take place. Next, the teacher incorporates *systematic* teaching, or the SCREAM variables to promote effective instruction and then *systematically* evaluates learning. The SCREAM variables include structure, clarity, redundancy, enthusiasm, appropriate rate, and maximized engagement.

Structured teaching is an effective approach based on the learning styles and characteristics of students with an autism spectrum disorder. Structured teaching includes organizing the environment, the teaching method, and the use of visual schedules (Schopler, Mesibov, & Hearsey, 1995). Structure may include the use of colored folders to designate specific classes, written or visual schedules, and the use of planners.

Clarity

Students with HFA/AS may have difficulty with verbal information. Avoid lengthy directions and information that is vague. Limit directions to essential words. Auditory information/prompting should be kept to a minimum, as it can be too overwhelming for some students. Written rules/directions can help the child understand what is expected of him at all times. Directions can be written on the board or can be written and placed on the student's desk for easy access. Reference to the rules/directions can be used rather than verbally telling him what to do or what not to do.

Redundancy

Repetition can be very successful for this population especially if the repeated lesson is presented in a unique way that motivates the student. Use the computer for additional opportunities for extra practice and limit the use of worksheets. Many students on the autism spectrum frequently like repetition because it is familiar. They know what to expect and how to respond.

Content information also may need to be repeated to be fully comprehended. If the teacher finds that a student with HFA/AS has difficulty maintaining attention or focus, the teacher may want to audiotape information and lectures that a student can listen to repeatedly. The student also may take the tapes home and listen to them as part of his homework.

ENTHUSIASM

Engaging the student with HFA/AS can be especially challenging especially if the topic does not include the student's specific interest. Enthusiastic teachers have been found to be effective in motivating students with autism. Some students with HFA/AS may have difficulty understanding and reading subtle teacher emotions and are more likely to understand the happy, animated teacher who expresses joy with his or her entire being.

APPROPRIATE RATE

It may be difficult for the general education teacher to find the appropriate pace for instruction with students on the autism spectrum. Students may become bored if the lesson progresses too slowly and yet may become frustrated if the lesson proceeds at a rapid pace. Usually the student's behavior will indicate if the lesson's pace is inappropriate.

MAXIMIZED ENGAGEMENT

To ensure that students with HFA/AS remain engaged, utilize their topic of interest. Materials also must be appropriate for their academic level and be challenging, yet not too overwhelming to cause frustration. For some students with HFA/AS, maximized engagement may mean that the student works alone; for others, it may mean that the student works with peers.

Optimizing Success: The Use of Visual Strategies

Due to the visual strengths of individuals on the autism spectrum, visual (e.g., picture, written) schedules, rules, directions, and tasks can be used effectively in the classroom to promote learning. They may be more effective than auditory-based directions and have been shown to increase time on task (Bryan & Gast, 2000), social engagement (Morrison, Sainato, BenChaaban, & Endo, 2002), and academic achievement.

Visual supports will assist in organizational skills and concept understanding especially of more abstract topics (e.g., war, courage). Computer software programs such as Inspiration™ and Kidspiration™ incorporate visual learning and technology to help students to clarify thoughts, organize and analyze information, integrate new knowledge, and think critically. Students see how ideas are connected and realize how information can be grouped and organized. With visual learning, new concepts are more thoroughly and easily understood when they are linked to prior knowledge. Through the use of webs, idea maps, concept maps, and diagrams, students can learn to structure ideas and facts.

Other visual supports include the following: physical objects (globes, models), charts, graphs, photographs or drawings, gestures (e.g., the teacher holds up three fingers when instructing students to take a 3-minute break), calendars, and mnemonics (linking a picture to a topic). Even the written word can serve as a visual guide and includes activities such as writing assignments on the board, writing assignments in a planner or journal, and writing/drawing one's thoughts and feelings (Kluth, 2003).

For example, Alice loved historical facts; she could recite what took place centuries ago. But, Alice had limited understanding of time and its relationship to the past. Her fourth-grade teacher decided to create a large visual timeline for Alice. She took butcher paper and placed it around two walls of the classroom. The timeline began with the year 1200 and continued to 2009. As Alice recalled an important date and fact, she drew a picture of it or wrote about it and placed it on the timeline. The teacher then was able to discuss with Alice how certain events came "first" and others "later." As the year continued and Alice collected even more important historical facts, she continued to add them to her timeline.

Optimizing Success: Student Strengths and Gifts

Some students will have an all-encompassing preoccupation with a specific topic or object of interest. Topics may include trains, dinosaurs, cartoon characters, maps, or Barbie. As a teacher, you will note these areas of interests and reflect on how they can be used to improve student achievement and highlight the strengths of the student. Because interests for students with HFA/AS sometimes become all encompassing, it takes a creative teacher to understand how those interests can be utilized to promote academic success.

Joey is a good example of such interests. Joey loved cement mixers. He would run to the window any time one passed by the school. He collected them, talked about them, and even slept with his toy versions. Joey's teacher knew that he would have to include cement mixers into the curriculum for Joey to become motivated to learn. One day, he made 60 copies of pictures of cement mixers in varying sizes. He then placed Joey's math problems inside the cement mixer pictures. He also placed reading passages inside the pictures. Immediately he saw success, as Joey eagerly did his math and read his passages. His work was completed just like that of his peers. Over time, the teacher began to fade the cement mixer from the pages until only a glimpse of the picture was present. What began as an irritating interest became an effective tool for instruction.

Optimizing Success: Peer Support

To promote social learning for students with ASD, research indicates a shift from adult-directed instructional strategies to peer-directed interventions (Rogers, 2000). Although research exists on peer supports to promote social learning, limited research exists on peer supports in the academic realm. In the elementary grades, typically developing peers frequently are utilized as peer supports. Young children may naturally know how to talk with a child with HFA/AS, how to calm her, and how to work with her in classroom activities. They also may be more tolerant of these students' obsessive interests and repetitive conversations. Effective teachers inform typically developing young children about HFA/AS as questions arise and are there as a support system as the young student with HFA/AS interacts with classmates.

In the elementary grades, many teachers have students begin group work. Group work can be difficult for students with HFA/AS, even with peers that they know. When working in groups or as peer tutors, teachers need to ensure that a hierarchical status does not develop where the nondisabled student is seen as superior to the student with HFA/AS. For this reason, all students, including those with HFA/AS, should serve as peer tutors.

Strategies that promote peer interaction for other students with disabilities also are effective when addressing peer supports for students with HFA/AS. Causton-Theoharis and Malmgren (2005) provided 10 specific strategies to encourage peer-to-peer interaction:

- Ensure that the student is in a rich social environment.
- Highlight similarities between the student with autism and his or her peers.
- Redirect conversation to the student with HFA/AS.
- Directly teach and practice interaction strategies in natural settings.
- Use instructional strategies that promote interaction.
- Teach others how to interact with the student with autism.
- Make rewards for behavior social in nature (e.g., playing a preferred computer game with a peer).
- Give the student responsibilities that encourage peer interaction.
- Systematically fade direct support.
- Make independence a goal.

Peer-to-peer interaction frequently involves a medium of exchange, for example, a material, task, or interest that links students together. In the general education classroom, the medium of exchange may be the general education curriculum, specific assignments, and group work. In some instances the medium of exchange may be the student's interest.

Many young children first learn about group work in elementary grades. It is a learning experience to work with others, share work assignments, and socialize. Although this may come naturally to many children, group work can be anxiety provoking and frustrating for students on the autism spectrum. Because these students tend to work best in structured environments, the teacher should assign children with HFA/AS specific roles within the group. In specific content areas such as science and social studies, some students with HFA/AS may achieve more learning on their own than with a group engaged in a hands-on activity.

For example, Charlie loved school, but frequently sat alone to do his work. Because his teacher wanted group work during math instruction, she placed Charlie's desk in a square with three other students who also loved math. She always made sure Charlie had a specific task within his group. Sometimes the teacher assigned him to be the "recorder" and take notes; other times he was the "go-getter" who gathered the math manipulatives. She created small cards with the name and visual representation of the duty of each role. For example, if Charlie received the card with "recorder," it also included a picture of a pencil and paper as a reminder of what he was to do.

Optimizing Success: Plan for Transitions

Two types of transition issues can be an issue for students with HFA/AS. The first is the transition(s) that take place within the school day. The second is the transition that takes place as the child moves from one grade or school to another. The following section will discuss both types of transitions.

TRANSITIONS WITHIN THE SCHOOL

Students with HFA/AS find the world confusing and difficult to understand. When they become engaged in an activity that they understand and enjoy, they are more apt to continue it and can pursue an enjoyed activity for hours. Unfortunately, schools demand that classes and topics frequently change—just as the student gets involved in his math problems, it is time to put the book away and move to English. Although this transition seems simple, it can be overwhelming to an individual who prefers the world remain constant. Transitions may be more problematic at the beginning of the school year as students become accustomed to new schedules and teachers. Visuals can be especially effective in assisting the student to see that a transition is taking place.

The difficulties may be seen as the student changes activities or changes environments. Kluth (2003) suggested the following to minimize frustration of making a transition:

- Give the student reminders regarding the amount of time left in an activity. The Red Visual Timer can be especially effective as it visually shows time elapsing.
- Especially in elementary grades, teachers may have a transitional activity the student completes, such as singing a short song; older students may be given a few minutes to write in a journal and reflect on the activity/ class that is ending.
- Peers can be used to remind a student that a transition is about to take place and may escort the student to the next class or help him or her get the materials needed for the next activity.

- ♦ Create transition rituals that take place at the beginning and the end of the activity/class.
- ♦ Give the students something to carry that is an indicator or reminder of the next class. For example, if the students are going to music, the student may carry sheet music or his instrument to class.

When students reach middle school, they may be changing classes for the first time. They will now have several teachers as opposed to one and may be supported by various special education professionals as well. Because transitions are difficult for students with autism, they may need a few minutes to compose themselves and orient themselves to the new environment. Strategies such as journal writing may help the student to make the transition. The student could be assigned a role upon entering the class; for example, he could be in charge of wiping the chalkboard, emptying the pencil sharpener, or turning on the computers.

Transitions Between Grades/Schools

Students may have high anxiety as they consider a move to a new grade or a new school. The student should have the opportunity to visit and meet his or her new teacher before the change occurs. Take a picture of the new teacher and the new classroom and/or school. In addition, take pictures of office staff, the school nurse, principal, cafeteria, and even the bathrooms. Parents can refer to these pictures and remind the student of the changes that will be taking place. When possible, videotape the new school as the videographer walks in the front doors and walks down the hall to the classroom. Although typical video modeling exhibits a person going through a task (in this case, walking into a new school and new classroom), this type of "perspective" video presents the information as though the viewer is actually in the video. If the high school has a media department, this could be a student project.

Cameron's story provides a good example of how students' difficulties with transitions can be managed effectively. Cameron had enjoyed elementary school but was anxious about the move to middle school. His new teachers created a mock schedule and had his parents walk him through the empty building prior to the start of school to acquaint Cameron with his new rooms and the idea of walking from one room to another. The middle school faculty had talked with his previous teacher and discovered that mornings were especially difficult for Cameron. With that information, they were able to have one of Cameron's favorite classes, math, as his first class of the day. They decided that if the crowded hallways became too difficult for Cameron to manage that they would allow him to change classes 5 minutes prior to the end of the class. That way he could walk through empty hallways and avoid the noise and confusion of his peers.

Optimizing Success: Encourage Independence

All students should have an opportunity to make choices and decisions in their lives. Frequently for students with HFA/AS, decisions are made for them, usually by adults in their lives. Although these individuals have the best intentions, students need to make their own decisions and be responsible for the consequences of those decisions. In elementary school, the teacher can encourage the student to make decisions and to learn that he can impact his environment. Well-meaning adults (e.g., teachers, paraprofessionals, parents) should not become "hovercrafts" who linger over the student with HFA/AS ready to tell him or her what to do and when to do it. Paraprofessionals should not translate directions nor do student work. If assistance is required, it should be minimal and support should be faded as the student increases independence. Even if the student has a mild cognitive impairment and difficulty with language, it is important to take the time to show the child how to strive toward independence. The general education teacher should remember that many students with HFA/AS eventually will leave high school and pursue higher education. It will be in their best interest to make them independent self-advocates who are prepared for life after school.

When John came to Edgerton High School, his teachers were stunned to see his dependency on staff. He constantly waited for his teacher or a paraprofessional to assist him before he started his work. When his team read his previous IEPs they discovered that John was accustomed to supports throughout his day. He was academically able to do the majority of his high school work but would always wait for adult assistance. He would not even use peer assistance, stating that he preferred to work with an adult. The general education teacher interviewed John and had him talk about his future goals. John stated that he wanted to be an engineer like his father. Over the next few weeks, the teacher had John investigate the work of an engineer to help him see that much of the work of an engineer is done without the close support of others. They knew that John saw himself as needing the support of others and not as an independent adolescent. With John, they wrote an affirmation that stated his ability to work alone. He had this affirmation written on his desk and in his planner to remind him to work independently: "I am able to work by myself. I am now a teenager and I need to do my own work."

Optimizing Success: Collaboration

The success of students with HFA/AS is dependent on the collaboration of the general education teacher, special education teacher and staff, and related service personnel. Simpson and colleagues (2003) have developed an Autism Spectrum Disorder Inclusion Collaboration Model that promotes successful inclusion of all students with ASD. Their model is based on the following principles: a coordinated team approach, curricular modifications, general education support, instructional strategies, coordinated team commitment, home-school collaboration, attitudinal and social support, and evaluation of inclusive practices. They also believe that successful inclusion is dependent on professionals (general education teachers, staff, and administration) who are agreeable to including qualified students with ASD and on the general education teacher who assumes primary responsibility of teaching. Although the general education teacher may assume primary responsibility of teaching, it should always occur in collaboration with trained professionals who are there for support.

TEACHING THE "BIG IDEA"

All students benefit from understanding the "big picture" as it relates to understanding new information in the curriculum. Students with HFA/AS may see the details of information but fail to see the gestalt or the big picture. It is important to determine the big idea that your students need to know and identify the essential questions associated with the big idea. The essential questions help students to go beyond factual information to understand concepts, processes, and ideas. Once students see the big idea they are able to connect ideas across curricula areas. For example, Jamie was knowledgeable about math and specific historical facts about Franklin D. Roosevelt. She knew that Roosevelt was the 32nd president of the United States and that he was born on January 30, 1882. She also knew that he died on April 12, 1945. Although these facts are important, Jamie failed to see Roosevelt in terms of the big idea and his global influence. Her teacher used "math formulas" to help her better understand some ideas that were linked to Roosevelt and events have an impact on other (future) events. For example, Jamie wrote the following formula to understand the Great Depression:

Depression = closed banks = people scared = no jobs = life was hard!

Because she also liked Roosevelt, Jamie wrote the following formula to remember his life:

Roosevelt = Japanese attack = WWII leader = D-Day = exhausted = dies 4/12/45

Teachers can identify the "big ideas" that they feel are important for students with HFA/AS to understand but will need to make these big ideas concrete and connected. To make ideas more concrete, summarize the major concepts and put each one on a card. For example, one concept might be that "all things change." Write this on a card. As you go through the school year, see if the student can identify ideas that fall within this concept.

Big Idea	Essential Questions	Objectives
Sometimes people don't get along	What is conflict? What causes conflict?	Create a plan for getting along with another person
The future is shaped by the past	What causes war? Why do people fight?	Write a peace treaty Develop a pictorial timeline for the past 50 years
Friendships affect us in many ways	Who is a friend? How do you keep a friend? Why do some friends leave?	Describe the relationship between literary characters (Frog and Toad) Describe a television character and his or her friend

FIGURE 3.3. Big idea, essential questions, and objectives sample.

Developing Essential Question(s)

Questions are related to the big ideas and are centered around major concepts, problems, interests, or themes relevant and authentic to students' lives and their surroundings. Questions are open-ended, nonjudgmental, and meaningful. Questions focus on understanding big ideas, and suggest areas of investigation and inquiry. One big idea, for example, may be "The future is shaped by the past." A specific topic within this big idea could be World War II. Essential questions that may follow could be "Could a war similar to World War II happen again?" and "Does war have anything to do with my life today?" From these topics, you can identify subtopics that are more concrete: leaders, dates, and famous battles. Develop activities that are focused on tasks that will help students find answers to these questions that leads to deeper understanding (see Figure 3.3).

ACCOMMODATIONS AND MODIFICATIONS

Once the major concepts have been identified, some students will require accommodations or modifications to access the curriculum and the big ideas. King-Sears (2001) described steps for teachers to consider when analyzing the curriculum for students with special needs and deciding if accommodations and modifications are required.

The first step is to analyze the general education curriculum as it already is and determine what features are "user-friendly" and which may need to be modified or adapted. Are there materials already available that address students with diverse learning styles? What aspects of universal design are included in the present curriculum? Story, Mueller, and Mace (1998) described universal design as the design of products and environments that are usable by all people, to the greatest extent possible, without the need for adaptation or specialized design. If curricula materials already address universal design then perhaps no adaptations or modifications are necessary. Unfortunately, universal design appears to still be in a state of infancy in regards to public school education. Simmons and Kameenui (1996) described a model of universal design for curriculum that focuses on the big ideas and instruction that may include scaffolding to enable students to reach higher levels of understanding.

Teachers should then see how the present curricula materials can be enhanced for students with disabilities and determine what will be done if further changes to the curriculum are required. Giangreco and Doyle (1996) suggested accommodations and modifications to the curriculum when more changes are required.

Accommodations

If accommodations are considered, the curriculum content and the difficulty do not change. To make accommodations, the teacher examines (and perhaps changes) the input and output methods used by the student. If the student has difficulty reading text, it may be provided on a tape recorder. An accommodation does not change the content of the subject matter or the performance expectations; students will learn what others are learning and will be assessed by the same standards. Accommodations may include graphic organizers, more frequent breaks, increased time for assignments, different assignments, and use of adaptive technology (calculators, spell checker, etc.). Because many students with HFA/AS have difficulty with future-oriented goals, one accommodation may be to have projects broken down into component parts with specific due dates. To make accommodations, the teacher examines (and perhaps changes) the input and output methods used by the student. If the student has difficulty reading text, it may be provided on a tape recorder. In regards to answering information, a student with ASD may asked to match terms and their definitions as opposed to defining the terms from memory (King-Sears, 2001).

The presentation of materials may be accommodated as well. This includes the teaching approach (visual, tactile, kinesthetic), preteaching certain instruction, highlighting important information, priming (providing information before the class sees it as a whole), dictating or typing answers, and allowing different homework assignments.

Teachers should consider whether homework is really important for the student with HFA/AS. If he or she has been successful in "keeping it together" all day, especially when in middle school or high school, the student with HFA/AS may need time at home to decompress and relax before the next day. Some students with Asperger's syndrome may have meltdowns at home as they enter into an environment that is safe and release the emotion of the day. If homework is asked of the student it should be enticing and rewarding for the student, perhaps utilizing his area of interest.

As the student progresses in school, data should be collected on the effectiveness of the accommodations because it frequently will change over time (Elliott

& Marquart, 2004). Although the student may require extensive use of a planner or organizer at the beginning of high school, his or her dependency may lessen over time. However, for many students with executive functioning issues, the accommodations that involve organization may need to be in place for a lifetime.

Modification

When the curriculum is modified, the student either receives different or less information from the curriculum; the subject matter is altered, performance expectations vary, and assessment of information is changed. Modifications may be slight or may be extensive. For example, first graders typically may learn the names of 10 explorers. If a child needs the curriculum modified, he may be asked to learn only one or two explorers. Students with HFA/AS frequently are intellectually capable of grasping the curriculum; other aspects of their school day, such as the social piece required to learn with others, may more directly affect their success in accessing information.

Some teachers will be unsure about grading. If the curriculum expectations are different, then examinations or assignments may be weighted as well. Any modification to grading, especially on report cards that are sent to families, should be reflected in writing so parents are aware that the grade is modified.

The IEP team will decide whether modifications are required but all team members should recognize the consequences of instructional modifications, mainly that students will be unable to successfully take standardized tests in that curricular area. The need for modifications also should be reviewed yearly because that need may change over time.

Environmental Accommodations

Elementary and secondary classroom factors can affect learning for students with AS. The general education teacher should be aware that frequently simple environmental accommodations can be made to promote learning.

In elementary grades, classrooms may be especially stimulating with colorful artwork, posters, projects, and books displayed on the walls and even on the ceiling. When possible, teachers can slowly add posters, pictures, and projects to the walls as the year progresses. Also be aware of classroom lighting. Overhead fluorescent lighting can be irritating to students with HFA/AS. Some students may wear a baseball cap in the classroom (and the cafeteria) if the lighting affects their sensory system. Sounds of fans, blowers, and heaters, while not noticed by other students, may be heard at the same level as the teacher's voice. Talk with students to gain a better understanding of the sounds that may be irritating to them.

Students with HFA/AS may require more frequent breaks and opportunities to move their bodies throughout the day. Therefore, a seating arrangement close to the door may be advantageous. Although this may be beneficial for some students in need of breaks, placement close to the door can become distracting if the door is left open and the student pays more attention to what is happening in the hallway as opposed to inside the classroom. Other students will benefit by having a seat closer to the front of the room that results in quick access to the teacher. Teachers should talk to the student and to discover his or her seating preference and keep that in mind when deciding seating arrangement. Does the seating arrangement allow for easy cueing and monitoring? Students also should be seated away from high-traffic areas such as the book center. If the student receives support from another professional such as the special education teacher or related service personnel (speech pathologist, occupational therapist) then the teacher needs to ensure that these professionals can easily access the student with minimal distractions to the class.

SCIENCE AND SOCIAL STUDIES

Although few studies address students with Asperger's and science, research on science and students with mild and moderate disabilities exists. Most of these studies include students with learning disabilities, emotional impairments, and cognitive impairments (Mastropieri et al., 2006) and highlight the importance of specific learning strategies for students with disabilities. A learning strategy is defined as an individual's approach to a task. It includes how a person thinks and acts when planning, executing, and evaluating performance on a task and its outcomes (Deshler & Schumaker, 1988).

In elementary school, children frequently are given the opportunity to discover science and *construct* their own knowledge regarding the universe through investigative inquiry. This type of learning emphasizes understanding through hands-on experiences that are concrete and meaningful (Scruggs & Mastropieri, 2007). A second approach is content-driven and involves fewer hands-on experiences and more rote learning through texts. Scruggs and Mastropieri give convincing arguments for both approaches, concluding that *constructivist* and *content-driven* approaches are both effective and that science learning can include a variety of approaches.

The majority of research in science and social studies has not addressed students with HFA/AS. So, how does a teacher decide which method to use with this population? If we look closely at the characteristics of students with HFA/AS (e.g., concreteness and difficulty with the abstract) an argument could be made that a constructivist approach would be appropriate. At the same time, other characteristics (e.g., good rote memory and inflexibility of thought) may signify that the teacher should use a content-driven approach that focuses on the text and memorization of facts. Because research on how students with HFA/AS learn science or social studies is not as prominent, teachers will need to experiment with both approaches and choose the one that best meets the learning style of the student.

Textbooks frequently are used to teach social studies in elementary and secondary classrooms. Recent studies have explored the use of technology in teaching social studies for students with disabilities but most include students with learning disabilities. Boon, Fore, Ayres, and Spencer (2005) examined the effects of a cognitive organizer, Inspiration 6 software, to promote learning in social studies for students with mild mental retardation and emotional disabilities. Results indicated that the use of Inspiration software improved motivation, a frequent concern when teaching students with ASD. Although there is no research on Inspiration 6 software for students on the autism spectrum, the concreteness of the program and its use with a computer make it a viable option for teaching students with HFA/AS.

FOSTERING LITERACY DEVELOPMENT

Deficits in executive function may affect a child's ability to read. This may be demonstrated by poor executive control of language fluency processes required for automatic naming. Many students with HFA/AS tend to be learners who acquire information visually more readily than orally. In their book, *Teach Me Language,* Freeman and Dake (1997) presented information that can be used by general education teachers to assist elementary and secondary students with HFA/AS. Because many students are visual learners, the book presents exercises and activities that promote vocabulary and organizational thought. Freeman and Dake stated that the only prerequisites to using the activities in the manual are that the child be a visual learner, be relatively compliant, and have some form of communication. Although the information may be presented as drills by a language therapist, other professionals, such as the general education teacher, can present the information, providing prompts as needed and then fading the prompts over time.

Teach Me Language includes activities that increase general knowledge by visually showing a way to present information. Freeman and Dake (1997) suggested that general knowledge is the foundation for other learning and that

> Children who do not pick up information incidentally miss much of the information that is naturally absorbed by normally developing children from birth. It is unreasonable and unrealistic to expect children with autism to become interested in age-appropriate information when they have a limited foundation upon which to interpret this information. Therefore, it is necessary to teach basic, general information in a way that these children can absorb and become interested in it. This technique provides a "hook" into age-appropriate information that all children are bombarded with every day. (p. 105)

Topic:	eagles
Main Idea:	eagles are big birds
Details:	nests
	long beak
	feathers
	swoops
	trees
	hunt-sky

FIGURE 3.4. Outline for topical information.

Note. From *Teach Me Language* (p. 114) by S. Freeman & L. Dake, 1997, Langley, BC: SKF Books. Copyright © 1997, SKF Books. Reprinted with permission.

Topics include animals, occupations, geography, planets, habitats, and places in the community. Using a visual format and drill, the teacher reads to and with the child, introducing new vocabulary and connecting information from one area (such as animals) to another area (such as geography). An example of an early exercise, an outline for topical information, is presented in Figure 3.4. Although the child may be reading, pictures may be included beside each word.

A simple outline can help a student learn how to comprehend and organize information. After reading a paragraph on a specific topic, the student then can give elaborating detail from the paragraph as presented in Figure 3.5. Some students may still have limited vocabularies in regards to specific nouns and verbs. Freeman and Dake (1997) suggested the Verb Game (see Figure 3.6) to increase the numbers of verbs in a student's vocabulary. The cards can be sent around the room as each child attempts to add a verb that goes with the corresponding noun. For example, one card states "_____ the ball." The first student might say "Bounce the ball" and then pass the card to the next student who may say, "Catch the ball." The exercise can be used with a small group or whole class to see how many verbs can be linked to the corresponding noun.

A second program, R.O.P.E.S., also utilizes graphic presentations to increase student knowledge. In regards to executive dysfunctions, the authors state that the deficits highlight what students need to learn (Schetter, 2004):

- **R**ecalling and restating information in meaningful ways;
- **O**rganization and planning skills;
- **P**rioritizing and goal-directed behavior;

My Topic: Farmers

Tell me about: farmers

Main Ideas:

        grows things

               corn, beans, peas

        works farm

               gets dirt ready

        uses tractor

               hay

        cows

               gets milk

FIGURE 3.5. Simple outline with elaborative statement.

Note. From *Teach Me Language* (p. 116) by S. Freeman & L. Dake, 1997, Langley, BC: SKF Books. Copyright © 1997, SKF Books. Reprinted with permission.

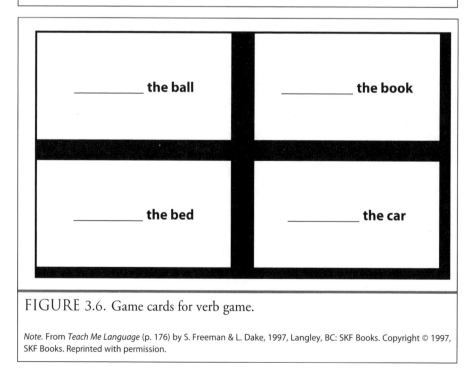

FIGURE 3.6. Game cards for verb game.

Note. From *Teach Me Language* (p. 176) by S. Freeman & L. Dake, 1997, Langley, BC: SKF Books. Copyright © 1997, SKF Books. Reprinted with permission.

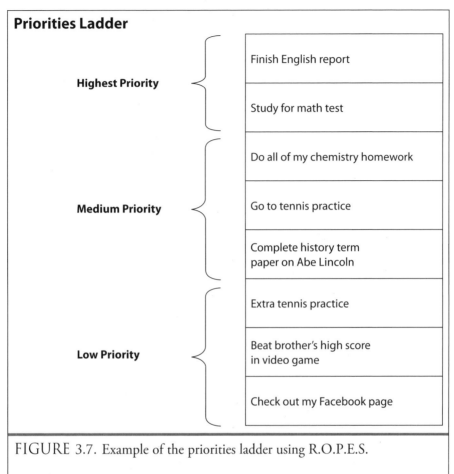

Priorities Ladder

Highest Priority	Finish English report
	Study for math test
Medium Priority	Do all of my chemistry homework
	Go to tennis practice
	Complete history term paper on Abe Lincoln
Low Priority	Extra tennis practice
	Beat brother's high score in video game
	Check out my Facebook page

FIGURE 3.7. Example of the priorities ladder using R.O.P.E.S.

Note. Adapted from Schetter (2004).

- ◆ Evaluating situations, actions, and outcomes; and
- ◆ Self-management.

Their cognitive behavioral approach is specifically for individuals with HFA/AS and other behavioral disorders and emphasizes the use of Venn diagrams, sequential organizers, and cluster organizers. An example of a visual that uses R.O.P.E.S., the Priorities Ladder, is presented in Figure 3.7.

NURTURING CREATIVITY IN THE FINE ARTS

Although art develops the creative side of many children, it can be a difficult subject for some children with ASD. If the child prefers structure and direction it may be difficult for him to express himself with art materials and view his own creations. However, art is the perfect medium for children with ASD to explore because it can help them to express their feelings and thoughts. The use of materials in new ways can enable children with ASD to see how materials can be used in alternative methods, thereby improving their flexibility of thought.

The theatre also may serve as an outlet for creativity and enable students with AS to learn about others by assuming different roles. Scripts are easily memorized, and students with AS may assume the personality of another even more easily than they do their own. Encourage students with HFA/AS to participate in school plays and debate. Some students may prefer to be behind the scenes but it can be a way for them to establish friendships with others while learning more about themselves and the arts.

CASE STUDY

Jane had been teaching fifth grade for more than 10 years. She felt confident, knowledgeable, and passionate about teaching. This year, however, she was faced with a new challenge: Peter, a student with Asperger's syndrome formerly taught in the resource room, was now in her general education classroom. Immediately Jane was taken with this young man who appeared wise beyond his years. By fifth grade, most students are comfortable with their classroom and friends and are looking forward to their transition to middle school. Peter, on the other hand, appeared awkward and out of place. While others talked easily, he appeared uncomfortable, preferring to stand alone at the back of the room.

Jane had met with Peter's previous teacher in August to discuss his academic progress and to brainstorm ways to assist him in the general education classroom. Because the former teacher found Peter to be easily distractible, Jane decided to have him sit in the front, at the end of the row, which would make it easier for him to access the door when he needed a break.

Jane had read that individuals with Asperger's syndrome frequently had intense interests and Peter was no exception. His former teacher said that Peter loved Sponge Bob Square Pants and topics regarding the weather. Jane was surprised to see that this 11-year-old boy was still interested in a topic of interest to much younger children. Within the first few weeks of school, the other children began to make fun of Peter and his unusual interest. Jane wanted to understand what aspect of Sponge Bob Square Pants was so appealing to Peter.

Because Peter was very verbal and always eager to talk, Jane decided to interview him to get a better understanding of his strengths, needs, and unusual interests. She composed a list of questions to ask Peter and conducted the informal interview one morning before school. She learned a lot about his love of books and science and his fear of making friends. He talked eagerly about Sponge Bob Square Pants as someone who always knew what to say and what to do. He said it also was easy for him to understand Sponge Bob and that he frequently did not understand his peers.

As Jane thought about their talk, she felt comfortable that Peter would have an opportunity to shine during science, especially because she implemented a hands-on approach to science. She also used a lot of group work and felt that this would provide opportunity for Peter to become acquainted with a few students more intimately and to demonstrate his gift in the sciences.

Although Peter was a good reader, it became evident that he had difficulty with comprehension and understanding more abstract issues about science. He was phenomenal at memorizing facts but had more difficulty in seeing how those facts translated to larger concepts. Jane began using software that provided graphics and organizational diagrams for Peter and for other students who had difficulties linking ideas together.

In addition to structured group work, Jane decided to assign Peter two peer supports who would assist Peter throughout the day. She rotated the peer supports approximately every 6 weeks so that all students had an opportunity to meet Peter. Likewise, Peter became a peer support to other students in the class. Because Peter was considered a science expert, he supported his classmates who needed further instruction in science.

As the year continued, Jane had occasional challenges with Peter that she could not solve. For example, Peter had a tendency to ask too many questions while she was talking. Other students recognized that they dare not talk while the teacher was talking but Peter failed to understand that social rule. For these problems, she would meet with the special education teacher. In this case, the special education teacher suggested that Jane give Peter three cards with question marks on them. Each time Peter asked a question, he relinquished a card. When he had no more cards, he could not ask any more questions. Instead, he was to write any further questions on paper and give them to the teacher at the end of the school day.

Jane and the special education teacher had regular monthly meetings with the special education team but frequently met informally as problems arose. Jane also attended Peter's IEP meetings and found them to be very insightful. At the IEP meeting she discovered that Peter had a long history of dysgraphia, disorganization, and reading comprehension problems. She shared her thoughts about Peter's strengths and areas in which Peter fell behind his peers.

By the end of the year, Jane felt comfortable as Peter's teacher. She talked to Peter to discuss his move to middle school the following year. She went to the middle school and took pictures of the classrooms, cafeteria, and hallways. Prior to next September, Peter would have an actual visit to his new school. Jane knew that the next year would be a difficult one for Peter but she felt confident that with continued support Peter would continue to grow academically and socially.

CONCLUSION

The student with HFA/AS can face numerous challenges in school that can be met successfully with a collaborative staff who understand that the curriculum is meant for all students. Many students on the autism spectrum are intellectually capable of academic work but issues regarding limitations in executive function may hinder successful outcomes. As previously noted, research on how students with HFA/AS access the general education curriculum is limited. The general education teachers will become the "researchers" as they explore various strategies to see what works best for their students. It will be a challenging learning process, but one that ultimately will lead to success for both teachers and students.

REFERENCES

Arick, J. R., Krug, D. A., Fullerton, A., Loos, L., & Falco, R. (2005). School-based programs. In F. R. Volkmar, R. Paul, A. Klin, & D. Cohen (Eds.), *Handbook of autism and developmental disorders. Volume 2: Assessments, interventions, and policy* (3rd ed., pp. 1003–1028). Hoboken, NJ: Wiley.

Attwood, T. (2007). *The complete guide to Asperger's syndrome.* London: Jessica Kingsley.

Bellini, S. (2008). *Building social relationships.* Shawnee Mission, KS: Autism Asperger Publishing.

Boon, R. T., Fore, C., Ayres, K., & Spencer, V. G. (2005). The effects of cognitive organizers to facilitate content-area learning for students with mild disabilities: A pilot study. *Journal of Instructional Psychology, 32,* 101–117.

Bryan, L. C., & Gast, D. L. (2000). Teaching on-task and on-schedule behaviors to high-functioning children with autism via picture activity schedules. *Journal of Autism & Developmental Disorders, 30,* 553–567.

Causton-Theoharis, J. N., & Malmgren, K. W. (2005). Increasing peer interactions for students with severe disabilities via paraprofessional training. *Exceptional Children, 71,* 431–444.

Delis, D. C., Kaplan, E., & Kramer, J. H. (2001). *Delis-Kaplan Executive Function System (D-KEFS).* San Antonio, TX: Psychological Corporation.

Deshler, D. D., & Schumaker, J. B. (1988). Learning strategies: An instructional alternative for low-achieving adolescents. *Exceptional Children, 52,* 583–590.

Dunlap, G., Kern, L., & Worcester, J. (2001). ABA and academic instruction. *Focus on Autism and Other Developmental Disabilities, 16,* 129–136.

Elliott, S. N., & Marquart, A. M. (2004). Extended time as a testing accommodation: Its effects and perceived consequences. *Exceptional Children, 70,* 349–367.

Freeman, S., & Dake, L. (1997). *Teach me language.* Langley, BC: SKF Books.

Giangreco, M. F., & Doyle, M. B. (1996). Curricular and instruction considerations for teaching students with disabilities in general education classrooms. In S. E. Wade (Ed.), *Inclusive education: A casebook and readings for prospective and practicing teachers* (pp. 51–69). Mahwah, NJ: Lawrence Erlbaum Associates.

Graham, S., & Harris, K. R. (2005). *Writing better: Effective strategies for teaching students with learning difficulties*. Baltimore: Paul H. Brookes.

Griffith, E. M., Pennington, B. F., Wehner, E. A., & Rogers, S. J. (1999). Executive functions in young children with autism. *Child Development, 70*, 817–832.

Gutstein, S. E., & Sheely, R. K. (2002). *Relationship development intervention with young children: Social and emotional development activities for Asperger syndrome, autism, PDD and NLD*. London: Jessica Kingsley.

Heaton, R. F., Chelune, G. J., Talley, J. L., Kay, G. G., & Curtis, G. (1993). *Wisconsin Card Sorting Test manual: Revised and expanded*. Odessa, FL: Psychological Assessment Resources.

Hill, E. L. (2004). Executive dysfunction in autism. *Trends in Cognitive Science, 8*, 26–32.

Individuals with Disabilities Education Improvement Act, PL 108-446, 118 Stat. 2647 (2004).

Janney, R. E., & Snell, M. E. (1997). How teachers include students with moderate and severe disabilities in elementary classes: The means and meaning of inclusion. *Journal of the Association for Persons with Severe Handicaps, 22*, 159–169.

King-Sears, M. E. (2001). Three steps for gaining access to the general education curriculum for learners with disabilities. *Intervention in School and Clinic, 37*, 67–76.

Kluth, P. (2003). *"You're going to love this kid!" Teaching students with autism in the inclusive classroom*. Baltimore: Paul H. Brookes.

Mastropieri, M. A., & Scruggs, T. E. (2007). *The inclusive classroom: Strategies for effective instruction* (3rd ed.). Upper Saddle River, NJ: Pearson.

Mastropieri, M. A., Scruggs, T. A., Norland, J. J., Berkeley, S., McDuffie, K., Tornquist, E. H., et al. (2006). Differentiated curriculum enhancement in inclusive middle school science: Effects on classroom and high-stakes testing. *Journal of Special Education, 40*, 130–137.

Meltzer, L., Pollica, L. S., & Barzillai, M. (2007). Executive function in the classroom. In L. Meltzer (Ed.), *Executive function in education* (pp. 165–193). New York: Guilford.

Moore, S. T. (2002). *Asperger syndrome and the elementary school experience: Practical solutions for academic & social difficulties*. Shawnee Mission, KS: Autism Asperger Publishing.

Morrison, R. S., Sainato, D. M., BenChaaban, D., & Endo, S. (2002). Increasing play skills of children with autism using activity schedules and correspondence training. *Journal of Early Intervention, 25*, 58–72.

National Research Council. (2001). *Educating children with autism*. Washington, DC: National Academy Press.

No Child Left Behind Act, 20 U.S.C. §6301 (2001).

Ozonoff, S., & Schetter, P. L. (2007). Executive dysfunction in autism spectrum disorders. In L. Meltzer (Ed.), *Executive function in education* (pp. 133–160). New York: Guilford.

Pressley, M. (2005). *Reading instruction that works: The case for balanced teaching* (3rd ed.). New York: Guilford.

Prior, M., & Ozonoff, S. (2007). Psychological factors in autism. In F. Volkmar (Ed.), *Autism and pervasive developmental disorders* (2nd ed., pp. 69–128). New York: Cambridge University Press.

Reed, T. (2002). Visual perspective taking as a measure of working memory in participants with autism. *Journal of Developmental and Physical Disabilities, 14*, 63–76.

Rogers, S. J. (2000). Interventions that facilitate socialization in children with autism. *Journal of Autism and Developmental Disorders, 30*, 399–409.

Schetter, P. (2004). *Learning the R.O.P.E.S. for improved executive functioning: A cognitive-behavioral approach for children with high-functioning autism and other behavioral disorders.* Woodland, CA: Autism and Behavior Training Associates.

Schmidt, C., & Heybyrne, B. (2004). *Autism in the school-aged child.* Denver, CO: Autism Family Press.

Schopler, E., Mesibov, G. B., & Hearsey, K. (1995). Structured teaching in the TEACCH system. In E. Schopler & G. B. Mesibov (Eds.), *Learning and cognition in autism* (pp. 243–267). New York: Plenum.

Scruggs, T. E., & Mastropieri, M. A. (2007). Science learning in special education: The case for constructed versus instructed learning. *Exceptionality, 15,* 57–74.

Simmons, D. C., & Kameenui, E. J. (1996). A focus on curriculum design: When children fail. *Focus on Exceptional Children, 28,* 1–16.

Simpson, R. I., de Boer-Ott, S. R., & Smith-Myles, B. (2003). Inclusion of learners with autism spectrum disorders in general education settings. *Topics in Language Disorders, 23,* 116–133.

Story, M. F., Mueller, J. L., & Mace, R. L. (1998). *The universal design file: Designing for all people of all ages and abilities* (Rev. ed.). Raleigh, NC: Raleigh Center for Universal Design.

Wagner, S. (2002). *Inclusive programming for middle school students with autism/Asperger's syndrome.* Arlington, TX: Future Horizons.

Watson, L. R., & Marcus, L. M. (1999). Diagnosis and assessment of preschool children. In E. Schopler & G. B. Mesibov (Eds.), *Diagnosis and assessment in ASD* (pp. 271–301). New York: Plenum Press.

CHAPTER 4

SOCIALIZATION AND CHILDREN WITH AUTISM SPECTRUM DISORDERS

KATHI WILHITE, MARSHA CRAFT TRIPP, LORA LEE SMITH CANTER, & KIM FLOYD

Relationships are all there is. Everything in the universe only exists because it is in relationship to everything else. Nothing exists in isolation. We have to stop pretending we are individuals that can go it alone.

—Margaret Wheatley

SOCIAL DEVELOPMENT

We, as human beings, are indeed social creatures. Being able to interact with others and develop socially not only helps promote personal growth in all developmental areas, it also helps us lead more enriching and satisfying lives. Social development, beginning in the early years of life, is critically important (Hartup, 1992; Katz & McClellan, 1997). From infancy, children interact with the physical and social world around them and begin to build relationships through active engagement and interdependence with others (Ladd & Coleman, 1993; Odom & McEvoy, 1988). These early interactive relationships form the foundation of social development, and this foundation continues to grow and expand as individuals learn, develop, and move toward social competence.

It generally is accepted that achieving social competence is a significant component of human development. However, there is no consensus on a universally accepted definition of the term *social competence*. There is agreement that social competence is a developmental construct involving the ability of individuals to meet the challenges of initiating and maintaining interactions and positive relationships with others (Guralnick & Neville, 1997; Hubbard & Coie, 1994; Katz & McClellan, 1997). As a developmental construct, social competence is manifested in different ways during distinct developmental periods (i.e., social competence may begin with infants' attachments with caring adults, progress to toddlers' emerging interactions with age-mates, and continue to more complex and involved peer interactions such as acceptance and friendships). Consistent components of social development include initiating and maintaining successful interactions and engaging in mutually satisfying relationships with others (Katz & McClellan, 1997). Additional dimensions of social competence include the effectiveness and situational appropriateness of social skills (Guralnick, 1990).

Promoting and maintaining appropriate social development among children is an important issue for parents and educators. Consider the experience many parents and educators have had when seeing the joy of children's play transformed into a poignant and troubling event as an isolated or ostracized child stands alone in a sea of smiling and laughing faces on the playground. Further, observers of this scene may notice that the lone child seems unaffected by the lack of interaction or may even appear to invite negative peer exchanges. A lonely outcast surrounded by age-mates who are connecting and interacting is troubling to watch. Additionally, the child exhibiting poor social skills and experiencing poor peer interactions is likely to have continuous, severe problems in overall social development. The solitary child on the playground may always fall short of acquiring the social competence needed to function in society. Children who have developed competence in socialization will demonstrate skills such as being generous, initiating and responding to others, sharing, following directions, cooperating, showing empathy, and monitoring and evaluating their own behavior (Raver & Zigler, 1997). Researchers have argued that the social competence children develop is important for leading a productive life (e.g., Disalvo & Oswald, 2002) and peer related social competence, in particular, may enhance children's overall development (e.g., Brown & Conroy, 1997, 2001; Guralnick, 1993; Guralnick & Neville, 1997; Ladd & Coleman, 1993).

The development of social competence occurs naturally for most children; however, some children, such as children with developmental delays, experience difficulties with the basic social skills, such as peer relationships, that comprise social competence (Odom, McConnell, & Chandler, 1993; Odom, McConnell, & McEvoy, 1992). Children with developmental delays are at greater risk for experiencing problems in other developmental areas (e.g., cognitive, language) and may be at greater risk for experiencing social maladjustment later in life (Deater-Deckard,

2001; Hartup, 1992; Ladd & Coleman, 1993; Parker & Asher, 1987; Rubin, Bukowski, & Parker, 1998). Children with developmental delays have lower rates of social interaction (Brown, Odom, Li, & Zercher, 1999; Guralnick & Groom, 1987) and fewer friendships (Guralnick, Gottman, & Hammond, 1995; Guralnick & Groom, 1987) than comparable peers without developmental delays. In addition to having fewer social interactions, researchers also have determined that there are differences in the quality of social interactions between children with and without developmental delays. Guralnick and Groom reported that children without developmental delays had more frequent and qualitatively more sophisticated levels of peer interaction than did children with developmental delays. Guralnick, Connor, Hammond, Gottman, and Kinnish (1996) found that children with communication delays had fewer positive interactions and were less successful in initiating interactions than their peers without developmental delays. When Brown and Crossley (2000) observed children with developmental delays during free play in an integrated preschool setting, they found that children with developmental delays spent less time verbally interacting with their peers and participating in group play than did children without developmental delays. Preschool-aged children with developmental delays also have been found to have less sophisticated forms of play than typically developing peers (Odom & McEvoy, 1988). Odom and his colleagues (1999) argued that children who experience delays in acquiring social skills may be at greater risk for peer rejection, thus continuing to limit the further acquisition of social skills needed to develop social competence.

ASD and Social Skills

The category of autism spectrum disorders (ASD) is considered to be one of pervasive developmental delay. Children identified as ASD exhibit a full array of cognitive functioning levels ranging from high intellectual abilities to severe intellectual deficits. The impact of ASD on day-to-day life activities also is quite varied. One child with ASD may have relatively mild impairment while another may have extremely severe impairment. Although the extent and impact may differ, children with ASD will have developmental delays.

Children who have ASD do not follow the typical pattern of social skill development and are not likely to independently develop the social behaviors that are the building blocks of social competence (Hall, 2009; Heflin & Alaimo, 2007). According to Connor (2002), current research outlines three core social skill development features, known as the autistic "triad," by which children with ASD often are identified. The first core social skill deficit present in children with ASD is inhibited peer interactions and social relationships. A child with ASD may appear to want to be alone and resist any invasion of his space by others. These children often cannot give or read appropriate social signals and may even appear to be actively antisocial. The second area of skill deficit in the triad is limited communication.

Children with ASD may have little to no verbal communication skills. For those with verbal communication, their vocabulary knowledge and articulation skills may be adequate but there often is poor use of language and poor understanding of nonverbal social cues that may result in communication being one-sided. The third and final area of skill deficit is the lack of imaginative play or flexible thinking. The child with ASD may lack true interactive play, which is a critical element in the development of both language and social skills.

According to Wallin (2004), social impairments can be classified into the three broad categories of social avoidance, social indifference, and social awkwardness. Children in the category of socially avoidant include those who tantrum or shy away from or attempt to escape social situations. Occasionally these children avoid social situations because of hypersensitivity to certain sensory stimuli. Therefore sensory needs must be addressed prior to attempts to teach social skills. A child who constantly is overwhelmed by the environment is not likely to be a successful participant in any instruction or intervention. Social indifference is common in many children with ASD. Children who are socially indifferent are those who do not actively seek social interaction, but at the same time, do not aggressively avoid such interaction. Finally, children with ASD who are socially awkward typically are functioning at a higher cognitive level. These children may try very hard to gain and keep friends, but are hindered by a lack of reciprocal skill in conversation and interest. Children who are socially awkward may focus on their favorite topic or topics to the exclusion of most everything else. They do not learn social skills and taboos by observing others. These children often are naïve, gullible, and unaware of the feelings of others. Participating in a normal "give and take" conversation is a difficult endeavor for the socially awkward child.

In order to participate successfully in a school environment, children must exhibit behaviors that encourage appropriate interactions with peers and adults. Given that individuals with ASD have impairment in social interaction, it is necessary that appropriate social skills be taught, encouraged, and generalized (Bellini, 2008).

ASD and Communication

One defining characteristic of ASD is impairment in the area of communication, as noted in the text revision of the American Psychiatric Association's *Diagnostic and Statistical Manual of Mental Disorders-Fourth Edition* (*DSM-IV-TR*; 2000). Scheuermann and Webber (2002) defined basic communication as "any set of interactions . . . that transmits information" (p. 166). In infancy, communication is accomplished through the use of eye gaze, gestures, and vocalizations such as cooing, babbling, and crying (Heflin & Alaimo, 2007). In contrast, infants with ASD may not follow the gaze of another, point to objects, or look toward someone who is talking (Hall, 2009). There is a predictable pattern of important developmental milestones in the typical development of communication. For children with ASD, this pattern may be disrupted, absent, or sporadic. Limited communication skills inhibit the ability of a child to express needs or preferences or to interact with others (Scheuermann & Webber, 2002). Developing a functional form of communication is critical in the development of basic socialization.

As in most all aspects of ASD, there is a wide range of communication impairment in children identified with this disorder. Some children with ASD will not develop verbal communication. Those who do gain verbalization may not use sounds or words as a means of communication; rather, verbalization may be echolalic or self-stimulatory. Children with ASD may display challenging behaviors that function as a means of communication. When communication skills that meet the function communicated by the behavior are taught, the challenging behaviors have been shown to decrease (Carr & Durand, 1985).

For those students with ASD who do develop functional verbal skills, communication can be considered as pedantic, lengthy, and "bookish" (Wing, 1981) and may be characterized by a lack of spontaneous conversation. Little descriptive language may be used, while there may be an overuse of stereotyped phrases. Children with ASD often exhibit a lack of understanding of the meaning of language and the function of communication (Attwood, 1998). These children may talk "at" people instead of "to" people. Their speech may be monotone or stilted with an unnatural tone of voice and their face may remain expressionless. Inappropriate gazing or body language may be noted and there may be a tendency to infringe on the personal space of others. Even with functional verbal language, children with ASD exhibit a lack of ability in initiating and sustaining conversation (Williams, 1995). Inappropriate communication also may include too much information, the use of socially inappropriate style (Bishop, 1989), repetitive questioning (Tantum, 1991), and/or the lack of ability to monitor conversation and listeners' informational needs (Fine, Bartolucci, Szatmari, & Ginsberg, 1994).

The Relationship of Communication and Social Skills

The ability to communicate with another person is essential for social interaction. One of three distinguishing characteristics, deficient communication is a hallmark of ASD, making socialization, another distinguishing characteristic of ASD, a challenge. Communication and socialization limitations exist for all children with ASD, regardless of the absence or presence of verbalization.

Children with ASD who have little or no meaningful spoken language present unique challenges for the teaching of social skills. However, as Bellini (2008) states, "Nonverbal communication is the foundation of successful social interactions" (p. 37). Nonverbal communication skills can be a positive starting point for introducing basic social skill development to children with ASD who do not have functional verbal skills. According to Bellini (2008) and Quill (1995), beginning level nonverbal communication skills related to the initial development of social skills include social attention (i.e., establishing and maintaining eye contact); reciprocal interaction (i.e., recognition of the meaning of a specific gesture from others); the use of gestures to communicate a need, want, or preference; imitation; and facial expressions (i.e., identifying the facial expressions of others and exhibiting facial expressions appropriate to the emotion felt). These beginning-level nonverbal communication skills can be taught, practiced, and generalized, thereby paving the way for beginning social interactions.

Children with ASD who do exhibit verbalization may have highly articulate, verbose, expressive language skills with large vocabularies. This is especially true in their specific areas of interest. These language skills can be misinterpreted as being advanced communication skills. Therefore when the child has difficulty understanding and using appropriate social communications, they may be seen as being manipulative or purposefully causing problems. Children with ASD typically lack the social communication skills necessary for minimal conversation interactions in areas such as conversational discourse, understanding and using nonverbal communication, and narrative discourse. A child with ASD may be able to perform routine social interactions such as greeting people but may not be able to engage in an extended, two-way communication. He or she may have difficulty initiating, participating in, or taking turns in a two-way conversation. A verbal child with ASD may exhibit excessive questioning. Children with ASD often have trouble interpreting another person's tone of voice, facial expressions, and body postures. Personal space boundaries and eye contact may present challenges. Children with ASD may not notice expressions that another person exhibits such as anger, a condescending attitude, sarcasm, sadness, or boredom. Some children may talk in monotone and have little change in pitch, volume, rhythm, or voice inflection. Challenges with narrative discourse skills manifest in difficulty in relating past events, summarizing a story, putting events in the order that they happened, or retelling a movie or TV show. Children with deficient narrative discourse skills may be very repetitive. The appropriate social application of conversational skills, nonverbal interactions, and narrative discourse skills can be taught and practiced, and to some extent, generalized. The first step in teaching both social and communication skills for nonverbal and verbal children is the assessment of the existing skill level in each area.

ASSESSING SOCIAL AND COMMUNICATION SKILLS

In assessing social and communication skills in children with ASD, it is important to first consider the skill progression of typically developing children. The typically developing child sets the standard of functioning in the general education environment. Using a set of developmentally sequenced skills allows for the determination of what skills a child already possesses and provides information about the next skills to be taught. Consideration of the typical developmental sequence also allows for the identification of skills that may have been missed or may have developed outside of the typical skill development sequence.

According to Quill, Bracken, & Fair (2000), three basic purposes of skill assessment are "to provide an estimate of developmental functioning, to describe skills needed for planning intervention and to document development and progress over time" (p. 39). Assessment can be done in a variety of ways, most frequently falling into either formal or informal types. Formal assessments are standardized, norm referenced, have required administration structures, and provide scores that can be compared to the scores of typically developing peers (Quill et al., 2000). Formal assessments often are required components of diagnosis and determinations of eligibility for specific services. Because they provide the typical developmental sequence in the area(s) being assessed, formal assessments also can be beneficial in planning intervention and instruction. Informal assessments often provide much of the information base on which intervention and instruction is built, making informal assessments especially useful for progress monitoring.

Many assessments used with children with ASD evaluate both social skills and the use of communication in socialization. A few of the more commonly used assessment tools include autism-specific scales such as the Autism Diagnostic Observation Schedule (ADOS), Autism Diagnostic Interview–Revised (ADI-R), and Childhood Autism Rating Scale (CARS; Quill, 2000a). Hall (2009) discusses additional assessment instruments for measurement of social and communication skills in children with ASD, including the Social and Communication Questionnaire (SCQ) and the Diagnostic Interview for Social and Communication Disorders (DISCO). Quill (2000a) has developed the Do-Watch-Listen-Say Assessment of Social and Communication Skills With Autism, an assessment tool for both social and communication skills that is contained within the larger framework of a curriculum designed to further the development of these skill areas.

In addition to the assessment of child-specific skills, it is critical that thorough assessment is conducted on the environment in which a skill is to be used. Given that most children with ASD do not inherently generalize skills from one setting to another, an ecological assessment will assist in the identification of the social requirements including the activities that occur in the specific environment; the structure of the activities (e.g., teacher directed, independent, small group); and the types of social interactions appropriate to the environment (e.g., peers, adults, conversation, requests, responses; Scheuermann & Webber, 2002).

Assessing the social and communication skills of a child allows for the identification of skills not yet present and/or skills not yet consistently performed. This information, coupled with the assessment of the environment(s) in which the child will use the skill, provide the basis on which social skill instruction, intervention, and strategies can be determined, implemented, and monitored.

Using Assessment Data to Guide Intervention and Instructional Decisions

Bellini (2008) states

> you cannot teach social skills to children until you know what needs to be taught! Not all children need the same intervention strategies, and not all children need to be taught the same skills. Too often we begin social skill intervention without fully evaluating the child's specific needs. (p. 58)

Therefore, assessment can provide information as to the specific social and communication skills that are exhibited by a child and skills that are deficient or are not observed to be present. In some cases, children may show deficiencies in the same skill but be in need of very different types of intervention and instruction. The two children described below, Al and Brian, illustrate this distinction.

Al was assessed and as a result of that assessment it was determined that he was deficient in the social skill of responding to greetings. Further assessment revealed that Al has not yet developed the specific skill of responding to greetings. In this case (skill deficit), the skill needs to be taught to Al. Brian was assessed and as a result of that assessment it was determined that he was deficient in the social skill of responding to greetings. Assessment revealed that Brian has received instruction in this skill and has, in the environment of the social skill instruction, responded to greetings. In this case, the skill has been taught but the student is deficient in the performance of the skill (performance deficit). Intervention and instruction to generalize the skill to environments beyond the social skill instructional group is needed.

Once strategies and interventions have been determined and implemented, it is essential to monitor progress. Ongoing evaluation will let you know if the child is making progress, as well as provide ideas for adjustment to or a change in a strategy or intervention.

Children with ASD are as varied as the general population; what works for one child may not work for another. Evaluation of the effectiveness of instruction, intervention, strategies, and/or specific social skill programs is essential and can include a variety of data collection methods. Interviews and observations are two of the more commonly used tools to collect child-specific performance data in the areas of social skills and communication. Rating scales also may be useful tools to provide pre- and postdata on social skill development (Bellini, 2008).

STRATEGIES FOR INCREASING SOCIAL AND COMMUNICATION SKILLS

Children with ASD are not able to understand complex rules of social interaction; they are very naïve and egocentric (Williams, 1995). Although a person with ASD has social skill and communication deficits, there are strategies that have proven to be helpful in teaching these skills. There are a wide variety of programs and strategies to assist in meeting the variety of social and communication skill challenges presented by students with ASD.

Social Skill Programs

Most social skill programs have three major components: task analysis, sequential teaching, and generalization. There are a multitude of social skill instructional programs available. Three examples of programs that either target or contain social skill development are included for illustrative purposes only: the authors do not endorse any specific program(s).

Do-Watch-Listen-Say (Quill, 2000a), designed specifically for children with autism, contains a structured social skill instructional program based on a checklist assessment of a child's existing skill level. The program is designed to be used in natural contexts and provides a variety of activities for use in teaching social skills in the areas of play (including solitary play and social play) and group skills (including attending, waiting, turn-taking, and following directions). This program also provides a community planning guide and progress monitoring forms.

Skillstreaming (McGinnis & Goldstein, 1997) focuses on teaching desirable skills. Although not designed specifically for children with ASD, the structure of this program may provide assistance in teaching appropriate social skills to these children. Skillstreaming begins with observation of the child's skills and the completion of a skill checklist, followed by direct instruction including prompting, encouragement, and reinforcement. This program addresses many of the social skill issues that arise in the school setting. Skillstreaming is available in versions for early childhood (40 skills), elementary school (60 skills), and adolescence (50 skills).

Originally designed to assist children with special needs in the development of prosocial and friendship skills, *Connecting With Others* (Richardson, 1996) focuses on six basic skill areas: concept of self and others, socialization, problem solving, communication, sharing, and empathy and caring. A total of 30 lessons provide direct instruction and stress the "generalization of the skills and concepts taught to the real-world environment" (Richardson, 1996, p. 7). Instructional strategies include modeling, coaching, rehearsal, transfer training, and evaluation. *Connecting With Others* is available in versions for grades K–2, 3–5, 6–8, and 9–12.

Strategies for Social Intervention

A group of strategies, including Circle of Friends, joint action routines, cooperative learning groups, Social Stories™, Comic Strip Conversations™, music therapy, ecological assessment, augmentative and alternative communication, social autopsies, and Relationship Development Intervention (RDI), are well documented in the research as successful strategies for teaching social skills for children with ASD. Each of these strategies will be discussed more in depth in the following sections.

The Web toolbox in Figure 4.1 highlights a variety of Web sites, providing information on teaching social skills to children who need them. Some sites are category specific (e.g., deal with one category of special needs), but all sites could provide information that would help teachers improve their efforts to teach, increase, and maintain positive social skills. The bulk of these Web sites provide free information. A few of the sites are sponsored by people or organizations marketing specific products or services. Please note, the inclusion of for-profit sites does not indicate the authors' endorsement of any one particular product or service. Rather, the for-profit sites were included for two reasons: (1) each site had ample free resources available, and (2) to let educators know that there is indeed a very large group of available resources to purchase. It is our hope that teachers will use this Web toolbox as a base as they develop their own personal Web toolbox for social skill development.

CIRCLE OF FRIENDS

The concept of having a "circle of friends" has been used in many different types of settings. The Circle of Friends approach for social skills enhances the inclusion in a mainstream setting of any child (known as the focus child) who is experiencing difficulties in school because of a disability, personal crisis, or because of challenging behaviors. Friendships are a significant and important component of our lives. Although developing friendships is "natural" for most of us, children with ASD have difficulty with friendship development. This process can help children learn to build and maintain friendships and help them to develop their sense of belonging in the social sector.

Circle of Friends is not to be confused with "circle time," a routine that occurs in many preschool and elementary school classrooms. A circle of friends is a group created specifically to assist a child in developing appropriate social relationships. Creating and maintaining such circles does not require a major commitment of time from the teacher because the true work is done by the peers themselves. The adult's role is to meet with the circle for 20–30 minutes weekly to facilitate their problem solving in the early stages. This group is more than a social skills group. It has a specific focus that includes learning about social skills through peer relationships and direct instruction. A regularly scheduled Circle of Friends session will help a child develop an idea of what friendship is all about.

Title	URL Address	Description
Interactive Collaborative Autism Network	http://www.autismnetwork.org	This site is targeted to reach teachers, parents, and youth with autism and is maintained by the ICAN project. The site covers a wide array of topics (called *modules*) on characteristics, assessments, and interventions (academic, behavioral, communication, environment, sensory, and social). These modules are comprehensive and informative with accurate and interesting information. The social module is well developed and gives very detailed information on specific interventions that teachers and parents can implement.
Cooperative Learning Network	http://www.lcandler.web.aplus.net/socialsk.htm	Cooperative Learning Network is a Web site maintained by a teacher, Laura Candler, and does a good job highlighting the steps in teaching social skills.
About.com: Special Education	http://specialed.about.com/lr/supporting_weak_social_skills_in_the_classroom/2912/2	This is a good site that lists articles written about supporting social skills in the classroom. There is a wide variety of articles providing a plethora of information about improving social skills for children that need it.
Polyxo.com: Teaching Children With Autism	http://www.polyxo.com/socialstories	This Web site has a wealth of practical and accurate information for teachers of children with autism. It provides a good deal of social stories and information on how to introduce them and use them in the classroom.
Lovaas Institute Blog	http://www.lovaas.com/blog/archives/15-Teaching-Social-Skills-to-Children-with-Autism.html	This Web site describes the steps in teaching social skills based on the Lovaas method. In addition, this site also gives a link to free research articles on the subject.
Teaching Social Skills to Kids Who Don't Have Them	http://maxweber.hunter.cuny.edu/pub/eres/EDSPC715_MCINTYRE/SocialSkills.html	This is an extremely helpful site for teachers wanting to teach social skills and offers a way to evaluate social skills curriculum.
NLD on the Web	http://www.nldontheweb.org	This site has links to research articles about working with children with nonverbal learning disabilities. It is not specific for autism but children with NLD have some similar deficits in social skills as do children with ASD.
Inclusive Solutions	http://www.inclusive-solutions.com	This site promotes the consulting and workshop endeavors of a private group of educational psychologists promoting their consulting and workshop services. In addition to being a for-profit Web site, there is a wealth of free accessible information to support inclusion, specifically social inclusion. In addition to useful links, this site also contains information on current research and literature supporting social inclusion, free ideas and strategies, details about person-centered planning, Circle of Friends information, and an online store for books, videos, inclusion packs, training equipment, toys, and T-shirts.
The West Virginia Autism Training Center: Model Preschool	http://www.marshall.edu/coe/atc/modelpreschool.htm	This Web site features a description of a Model Circle of Friends Preschool Program for young children with autism and their typically developing peers. The program incorporates best practices taken from the field of early childhood and autism.

FIGURE 4.1. When students need help with social skills: A Web toolbox.

Figure 4.1., Continued

Title	URL Address	Description
Social Stories	http://thegraycenter.org	Developed by Carol Gray, Social Stories and Comic Strip Conversations are used with children and adults with ASD. This center works to improve social understanding by helping individuals with ASD to communicate and interact more successfully with the people with whom they live and work.
The National Autistic Society	http://www.nas.org.uk	This Web site provides an autism helpline. This society is based in London. It provides information about the definition and characteristics of autism and Asperger's syndrome. You can retrieve current information about interventions and behavior management skills. Additionally there is information for parents about diet and other strategies.
Baltimore County Public Schools	http://www.bcps.org/ offices/special_ed/ altmsa_autism/Music-Therapy-Page.html	This is just one Web site of many that discusses specialized services for children within the autism spectrum. Music therapy services are provided in this school district to assist students to be functional participants in their educational environment. Music therapists provide direct and consulting services to a student when assessed to show that music therapy is needed to assist in gaining IEP progress.

The Circle of Friends can be made up of peers but also can include parents, other family members, coaches, and church members. The circle can help the child develop social skills including cooperation, problem solving, trust, and empathy. The members of the circle need to include those who are good models for the children. In beginning the circle, potential members are brought together to explain the purpose of the group. This does not mean that a child's disability, or other confidential information, should be shared. In meeting with the circle, the needs and interests of the identified child should be taken into account. Using the interest of the child serves to draw the child initially into the group. The facilitator of the group should understand the function of the circle and direct the group through new ideas.

Supporting friendships for children with ASD is more than placing the child around classmates. It requires a commitment and dedication from the leader and circle members to be concerned about the long-term happiness of the child. The child may not become "best friends" with every child in the circle, but hopefully the child can find at least one friend with whom a common bond can be established.

After reading the information above, research the concept of Circle of Friends in greater detail using the Web sites provided in Figure 4.1. Then develop a Circle of Friends for a child in your classroom. Become the facilitator of the group and train the members to be a support for the designated child in teaching specific social skills such as waiting for a turn to speak and learning social nuances. Select the skills that are pertinent to the child.

JOINT ACTION ROUTINES

A joint action routine (JAR) is a routine interaction between two or more people. Joint action routines look like the many activities that we participate in each day. However, in order to be a true JAR, the routine must be predictable, logical, and repeated over time. McClean and Snyder-McClean (1984) developed the concept of JAR. The goal of a JAR is to develop spontaneous conversation and increase social understanding.

In order to completely understand a joint action routine, Quill (2000b) used the analogy of a mini-theatrical performance. In every performance there is a title to the play. The actors are given roles and the roles all relate to one another in some way. The play has a beginning and an end and the plot has a specific sequence. A script is given to all of the actors and there are rehearsals where the lines are memorized and repeated. As with plays, a JAR consists of a unifying theme, joint focus, and specific roles; is repeatable over time; and may include planned variations. Effective routines have themes that are motivating and meaningful. A theme can be as simple as playing with a doll or as complex as role-playing a cell phone call. Most importantly, the theme can only be successful if the activity is meaningful and motivating to the child.

Joint focus suggests that the participants are willing to attend to the same event and respond accordingly. Interaction is required so there is an opportunity for social practice. Some activities, such as puzzles and games, lend themselves to shared attention or interaction, such as taking turns. These activities give the child the opportunity to share common vocabulary and concepts.

In most routines it is important that specific steps are defined. Examples of defined school routines include getting out homework or getting ready to go to lunch. Sometimes routines are more complex and require the child to play different roles within the same activity. The childhood game of playing post office is such an example. One time the child can be the customer and another time the child can be the postmaster. The introduction of variations allows the child to anticipate what to say or do in certain situations.

In a JAR, there is a logical sequence to the activity with specific steps that follow a particular order. Repetition and practice of the specific steps may be needed. In some instances a precise script is needed; other times the teacher may teach the child variations of phrases to say. Joint action routines are predictable by nature but there has to be planning for variation and expansion. Children with ASD can easily get into a routine of rote responses. Therefore, it is important to practice variations within the comfortable structure of a routine (see http://www.autismnetwork.org/modules/comm/jar/lecture02.html). Be sure to individualize and adapt the joint action routine based on the child's specific goals. In developing joint action routines, consider both the age appropriateness of the routine and the child's ability level. Don't forget to consider the child's interests.

Lesson Plan

Child's Name: Jason   **Date:** 9-5-08
Routine Name (Theme): School cafeteria
Props Needed: Pictures of food, tray, fork and spoon, milk, napkin, meal ticket
Roles: Student

> **Receptive/Expressive Vocabulary:**
> Picture cards of food items
> Names of food items
> Cafeteria workers
> Understanding of use of meal ticket

Basic Sequence:	**Planned Variation:**
Child walks in line to cafeteria	May be in line next to
Picks up tray, napkins, and utensils	different students
Proceeds through food line and	Variation of food choices
tells cafeteria worker what	Variation of milk choice
he wants on his plate	Different cafeteria workers
Proceeds to end of food line and picks	Different cashiers
up plate and sets it on tray	
Tells cafeteria worker "thank you"	
Picks up milk carton	
Give cashier his meal ticket to	
be entered in computer	
Tells cashier "thank you"	
Takes tray and sits at table next	
to his assigned buddy	
Takes tray to return area	
Puts napkin and milk carton	
into garbage can	
Puts tray on conveyor belt	
Returns to table and waits to return to class	

> **Language Target/Number of Opportunities:**
> Greeting
> Communicating order to cafeteria workers
> Response to simple requests
> Saying "thank you"
> Talking with buddy at table during lunch (simple conversation)

FIGURE 4.2. Sample lesson plan.

Figure 4.2 presents a sample lesson plan adapted from the work of McLean and Snyder-McLean (1984) that demonstrates a joint action routine. Teachers should select a student in their classroom who needs to learn a daily social routine, use the lesson plan in Figure 4.2, and develop a joint action routine for the student. Teachers should keep working with the student until the child has mastered the specific daily routine.

COOPERATIVE LEARNING GROUPS

Cooperative learning is the instructional use of small groups in which children work together so that all can learn. Groups are heterogeneous and every child has an equal opportunity for success. One important component that is beneficial for children with ASD is that in a true cooperative group the children arrange themselves so that they are positioned to face each other for direct eye-to-eye contact and face-to-face academic conversations. Another feature is that the children learn to engage in true interaction (Balkcom, 1992; Slavin, 1991).

Cooperative learning is designed for children to work cooperatively and collaboratively together as small teams. The essential components include cooperation, which involves positive interdependence; face-to-face promotive interaction; interpersonal and small-group skills; and group processing (Johnson, Johnson, & Holubec, 1993). In the group every child has someone who is committed to helping him or her as a person. Social skills for effective cooperative work do not appear magically but must be taught just as you would teach an academic skill. Therefore, the outcome of working in cooperative groups is not only academic but also the development of communication skills with one another (Johnson, 1991). Teachers can incorporate a jigsaw activity to teach cooperative learning. Just as in a jigsaw puzzle, each piece—each student's part—is essential for the completion and full understanding of the final product. If each student's part is essential, then each student is essential, and that is precisely what makes this strategy so effective. Go to http://www.educationworld.com/a_curr/strategy/strategy036.shtml to learn more about jigsaw activities. Review what the research says about the jigsaw technique and then develop a jigsaw activity to use in the classroom that will not only teach the academic skill, but also will allow students with ASD to develop social skills.

SOCIAL STORIES™

A social story is a simple method that may be used at home, at school, or in the community to teach or maintain social skills to children with ASD and related disabilities. They can be used to teach appropriate behaviors such as how to get along with peers and how to participate in conversations. Social stories provide an individual with accurate information about situations that may be difficult or confusing. The situation is described in detail and focus is given to a few key points: the important social cues, the events and reactions the individual might expect to occur in the situation, the actions and reactions that might be expected, and why. The goal of the story is to increase the individual's understanding of and comfort with a situation, and possibly suggest some appropriate responses for the situation. It is an intervention strategy that teaches children with ASD self-awareness as well as self-calming and self-management skills (Wallin, 2004).

The idea of social stories was developed by Carol Gray (1991) as a way to provide concrete information to help improve social skills and increase appropriate behaviors. A social story uses specific types of sentences to teach social skills. It is written for a specific child in a specific situation. The style and content will vary according to the age of the child and the given event.

A social story is an easy and effective way to teach children to handle problem situations such as transitioning from one subject to another, understanding social situations, or managing unstructured times such as changing classes in appropriate ways. When developing a social story, the topic is determined by observing the child and gathering information related to the situation that presents problems. It is helpful for the child to give input into the writing of the story. The story is reviewed with the child as often as needed.

It has been proposed that those with ASD may lack a *"theory of mind."* This deficit is essentially a lack of understanding that others have their own thoughts, feelings, plans, and points of view and results in difficulty understanding the expectations of others and an inability to predict what others will say or do in social situations. This theory of mind phenomenon appears to be unique to those with ASD and largely independent of intelligence.

Social stories address the theory of mind deficit. Children are given some perspective on the thoughts, emotions, and behaviors of others. Social stories help the child better predict the actions and assumptions of others and present information about social situations in a structured and consistent manner. They also give children direct contact with social information through pictures and text as opposed to speech or observation. Finally, social stories provide a distance between teaching the child about a social situation and the possible stresses of the social situation itself; they give the child a chance to practice the skills often and on his or her own terms (Wallin, 2004).

Social stories can be used to accomplish several specific purposes, such as to describe social situations and appropriate responses, to correct responses to a social situation in a nonthreatening manner, to personalize instruction for each child, to break goals into easy steps, to teach routines for better retention and generalization, to help the child cope with both expected and unexpected transitions, and to address a wide variety of problem behaviors (i.e., aggression, fear, obsessions; see http://www.autismnetwork.org/modules/social/sstory/lecture01.html#topic2).

A social story usually is a first person, present-tense story used to provide a child with as much information about a social situation as possible, so that he or she is better prepared to face and act appropriately in that situation. According to Gray (1991), there are four types of sentences used to present information in a social story: descriptive, perspective, directive, and control. **Descriptive sentences** objectively address the "w" questions: *where* the situation takes place, *who* is involved, *what* they are doing, and *why* they may be doing it. **Perspective sentences** give a peek into the minds of those involved in the story; they provide details about the emotions and thoughts of others. **Directive sentences** suggest desired responses tailored to the child. They tell the child what to do. **Control sentences** are authored by the child as something of a mnemonic device—a sentence to help him or her remember the story or deal with the situation. Control sentences are not used in every story and typically are used only with children functioning at a fairly high cognitive level.

According to Gray (1991), a good social story has several distinct characteristics. One directive or control statement should be used for every two to five descriptive and/or perspective statements. Choose the number of sentences to go on each page according to the child's functioning level. One to three sentences per page may be appropriate for some children; however, if the child is higher functioning, more sentences may be used. To facilitate the child's understanding of the social story, it may be helpful to address only one concept per page.

There are a variety of mediums for maintaining the social stories for a child. They can be written in book format, placed in a notebook, written on note cards, or maintained in a computer file. Photographs or pictures may help aid a child in understanding a social story; other children may be distracted by pictures or may have difficulty generalizing from a picture. Go to Carol Gray's official Web site for Social Learning and Understanding at http://www.thegraycenter.org/store/index.cfm?fuseaction=page.display&page_id=20. There are many sample social stories located at this Web site. Teachers can review these samples to help develop a story for a child who has a specific social need.

Comic Strip Conversations™

Developed by Carol Gray (1994), a comic strip conversation is a conversation between two or more people that incorporates the use of simple drawings. They provide a visual representation of a conversation in order to enhance the child's understanding of a social situation. The drawings use symbols, stick figures, and color. Colors can be used to express feelings such as green for happy, blue for sad, or black for anger.

The conversation usually begins with small talk and then progresses to talking about a particular situation. Information such as where and when the situation takes place, who is involved, and what is being said is included in the comic strip. The conversation then focuses on what people in the situation may be thinking. Finally, the conversation is summarized.

By seeing the different elements of a conversation visually presented, some of the abstract aspects of social communication are made more concrete and easier to understand. Comic strip conversations can help a child with ASD learn how to deal with specific social situations. They are most helpful when there is a need to convey important information, when there is a misunderstanding, or to solve a problem (Gray, 1994).

MUSIC THERAPY

Music therapy is the use of music to effect positive changes in the psychological and social functions of children with ASD. We can all think of songs that we learned as we were growing up; we can remember the alphabet because we learned the ABC song. We don't have to be music majors to enjoy music. We know that music also can be calming to us and that it has an emotional effect on us. Music therapy can address goals in the social-emotional and communication areas as well as other areas. Music is effective for children with ASD because it is a nonverbal form of communication (Staum, 2003).

Impairment in joint attention is typical of children with ASD. Responding jointly means focusing attention on an object selected by another person. One can initiate joint attention by directing another person to focus his or her attention on something. Joint attention also is the basis of shared enjoyment, which is not just having fun but the feeling that having another person participate in the activity with you makes the experience better than doing it alone. When both participants are having fun, they let each other know it through their gazes, smiles, and laughter. Shared enjoyment is central to a music therapy session (Thaut, 1999).

Most children with ASD have impairment in reciprocal social interaction. The ability to ask for clarification and repair a relationship when misunderstandings occur is a critical skill needed to develop friendships. Skillful use of the pace of music, including starting and stopping of the music during the session, can help to guide the child through the pace of social interaction. The music therapist uses music therapy to frame conversations with the child. The therapist also may use songs that teach specific communication skills such as greetings, when to say "excuse me," or listening or responding to a partner's topic.

One technique that those of us with few musical skills can use is known as piggybacking. This is coming up with new lyrics to a familiar song. Children with ASD often are able to learn a social skill more easily when it is taught to music and once learned, the music becomes a signal to use the skill. Nursery rhymes and children's songs are an effective way to highlight the message we want to teach. For older children, teachers may want to use a popular TV theme song or a rap or pop song. Go to https://www.bcps.org/offices/special_ed/altmsa_autism/Music-Therapy-Page.html and review some sample piggyback songs. Using these samples, teachers can develop their own songs and teach social skills to their students.

ECOLOGICAL ASSESSMENT AS A TOOL FOR TEACHING SOCIAL SKILLS

Most people can tell you how they learned a particular academic skill such as how to regroup in subtraction but they cannot tell you how they learned to "read" facial expressions of others; they just knew. Children with ASD don't just know. They have to learn just as they learn academic skills. That is what makes teaching social skills so difficult. One of the most important goals for children with ASD is to be able to participate to the fullest extent possible in natural environments with other children. Educators of children with ASD must have an astute knowledge of what is going on in the environment and what skills the child needs to know for successful participation.

An ecological assessment is a format that is designed to determine how a child without a disability performs a certain activity in a given environment in order to be able to teach that skill to a child with a disability. There are four components that make up an ecological assessment: (1) identification of behaviors or skills being performed, called an *ecological inventory*; (2) identification of natural cues and correction procedures; (3) identification of performance criteria; and (4) completion of the student repertoire inventory, which evaluates the child's ability to perform the skill identified in the inventory (Quill, 2000a; Simpson, Myles, Sasso, & Kamps, 1991).

The first step in completing this assessment is to go to the natural environment in which the activity being analyzed occurs. The sequence of skills performed by children without disabilities is observed and recorded. The communication skills that occur also are recorded. Figure 4.3 shows an example of this technique during a show-and-tell session in a kindergarten classroom.

Once the ecological assessment is completed, the next step is to determine what natural cues and correction procedures guide the nondisabled. This will assist the educator in teaching the steps to the child. Figure 4.4 provides an example of how teachers can explain natural cues to students.

The third step, identifying the performance criteria, will tell you when show and tell is happening and where the children are seated. It also will identify the average amount of time that a child takes to describe his item. This will aid the child with ASD in knowing how to engage the interest of peers without talking too long and becoming obsessed with the topic. Figure 4.5 shows how performance criteria can be created for the show-and-tell activity.

In the final step, the student repertoire inventory evaluates if and how the child performs each step in the ecological inventory indicated by a plus/minus sign. This occurs after the child is given the opportunity to attempt the skill in the naturally occurring situation. It is critical that the teacher complete the ecological assessment by direct observation. Figure 4.6 shows what a sample student repertoire inventory might look like.

Finally, Figure 4.7 provides a sample form that can be used in conducting an ecological assessment.

AUGMENTATIVE AND ALTERNATIVE COMMUNICATION

Augmentative and alternative communication refers to any system or method of communication that is used to replace or support speech for children whose verbal skills are limited or lacking. Augmentative communication is the use of any

Sequence of Skills	Communication: Nonverbal (NV) and Verbal (V)
Teacher puts her finger to her lips signaling a start of the activity and for everyone to look at her.	Teacher puts finger to lips. (NV)
Students stop what they are doing.	Student looks at teacher and observes NV cue. Student gets quiet and still and makes eye contact with teacher to demonstrate that he or she is attending to NV cue.
Teacher tells students to take out their show-and-tell item from their book bag.	Teacher gives V cue to students: "Take your book bag from under your desk and remove your show-and-tell item. When you are ready to show your item, raise your hand." (V)
The students remove their book bag from under their chairs. Students remove their show-and-tell item from their book bag. Student raises her hand.	
Teacher calls on student to go to the front of class.	"Hanna, come to the front of the class and briefly tell us what you have brought to school today." (V)
Student gets out of her chair and walks to the front of the class with her item. Student talks about the item using 3–4 sentences.	Hanna says: "This is my doll that I got for my birthday last week. Her name is Mia. She is an American Girl Doll. I like to brush her hair and put on her prettiest clothes. It is her ice skating outfit." (V) She holds up her doll so that everyone can see. (NV) Hanna smiles as she talks. (NV)
After the student finishes talking about the item, she returns to her seat. The student takes out book bag and puts item inside. The book bag is placed under her chair.	Hanna then walks back to her seat and takes out her book bag and puts her doll away. (NV)

FIGURE 4.3. Observation of skills and communication in a show-and-tell session in a kindergarten classroom.

aids or techniques that supplement existing vocal or verbal communication skills. Alternative communication is the use of communication techniques that are used by those without any vocal ability. Together these two types of communication are referred to as AAC.

Unaided techniques do not require any external equipment. This means that the individual uses gestures or signs for communication purposes. We all use gestures as we speak, some more than others. We nod our heads, use facial expressions for communication, or use our fingers to point. Children with ASD can express

Identification of Natural Cues and Stimuli

1. Make eye contact with teacher in order to attend to the nonverbal cues (her fingers to her lips) to be quiet and still.
2. When telling about the show-and-tell item, make an appropriate facial expression to demonstrate that you like what you have brought to school. Demonstrate this by smiling.
3. Look around at your classmates when you are talking. See if they are smiling. That will let you know if they are interested in hearing about your item. If they are not smiling, then only tell 2 things about your item. If they are smiling you may tell 4 things about your item.
4. Also, look at the teacher to see if she is smiling. This means that she approves of what you are saying.
5. When you finish and you return to your seat, look your classmates in the eye as you pass by them and smile.

FIGURE 4.4. Instructions for natural cues and stimuli for a show-and-tell session.

Identification of Performance Criteria

Show and tell takes place only on Friday. It takes place after everyone comes into the class first thing and after the morning announcements and the Pledge of Allegiance. Each child tells the following:
- What he or she brought for show and tell.
- Why he or she likes it.
- What you can do with it (e.g., build houses, race cars, fix hair on doll and change clothes, etc.).

FIGURE 4.5. Performance criteria for a show-and-tell session.

Student Repertoire Inventory

+ The student looks at teacher
+ The student takes book bag from under desk
+ The student takes out show-and-tell item (doll)
+ Student raises hand
+ Student walks up to front of class
− Student does not look at students when talking
− Student exhibits no facial expressions when talking about her doll
− Student becomes obsessed with topic and teacher has to thank student for sharing, indicating that time is up
+ Student walks back to seat
− Student begins playing with doll rather than returning it to book bag.

FIGURE 4.6. Sample student repertoire inventory.

Ecological Assessment	
Step 1	
Sequence of Skills	Communication: Nonverbal (NV) and Verbal (V)
Step 2	
Identification of Natural Cues and Stimuli	
Step 3	
Identification of Performance Criteria	
Step 4	
Student Repertoire Inventory (+, -)	

FIGURE 4.7. Blank ecological assessment form.

basic communication needs by these gestures or they can use sign language, which is much more complex.

Aided techniques require external materials or devices such as simple picture boards, voice output devices, or complex devices with computer capabilities. Aided techniques range from inexpensive to very expensive; however, they all have one thing in common and that is the use of symbols to communicate. Often photographs or line drawings are used. For example, cards with pictures of a hamburger, a slice of pizza, or a hot dog can be used with children to identify what kind of food that he or she would like to eat for lunch. To make such cards, teachers can go to their local school supply store and purchase unlined index cards that have a ring through the lefthand corner. A similar setup can be made by purchasing blank cards, punching a hole in the lefthand corner, and then threading a key ring through the corner. Locate pictures for communication purposes on the Internet. Copy these pictures to a file and print them when needed. Then cut out these pictures and glue them to the index cards. This makes a handy communication system when taking community trips or to use at home or school.

Social Autopsies

Lavoie (2005) noted that:

Most social skill errors are unintentional. It is universally accepted that a primary need of all human beings is to be liked and accepted by other human beings. Therefore, if a child conducts himself in a manner that causes others to dislike or reject him, can we not assume that these behaviors are unintentional and far beyond the child's control? Why would a child purposefully defeat one of his primary needs? (p. 2)

Social autopsies are designed to assist a child in understanding and interpreting a social mistake after it has occurred (Heflin & Alaimo, 2007). An additional benefit of social autopsies is the opportunity to teach the concept of cause and effect, a skill that often is difficult for children with ASD to grasp (Lavoie, 2005). A social autopsy is conducted with a child and a helping adult. There are four main components in conducting a social autopsy: (1) identifying the social mistake that was made, (2) determining if any harm was caused by the mistake, (3) deciding how to correct the mistake, and (4) planning to prevent the mistake from occurring again (Linn & Myles, 2004). Social autopsies must incorporate practice, feedback, and reinforcement to ensure success. Social autopsies often include a written framework completed by the child. However, if the child is not proficient with writing skills, dictation to the helping adult can be used (Heflin & Alaimo, 2007).

Relationship Development Intervention (RDI)

Relationship Development Intervention (RDI) is based on the concept of remediation through assisting a child with ASD to develop self-regulation and competence (Hall, 2009). Multiple techniques, such as spotlighting, scaffolding, and elaboration, are based on RDI concepts. The underlying thread of these techniques is the teaching of awareness or "mindfulness" (Hall, 2009). Spotlighting is a technique that assists a child with ASD to identify what is important about an event so that it is more likely that the child will retain a memory of the experience. Actions in spotlighting might include slowing speech for emphasis, exaggerating gestures or expressions, or pausing before saying something important. Scaffolding is familiar to teachers who often use this technique in academic instruction. In scaffolding, supports are provided to allow for the development of competence. As a skill reaches mastery level, supports are systematically removed. Elaboration gradually adds new experiences. Examples of elaboration might include using a known material in new ways, practicing a known skill with the addition of uncustomary background noise, or using a new modality in a familiar activity such as listening to a story that the child often reads to herself (Hall, 2009).

TEACHING TIPS TO ENHANCE THE DEVELOPMENT OF SOCIAL SKILLS

Most children with ASD want friends but don't know how to interact. They have to be taught how to react to social cues and taught appropriate responses to make in various social situations. Social judgment will only improve after rules for social situations have been taught, learned, and practiced (Williams, 1995).

There are numerous ways in which adults in an educational setting can enhance the development of social skills in children with ASD. "Engineered acceptance" (Williams, 1995) describes the creation of situations in which a child with a disability is strategically paired with others for a specific purpose. For example, a specific skill possessed by a child with ASD may be emphasized by creating a cooperative learning activity in which reading skills, vocabulary, or memory will be seen by other children as an asset. A peer in the class who has empathy for the child with ASD may be selected to be a peer buddy. The peer can model and engage the child with ASD in conversation as well as assist the child in other areas. The peer buddy also can engage the child with ASD in social activities such as sitting with the child at lunch or engaging in a playground activity together. Specific and structured activities to be shared with one or two classmates can be provided. Consider the use of activities involving cooperation or turn taking. Tasks or mini-projects to be completed using the computer, such as creating charts to be placed around the classroom, require the cooperation of two or more children. Duties to be completed at lunch or before or after school may be assigned to a team of peers on a rotating basis. The use of age-appropriate games can be very helpful in teaching and role-playing appropriate social behavior. Because the cognitive level of children with ASD varies, the developmental level of the child should be considered in the selection of activities, projects, or games.

Recognizing emotions, feelings, or thoughts of others based on facial expressions or other visual clues may require the provision of extensive practice. In teaching skills related to emotions in social situations, begin with a series of cartoon faces with clearly drawn facial expressions indicating anger, happiness, sadness, and so forth. Ask the child to identify the feeling and guess what caused this feeling (Connor, 2002). For a child with ASD who has difficulty identifying emotions from facial expressions and nonverbal cues, locate pictures from the sports page of a newspaper or from the Internet showing the emotions of players or fans. Ask the child to identify the emotion and tell why the person is experiencing that emotion. Prior to participating in games or other social situations, provide a child with ASD pictures of children participating in similar events or situations and ask what the people in the picture are doing and what they might be thinking or feeling.

Social rules for conversation include how to greet others, how to initiate a conversation, taking turns in a conversation, and maintaining appropriate eye contact (Connor, 2002). Enlist the assistance of parents or other helping adults in the teaching and practicing of basic social rules for conversation such as appropriate manners (e.g., please, thank you), eye contact with the person when engaging in conversation, maintaining an appropriate distance from another person when talking, and how to engage in social conversations. "Engineered conversation" strategies provide a controlled situation in which conversational skills can be observed, taught, and practiced. Model two-way conversation and let children role-play. Have children observe a live or videotaped two-way conversation followed by a discussion of the various aspects of the conversation. Be sure to give special attention to the nonverbal cues taking place during the conversation (Connor, 2002).

Adults in the school setting also can "engineer" a variety of environmental factors to assist a child with ASD in social situations and interactions. Children with ASD need to learn the basic "how to's" of living and getting along with others. According to Myles and Simpson (2001), this is known as "The Hidden Curriculum." These are things that other children seem to inherently know. Direct skill instruction is a good way to teach children how to behave and communicate in different situations. Skills might include how to tell when someone is joking or how to recognize how someone is feeling. The primary disadvantage of relying only on direct instruction in these types of skill areas is the lack of generalization to real-life situations. Strive to incorporate real-life situations into the teaching of social skills. Consider videotaping or audiotaping examples of both appropriate and inappropriate social behaviors in real environments for use in instruction. Provide visual reminders of socially appropriate behaviors through the use of individualized social rules cards that can be taped to a child's desk or notebook. These strategies can help to reinforce what is appropriate in social situations as well as assist in applying skills to real-life settings (Stokes, n.d.).

Children with ASD, even those considered to be functioning at a very high level, have difficulty "fitting in" with others. Assist a child in locating appropriate social opportunities. Encourage participation in clubs or organized activities. This is especially pertinent if there is access to a club or extracurricular activity that pertains to one of the areas of interest for the child. For example, if the child enjoys music, encourage participation in chorus or the school band. Match social interaction programs to the child's specific needs and settings. Programs for facilitating social interactions between socially competent children and children with ASD need to vary based on individual subject, setting, and needs ("Considerations," n.d.). Establish reasonable social interaction expectations. Keep in mind that it is unreasonable to expect social interaction programs to lead to intimate friendships between children. They are designed to increase social interaction and facilitate social skills development ("Considerations," n.d.).

Verbal children with ASD may unknowingly discourage social interactions by talking excessively on a topic of interest or repetitive questioning. In a group setting in the classroom, adopt the circle time strategy of limiting verbal contribution to whoever is in possession of some object while making sure that each child has the opportunity to hold the object (Connor, 2002). According to Connor, if a student engages in repetitive questions or obsessive topics of conversation, there are several specific strategies teachers can use to help limit this excessive conversation. Clearly state that questions will only be answered after an assigned task has been completed, agree to a later time when responses to questions will be given, select a particular place such as the playground where questions can be asked, or specify specific times when the obsessive topic can be introduced. Discussion time about a favored topic can be used as a reward for completing a particular assignment. Be sure to provide time, attention, and positive feedback when the child is not talking about the obsessive topic. Directing advice about when and for how long the child can discuss the favorite topic, perhaps with a signal to indicate when enough is enough, can be useful (Connor, 2002).

Children with ASD may be perceived by some peers as odd and may be subjected to negative treatment. It is important to provide both protection and information about situations that may arise with other children who may be unkind or uncaring. Protect children from being bullied or teased. Teach strategies for self-control when experiencing feelings of anger or frustration. Provide practice in the steps of stopping, counting to 10, considering options, and decision making (McGinnis & Goldstein, 1997).

CASE STUDY

Andrew is a 17-year-old senior in high school who was identified with Asperger's syndrome as a fifth grader. He was identified as having ADHD by his pediatrician when he was 5 years old and was prescribed medication. He was initially referred by the school system when he was 10 for testing because his teachers said that he was lazy, he refused to write, he was very stubborn, and he would not make eye contact or participate in class. The IEP team suspected an autism spectrum disorder after a lengthy meeting and comments made by the parents. He was evaluated by the local TEACCH Center and diagnosed with high functioning autism. Since that time he has had an IEP and has received consultant services in the regular classroom setting. The following is an interview with his mother concerning his social and communication skills.

1. **Describe the social interaction of Andrew as a preschooler as compared to his brother (who is 2 years older).** Andrew was seen as a very shy child. When he began talking he spoke very little and then he went from one word, to full sentences, to full paragraphs. He had an extensive vocabulary and his syntax and use of language was impeccable. His brother was very

social and outgoing and had a lot of friends. Andrew would only play with other children if they had the same interests that he had; otherwise he played alone.

2. **What about social interactions in elementary and middle school?** Andrew became totally withdrawn in about fifth grade. This was the year that he was so withdrawn that he would not talk even if called on by the teacher. He was depressed and had no interest in communicating with others.

3. **How were social skills taught to Andrew in elementary school?** Andrew was referred by his pediatrician to a psychiatrist. He participated in social skills training. This involved the development of social skills through role-playing and game playing. In role-playing, the counselor would ask him, "What do you think my next action should be?" She also worked with him in reading body language including facial expressions and body stance. She trained him on how to initiate basic introductory conversations.

4. **Did that change in high school?** When he went to high school, the principal knew that Andrew had an intense love for music. The principal met with the IEP team and Andrew signed up to be in the marching band and in the jazz band. Even though he initially had no friends, he at least was able to capitalize on his obsession of music. Andrew can play 17 different instruments. He is an outstanding bass guitarist. Not only is he well versed in music and all of the different musical groups and their style of music, but he also composes his own music. In the 10th grade, a new student moved into the school who had the same love for music as Andrew. Recognizing this, the principal scheduled them to have the same lunch. Since the 10th grade, these two have eaten lunch together, had band together, and socialized together. For the first time in his life, Andrew spent the night at a friend's house. He finally began to come back socially. He is highly respected by the band members. The band members look out for Andrew. They remind him to button his uniform and put his collar down. Recently one of the band members commented, "I'm just starting to get into that head of his and I find it very fascinating."

5. **How about his relationship with his brother at this stage in his life?** He and his brother (Matthew) are both in a rock band together. They play for local restaurants. They have played for special events at school. They go to concerts together. Recently they went to a Pearl Jam concert and spent the night and came back the next day. Matthew is the planner and the organizer. He is in tune to Andrew's mood swings. Matthew knows that Andrew has more musical talent and accepts that. He also is Andrew's protector and buffer. He has made it clear that "if you don't get along with my brother, then you will not get along with me." Andrew is confident in music but does not see himself as being as talented as he really is.

6. **Does he recognize his social limitations?** Yes, he limits himself to his immediate peer group. He doesn't remember a lot of things that have happened to him in his life. This can be good in some respects. But the flip side of this is that he doesn't see his benchmarks—how far he has come.

7. **Has he been able to apply his previous social skills training?** Somewhat. Recently, a member of another band was getting jealous of Andrew's band because they were both playing at a local restaurant. Andrew read the guy's body language and came home that night and told me about it. He said that he was afraid that there was going to be a scene at the restaurant. I was sorry about the animosity but was pleased that Andrew noticed and could read the other guy's body language. That would have never happened a few years ago.

8. **Does he have any problems with depression now?** Yes. He is on medication for depression and he is receiving professional counseling. In the 10th grade, he wrote a poem about darkness and sadness. His English teacher told me that it was written on such an intense level. I feel as if he lives in an emotional bubble. He absorbs everything but he doesn't let it out. Sometimes, I worry that he will commit suicide if he doesn't see himself fitting in as an adult.

9. **Do you ever see him cry?** I have not seen him cry since he was in the third grade. His best friend's mother told me that he recently cried when she was transporting her son and Andrew from school. Being around peers upsets him. He wants to be able to catch up socially and emotionally with them.

10. **How does he interact with you (his mother)?** We have come a long way since he was in elementary school. We can have conversations but it can be emotionally draining for both me and Andrew. It takes so long for him to make his point. He will make eye contact with me and he also can read my body language. He knows that if I give him a certain look then he needs to refrain from talking too obsessively or to stop whatever it is that he is doing in that particular situation. He also has developed that trust for me over the years. We can talk about music. He knows that I will not judge him and that we can agree to disagree. About a year ago, I faced a near-death experience. He did not cry but his fear showed up as frustration. He was not as nearly organized during this time period.

11. **What about his relationship with his father?** I realized after Andrew was identified as ASD, that his father also has Asperger's syndrome. They have many of the same characteristics, therefore it is difficult for the two of them to communicate.

12. **Does he maintain social interactions with other adults?** He will talk with his band director. He also will talk some with his principal. He will even let the principal walk by and tap him on the shoulder. He prefers talking

to adults rather than teens his own age. He thinks that most teenagers are shallow and have nothing important to say. He also can deal with adults better because he sees their emotions as being more on an even keel.

13. **How do the social skills he displays compare with the social skills of others his age?** He does not have the same interests as others. Again, he see their interests as being shallow: what movie to go see, where to go on Saturday night, what to wear, etc. His only same interest is that of music. But, his interest in music is at a much deeper level. He doesn't just listen for enjoyment sake as other teens do. He analyzes the music and can tell you the musical history behind the period of time when the music was written. Much of the music that he really likes was during the rock era, which was also during the period of time of the Vietnam War, the Kent State episode, Woodstock, and so on. He actually knows the words of the songs and the historical references. He enjoys the music of Bob Dylan, Neil Young, etc. He can have a give and take conversation about music, and the technical aspects of how movies and videos are made. He is not as obsessed about talking about his interest as he was when he was younger.

14. **How do you see him as an adult?** I am worried because he does not feel emotions as "normal" people do. He also is concerned that he does not feel those emotions. I am concerned that he will not be able to feel love, and the intense feeling of caring for someone else. He also doesn't feel the emotion of losing a loved one. He has told me that he sees himself as living alone as an adult. He would like to enter into a relationship with a female, but frankly, he doesn't see that happening. He definitely does not want to have children; he says that he doesn't want them to have the same problems that he has.

15. **Overall, from a communication standpoint, what would you recommend for other students with Asperger's syndrome?**

    a. I would recommend a system for social cues with the teacher that she can use. My suggestion is that she walk by and put her hand on the desk of the student to bring him back to attention or the task at hand.

    b. If the student appears to be lazy or obstinate that means that the student does not understand the assignment or what is going on in the classroom.

    c. Initiate touch very slowly. Begin by getting close to the student without touching.

    d. Give the student a chance to shine on topics of interest.

    e. Find out the student's sense of organization and don't make him change to fit your style of organization.

    f. Let the student know that he can trust you.

     g. Don't expect an emotional response from the student.

     h. Don't expect him to judge others.

     i. Always correct him one-on-one.

Now that you have read this case study, reflect on the following questions in regards to what you have learned about students with ASD thus far.

1. Based on your knowledge of students with ASD, what characteristics does his mother identify?

2. Were there any surprises for you in reflecting about his social and communication skills? If so, what were they?

3. What would you add to the list of recommendations that the mother made for working with students with ASD?

CONCLUSION

The impact of socialization challenges for students with ASD, both in school and in the larger community, is of critical importance. Socialization for most individuals, including those with ASD, is one of the primary means for satisfying the basic human need of belonging (Glasser, 1998). For children, being accepted and valued by peers and adults in the school setting is paramount to achieving a sense of belonging (Frey & Wilhite, 2005). Recognizing the impact of ASD on communication and socialization, assessing a child's communication and social skills, establishing a functional and reliable method of communication, providing direct instruction in deficient social skill areas, and incorporating daily strategies and supports to assist a child with ASD in the learning and performance of social skills are all essential steps in assisting these children to function successfully in the social environments of school and community.

REFERENCES

American Psychiatric Association. (2000). *Diagnostic and statistical manual of mental disorders* (4th ed., Text rev.). Washington, DC: Author.

Attwood, T. (1998). *Asperger's syndrome: A guide for parents and professionals.* London: Jessica Kingsley.

Balkcom, S. (1992). Cooperative learning Washington, DC: Office of Educational Research and Improvement. (ERIC Document Reproduction Service No. ED346999)

Bellini, S. (2008). *Building social relationships: A systematic approach to teaching social interaction skills to children and adolescents with autism spectrum disorders and other social difficulties.* Shawnee Mission, KS: Autism Asperger Publishing.

Bishop, D. V. M. (1989). Autism, Asperger's syndrome and semantic-pragmatic disorder: Where are the boundaries? *British Journal of Communication, 24,* 241–263.

Brown L. J., & Crossley, S. A. (2000). Delayed children's social interactions focus for intervention. *Australian Journal of Early Childhood, 25*, 27–35.

Brown, W. H., & Conroy, M. A. (1997). Promoting and supporting peer interactions in inclusive preschools: Effective strategies for early childhood educators. In W. H. Brown & M. A. Conroy (Eds.), *Inclusion of preschool children with developmental delays in early childhood programs* (pp. 79–108). Little Rock, AR: Southern Early Childhood Association.

Brown, W. H., & Conroy, M. A. (2001). Promoting peer related social-communicative competence in preschool children with developmental delays. In H. Goldstein, L. Kaczmarec, & K. English (Eds.), *Promoting social communication in children and youth with developmental disabilities* (pp. 173–210). Baltimore: Paul H. Brookes.

Brown, W., Odom, S., Li, S., & Zercher, C. (1999). Ecobehavioral assessment in early childhood programs: A portrait of preschool inclusion. *Journal of Special Education, 33*, 138–153.

Carr, E., & Durand, V. M. (1985). Reducing behavior problems through functional communication training. *Journal of Applied Behavior Analysis, 18*, 111–126.

Connor, M. (2002). *Promoting social skills among children with autism*. Retrieved from http://www.mugsy.org/connor38.htm

Considerations for social interaction with autistic students. (n.d.). Retrieved December 12, 2008, from http://www.teachervision.fen.com/autism/teaching-methods/8208.html

Deater-Deckard, K. (2001). Annotation: Recent research examining the role of peer relationships in the development of psychopathology. *Journal of Child Psychology, 42*, 110–125.

Disalvo, C. A, & Oswald, D. P. (2002). Peer-mediate interventions to increase the social interaction of children with autism: Consideration of peer expectancies. *Focus on Autism and Other Developmental Disabilities, 17*, 198–208.

Fine, J., Bartolucci, G., Szatmari, P., & Ginsberg, G. (1994). Cohesive discourse in pervasive developmental disorders. *Journal of Autism and Developmental Disorders, 24*, 315–329.

Frey, L. M., & Wilhite, K. L. (2005). Our five basic needs: Application for understanding the function of behavior. *Intervention in School and Clinic, 40*, 156–160.

Glasser, W. (1998). *Choice theory: A new psychology of personal freedom*. New York: HarperCollins.

Gray, C. (1991). *Social stories*. Retrieved from http://www.thegraycenter.org

Gray, C. (1994). *Comic strip conversations*. Arlington, TX: Future Horizons.

Guralnick, M. J. (1990). Social competence and early intervention. *Journal of Early Intervention, 14*, 3–14.

Guralnick, M. J. (1993). Second generation research on the effectiveness of early intervention. *Early Education and Development, 4*, 366–378.

Guralnick, M. J., Connor, R. T., Hammond, M., Gottman, J. M., & Kinnish, K. (1996). Immediate effects of mainstreamed settings on the social interactions and social integration of preschool children. *American Journal of Mental Retardation, 100*, 359–377.

Guralnick, M. J., Gottman, J. M., & Hammond, M. A. (1995). Effects of social setting on the friendship formation of young children differing in developmental status. *Journal of Applied Developmental Psychology, 17*, 625–651.

Guralnick, M. J., & Groom, J. M. (1987). The peer relations of mildly delayed and non-handicapped preschool children in mainstream playgroups. *Child Development, 58*, 1556–1572.

Guralnick, M. J., & Neville, B. (1997). Designing early intervention programs to promote children's social competence. In M. J. Guralnick (Ed.), *The effectiveness of early intervention* (pp. 579–610). Baltimore: Paul H. Brookes.

Hall, L. J. (2009). *Autism spectrum disorders: From theory to practice.* Upper Saddle River, NJ: Pearson.

Hartup, W. W. (1992). Peer relations in early and middle childhood. In S. F. Warren & A. K. Rogers-Warren (Eds.), *Handbook of social development* (pp. 257–281). New York: Plenum Press.

Heflin, L. J., & Alaimo, D. F. (2007). *Students with autism spectrum disorders: Effective instructional practices.* Upper Saddle River, NJ: Pearson.

Hubbard, J. A., & Coie, J. D. (1994). *Emotional correlates of social competence in children's peer relationships.* Retrieved November 4, 1992, from http://www.udel.edu/psych/fingerle/article1.htm

Johnson, D. (1991). *Human relations and your career.* Englewood Cliffs, NJ: Prentice-Hall.

Johnson, D., Johnson, R., & Holubec, E. (1993). *Cooperation in the classroom* (6th ed.). Edina, MN: Interaction Book Company.

Katz, L. G., & McClellan, D. E. (1997). *Fostering children's social competence: The teacher's role.* Washington, DC: National Association for the Education of Young Children.

Ladd, G. W., & Coleman, C. C. (1993). Young children's peer relationships: Forms, feature and functions. In B. Spodek (Ed.), *Handbook of research on the education of young children* (pp. 219–223). Hillsdale, NJ: Lawrence Erlbaum Associates.

Lavoie, R. (2005). *Social skill autopsies: A strategy to promote and develop social competencies.* Retrieved from http://www.ldonline.org/article/14910

Linn, A., & Myles, B. S. (2004). Asperger syndrome and six strategies for success. *Beyond Behavior, 14,* 3–9.

McGinnis, E., & Goldstein, A. P. (1997). *Skillstreaming the elementary school child: New strategies and perspectives for teaching prosocial skills.* Champaign, IL: Research Press.

McLean, J., & Snyder-McLean, L. (1984). Recent developments in pragmatics: Remedial implication. In D. J. Muller (Ed.), *Remediating children's language* (pp. 55–82). San Diego, CA: College Hill.

Myles, B., & Simpson, R. (2001). Understanding the hidden curriculum: An essential social skill for children and youth with Asperger syndrome. *Intervention in School and Clinic, 36,* 279–291.

Odom, S. L., & McEvoy, M. A. (1988). Integration of young children with handicaps and normally developing children. In S. Odom & M. Karnes (Eds.), *Early intervention for infants and children with handicaps: An empirical base* (pp. 241–248). Baltimore: Paul H. Brookes.

Odom, S. L., McConnell, S. R., & Chandler, L. K. (1993). Acceptability and feasibility of classroom-based social interaction interventions for young children. *Exceptional Children, 60,* 226–236.

Odom, S. L., McConnell, S. R., & McEvoy, M. A. (1992). Peer social competence intervention for young children with disabilities. In S. L. Odom, S. R. McConnell, & M. A. McEvoy (Eds.), *Social competence of young children with disabilities: Issues and strategies for intervention* (pp. 3–35). Baltimore: Paul H. Brookes.

Odom, S. L., McConnell, S. R., McEvoy, M. A., Peterson, C., Ostrosky, M., Chandler, L. K., et al. (1999). Relative effects of interventions supporting the social competence of young children with disabilities. *Topics in Early Childhood Special Education, 19,* 75–95.

Parker, J. G., & Asher, S. R. (1987). Peer relations and later personal adjustment: Are low-accepted children at risk? *Psychological Bulletin, 102,* 357–389.

Quill, K. A. (Ed.). (1995). *Teaching children with autism: Strategies to enhance communication and socialization.* Albany, NY: Delmar.

Quill, K. A. (2000a). *Do-watch-listen-say.* Baltimore: Paul H. Brookes.

Quill, K. A. (2000b). *Joint action routine.* Retrieved from http://www.autismnetwork.org modules/comm/jar/index.html

Quill, K. A., Bracken, N., & Fair, M. (2000). *Children with disabilities.* Baltimore: Paul H. Brookes.

Raver, C. C., & Zigler, E. F. (1997). Social competence: An untapped dimension in evaluating Head Start's success. *Early Childhood Research Quarterly, 12,* 363–385.

Richardson, R. (1996). *Connecting with others.* Champaign, IL: Research Press.

Rubin, K. H., Bukowski, W., & Parker, J. G. (1998). Peer interactions, relationships, and groups. In W. Damon & N. Eisenberg (Eds.), *Handbook of child psychology: Vol. 3* (5th ed., pp. 619–700). New York: Wiley.

Scheuermann, B., & Webber, J. (2002). *Autism: Teaching does make a difference.* Belmont, CA: Wadsworth Group.

Simpson, R. L., Myles, B. S., Sasso, G. M., & Kamps, D. M. (1991). *Social skills development for students with autism.* Reston, VA: Council for Exceptional Children.

Slavin, R. J. (1991). Syntheses of research on cooperative learning. *Educational Leadership, 48,* 71–82.

Staum, M. J. (2003). *Music therapy and language for the autistic child.* Retrieved August 9, 2003, from http://www.autism.org/music.html

Stokes, S. (n.d.). *Children with Asperger's syndrome: Characteristics/learning styles and intervention strategies.* Retrieved December 12, 2008, from http://www.specialed.us/autism/asper/asper11.html

Tantum, D. (1991). Asperger's syndrome in adulthood. In U. Frith (Ed.), *Autism and Asperger syndrome* (pp. 147–183). Cambridge, England: Cambridge University Press.

Thaut, M. H. (1999). Music therapy with autistic children. In W. B. Davis, K. E. Gfeller, & M. H. Thaut (Eds.), *An introduction to music therapy: Theory and practice* (2nd ed., pp. 180–196). Dubuque, IA: McGraw-Hill.

Wallin, J. (2004). *Social stories.* Retrieved from http://www.polyxo.com/socialstories/introduction.html

Williams, K. (1995). Understanding the student with Asperger's syndrome: Guidelines for teachers. *Focus On Autistic Behavior, 10,* 9–16.

Wing, L. (1981). Asperger's syndrome: A clinical account. *Psychological Medicine, 11,* 115–129.

CHAPTER 5

BEHAVIORAL INTERVENTIONS FOR CHILDREN AND YOUTH WITH AUTISM SPECTRUM DISORDERS

STACEY JONES BOCK, JEFFREY P. BAKKEN, & NICHELLE KEMPEL-MICHALAK

CHILDREN and youth with autism spectrum disorders (ASD) are being included in the general education environment at an increasing rate (Conroy, Asmus, Sellers, & Ladwig, 2005; Hundert, 2007; Kluth, 2003; Simpson, de Boer-Ott, & Smith-Myles, 2003; Smith-Myles, Simpson, & de Boer-Ott, 2008; Webber & Scheuermann, 2008). This is due in part to two driving forces: the overall increase of children being diagnosed on the spectrum (Centers for Disease Control and Prevention, 2007) and changes to the least restrictive environment (LRE) provision in the 1997 Reauthorization of the Individuals with Disabilities Education Improvement Act (IDEA; Simpson et al., 2003). These forces have required schools to react responsibly and creatively to formulate effective plans for including students with disabilities.

Many children with and without disabilities can exhibit challenging behaviors. Children and youth with ASD, in particular, exhibit behaviors that often interfere with their participation and provide disruption to the participation of other children in the education environment (Conroy et al., 2005). This chapter will serve as a guide to teachers supporting students with ASD in the general education environment. The chapter will review the common behavioral characteristics of children and youth on the autism spectrum, provide a description of the process for how teachers can determine the function of the child's behavior, discuss the steps for completing a functional behavior assessment, and offer a procedure for writing a supportive behavior intervention plan.

Behavioral Characteristics

Describing the behavioral characteristics of children and youth with ASD can be a difficult task. As the saying goes, "Once you have met one person with autism, you have met one person with autism." Every child on the autism spectrum is a unique individual; no two are alike. There are, however, common behavior characteristics that can be seen in children and youth with ASD to varying degrees. These common behavioral characteristics include stereotypic behavior, self-stimulatory behavior, distractibility, impulsivity, obsessive insistence on routine and the need for sameness, perseveration, and aggression (American Psychiatric Association, 2000; Conroy et al., 2005; Heflin & Alaimo, 2007; Simpson et al., 2003; Simpson, Smith-Myles, & LaCava, 2008; Webber & Scheuermann, 2008). Each of these behaviors directly impacts the learning and socialization of children and youth on the spectrum.

Stereotypic and Self-Stimulatory Behavior

Stereotypical behaviors often are seen as nonadaptive, meaning they have no obvious purpose or function for personal independence or social sufficiency (Sparrow, Balla, & Cicchetti, 1984). Stereotypic behaviors include repetitive motor movements such as hand flapping or rocking and verbalizations such as humming or the repetition of words or phrases (Fouse & Wheeler, 2005). Stereotypic behaviors also are seen as self-stimulatory in nature (Conroy et al., 2005). Even though they have no adaptive function, they may soothe or provide comfort to the child by creating predictability and routine (Simpson et al., 2008).

Distractibility and Impulsivity

Short attention span, inattentiveness, or an inability to attend to important things in the environment also are hallmark characteristics of children and youth with ASD. Children and adolescents on the spectrum often receive a comorbid diagnosis of attention deficit hyperactivity disorder (ADHD). There is much disagreement in the field as to whether it is a true differential diagnosis or only a strong characteristic found in some variants of ASD (Lecavalier, 2006).

Insistence on Routine and Need for Sameness

Children and youth with ASD often exhibit an insistence upon routine or a need for sameness (American Psychiatric Association, 2000). They like things to look the same and things to be done the exact same way every time. For instance, changing the classroom desk arrangement could be very unsettling to students with ASD. At times they also are inflexible with changes in their daily schedules or with changes in individuals within their environment. When unexpected changes occur, children and youth with ASD can react with protest, an unwillingness to cooperate, or even aggression.

Perseverative Behavior

Perseveration is the persistent repetition of a thought pattern or repetition of a behavior or activity for a long period of time (Heflin & Alaimo, 2007). It also includes an all-encompassing preoccupation or restricted pattern of interest (American Psychiatric Association, 2000). Common perseverative behaviors include ordering objects in the environment, creating seemingly nonfunctional rules, and all-encompassing preoccupations and restricted interests. Children and youth with ASD can become so obsessed with restricted interests that it literally takes over their life; they can have difficulty thinking, talking, or reading about anything else. They can get to the point that they seem lost in the preoccupation. It is easy to see how perseverative behavior can interfere with learning in the general education environment.

Aggressive Behaviors

Aggression is one of the most serious and debilitating behaviors a child or adolescent on the spectrum can exhibit. Aggression can be divided into two categories: physical aggression and verbal aggression. Physical aggression is any action applied to a person or object with intent to inflict harm or damage. Verbal aggression includes profanity, name calling, or threatening another individual (Fouse & Wheeler, 2005). Aggressive behavior secludes the child from the community and at times from his or her own family. Aggressive behaviors fall under a "no tolerance" policy for most schools.

Comparison to Typical Behavior

Children with ASD also exhibit many of the same behaviors that typically developing children exhibit. The difference lies in the intensity with which the child engages in the behavior. For example, a typically developing child may have an interest in a video game. The child may talk about it with his friends, play it after school, and formulate strategies for beating the game. A child with ASD also may have an interest in a video game. However, for the child with ASD, that interest can become an obsession. The child with ASD may not want to go to school because he wants to play the game. If he goes to school, he may repeatedly request the game or only engage in conversations that are focused on the game. In fact, he may exhibit aggressive behaviors if he is told he cannot play the game.

Behavioral Characteristics Summary

With the rise in the prevalence of ASD, inclusion of children and youth on the spectrum will only increase in the coming decades (Simpson et al., 2003). Every child on the autism spectrum is a unique individual; however, there are common behavioral characteristics that can be seen in varying degrees across the spectrum. Behavioral characteristics, such as stereotypies and perseveration, that are inherently a part of an autism spectrum diagnosis, can pose significant challenges to families and classroom teachers. In order to address these challenges, individuals supporting the child or adolescent with ASD must rely on evidence-based methods such as functional behavior assessment to replace the unwanted behaviors.

DETERMINING THE FUNCTION OF BEHAVIOR

"If a child doesn't know how to read, *we teach*." "If a child doesn't know how to multiply, *we teach*." "If a child doesn't know how to behave, *we* . . ." Why can't this last sentence be finished as automatically as the others? Traditionally, inappropriate behavior has been dealt with by using general interventions that were reactive and somewhat punitive in nature. These strategies were applied after the child had engaged in an inappropriate behavior in an effort to deliver a powerful enough consequence that the child would not engage in the inappropriate behavior again. Reactive strategies provided a "quick fix" for getting the child to stop the behavior. Unfortunately, reactive or punitive consequences only work for short periods of time, they rarely result in overall behavior change, and they do not address the purpose or the function of the child's or adolescent's behavior. For instance, if a child were to do something that he was not supposed to do such as throw a book across the room, he might be placed in time-out regardless of the purpose or function of the behavior. Unfortunately, without determining the function of a child's inappropriate behavior, the behavior could be unintentionally reinforced. The child may have thrown the book to get out of transitioning to another subject or to get out of completing an assignment.

The use of positive behavior supports, more specifically, functional behavior analysis, provides a proactive approach that identifies the communicative function of the child's behavior and ultimately provides information that is needed to develop an intervention that will replace the inappropriate behavior or prevent the behavior from occurring in the first place. Positive behavior support (PBS) is a construct that uses proactive, positive behavioral intervention procedures for analyzing the communicative intent of behavior and designing individualized programs that promote social growth and autonomy (Sugai et al., 2000). Functional behavior assessment (FBA) is the process of identifying the functions associated with a challenging behavior, the identification of a hypothesis for why the behavior occurs, and the development of an intervention that will replace the challenging behavior with a socially appropriate alternative (Scheuermann & Hall, 2008; Sugai et al., 2000).

Historical Foundation of Positive Behavior Support and Functional Behavior Assessment

To understand why functional behavior assessment (FBA) is an important and necessary process in behavioral support and behavioral change, it is necessary to understand historically how we arrived at this process. PBS and FBA have their roots in applied behavior analysis. Although PBS and FBA, in concept, are at least as old as behavioral psychology, the current trend toward widespread implementation in schools began in the 1990s (Horner et al., 1990).

FBA originally was used clinically in the 1960s and 1970s to try to understand why individuals with significant disabilities engaged in aggression and self-injurious behavior (Durand & Carr, 1985). FBA was an emerging concept but not the primary behavioral philosophy of the time. This was the age of psychoanalysis, which had an emphasis on getting rid of inappropriate behavior or moving the individual through the behavior by trying to understand where the individual was in the process of psychodevelopment. What developmental stage the individual was able to complete, what conflict was present in the psychological process, and how the individual could move to the next developmental stage were all important questions to the psychoanalyst. The primary intervention applied by the psychoanalyst was counseling.

In the 1970s and 1980s, FBA was still clinically present but behavioral modification was the guiding philosophy. Behavioral modification had an emphasis on eliminating the inappropriate behavior. Sometimes negative approaches were used to eliminate the inappropriate behavior—approaches that may have been punishing to the individual (Alberto & Troutman, 2006). What was important about this time in history is that we learned that negative behavioral approaches did not have long-term impact on behavioral change. We also learned that if we did not replace the inappropriate behavior then the individual would begin to exhibit an equally inappropriate behavior or worse.

In the 1990s, FBA stepped out of the clinics and into the classrooms. Furthermore, the reauthorization of IDEA in 1997 mandated the FBA process by law under certain circumstances (Scheuermann & Hall, 2008; Sugai et al., 2000). The mandate required that schools must perform an FBA for any student placed in an interim alternative education setting, at risk for suspension for up to 10 days, undergoing a change of placement to a more restrictive setting, or for any student whose behavior impeded his or her learning or the learning of others.

FBA is a valuable tool for educators and IEP teams (Scheuermann & Hall, 2008). Professionally, you should conduct an FBA whenever you can answer "yes" to any of the following questions:

- Does the child fail to respond to consequences?

- Have you ever thought the child is just being defiant?
- Is the child or adolescent exhibiting the behavior all of the time?
- Does the behavior cause the child or adolescent social isolation?

If you answered yes, functional behavior assessment is going to be the process for you. Most importantly, you should professionally perform an FBA anytime the behavior impacts the individual's or family's quality of life.

Steps for Completing a Functional Behavior Assessment

When adopting the FBA philosophy and committing to completing the process, there are three guiding principles that need to be embraced: (1) children engage in inappropriate behavior because it works for them—they are receiving a reward or a "pay-off"; (2) behavior serves a purpose that is functional for the individual, whether it is positive or negative; and (3) children with ASD, even children who have verbose expressive language, have significant issues with communication; therefore, they communicate using their behavior. FBAs are completed to determine the function of the child's or adolescent's behavior. Once we have identified the function we can design a behavior support plan that includes interventions that teach positive replacement behaviors to help the child meet individual needs in a more effective, socially desirable manner (Scott & Nelson, 1999). Sugai and colleagues (2000) identified six main steps involved in conducting an FBA and developing a behavioral support plan. The following steps were further defined and clarified using the work of Alberto and Troutman (2006); Cooper, Heron, and Heward (2007); and Scott and Nelson (1999). They include identifying the target behavior, collecting indirect information, developing a hypothesis, collecting observational data, and writing a behavior support plan.

The Team as a Part of the FBA Process

The Individual Education Program (IEP) team, which includes the student's parents, completes the FBA. When meeting as a team, meet at times that are convenient for the family, set up the environment and arrange the room to facilitate equal exchanges between all team members, state the goals and the agenda, and be sure to set starting and ending times for the meeting. Always remove jargon from the process so that everyone is on the same page.

One person should not be responsible for gathering all of the information and conducting the FBA; however, one person may be the case manager and oversee and coordinate the process. It also is important to consider who will be collecting the information. Who will be responsible for summarizing and displaying the information? When and how often will the information be collected? Who will meet, and when and how often will they meet, to review and discuss the information for decision making? Specifying and outlining this information with the team helps outline an action plan so everyone involved is aware of his or her responsibilities.

Step One: Identifying the Target Behavior

The first step in the FBA process is identifying and defining the target behavior. When identifying a behavior, it's important to prioritize and select only one or two behaviors to replace at a time. Targeting more than two behaviors at a time causes confusion and possibly makes the FBA process invalid. Priority can be determined based on the severity of the behavior, the level to which it impedes socialization, or by the degree to which it impacts the student and his or her family. For example, some behaviors are so severe, such as physical aggression, that they pose a safety concern for the student or the safety of other students. Physical aggression would likely receive a higher priority than the behavior of removing items from other student's desks.

After selecting a target behavior, the behavior must be operationally defined. Specifically defining the behavior using clear, observable terms makes the behavior more objective. An observer must be able to clearly determine whether the behavior occurred or did not occur. Another way to test the definition is to see if it passes the "stranger test." Could a complete stranger read the operational definition and identify whether or not the student had exhibited the behavior? If the answer is yes, then the behavior is clear, observable, and measurable. Observable behaviors are described by action verbs such as touching, walking, saying, or writing. These do not include feelings or intentions inferred from other behaviors. For example, the behavior "refuses to do work" is not operationally defined, observable, or measurable because the description can mean different things to different people. Operationally defining "refuses to do work" for one student may be "Joe crosses his arms across his chest, looks away from the teacher, and says, 'No, I'm not going to do that.'" For another student the definition may look a little different—"Bryan crawls under his desk, puts his head on his knees, and makes a humming vocalization." Would an observer have been able to identify Joe or Bryan from the original description of "refuses to do work?" Figure 5.1 contains examples of well-written and poorly written operational definitions.

When performing an FBA it also is important to obtain information from other people. By targeting a specific behavior, everyone involved in the process will be able to recognize and agree when the behavior is occurring. This also ensures objectivity. When a behavior is objective we are more likely to obtain an accurate recording of data and gain information that we can use to support the child.

Well-Written	Poorly Written
Jimmy hits peers with a closed fist and bites his arm leaving teeth indentions.	Jimmy displays aggressive behavior.
Taylor gets out of his seat and talks to peers during independent seatwork.	Taylor is off-task.
Kyle threatens peers by verbalizing, "I'm going to kill you" while pointing a finger gun.	Kyle is mean to his peers.

FIGURE 5.1. Examples of operational definitions.

Step Two: Collect Information About the Behavior Using Indirect Methods

Gather information about the target behavior through indirect methods. Indirect methods include interviews and a review of records. Interviews can provide valuable information about the student and the challenging behavior. An interview is used to ask parents, teachers, or anyone else who interacts with the child or adolescent specific questions about the behavior that's being exhibited, including what the behavior looks like, when it occurs, and what happens before and after the behavior occurs.

Using a structured interview format will help to ensure that each interviewee is asked the same questions. The Functional Assessment Interview Form (O'Neill et al., 1997) is one example of a comprehensive, semistructured interview tool used to help define the many variables that help predict a child's challenging behavior. This classic form begins with a description about the behavior, helps define the antecedents and consequences and other important information, and concludes with hypotheses and summary statements (see Figure 5.2 for an adapted version of this form). Another useful structured interview form is the Motivation Assessment Scale (MAS; Durand & Crimmins, 1992). The MAS is a 16-question structured form that identifies the function of the challenging behavior as either obtaining attention, escaping or avoiding nonpreferred activities, obtaining preferred items or activities, or providing sensory stimulation. It was designed to focus on one behavior at a time; therefore, separate MAS forms should be completed if there are multiple behaviors (Johnston & O'Neill, 2001). The MAS is shown in Figure 5.3.

Other indirect ways of gathering data include reviewing school records including IEPs, case study documents, previously completed functional assessments, behavior support plans, attendance data, daily logs, and portfolios of student work and achievement data. Paying close attention to personal and school-related environmental factors increases the likelihood that your hypothesis will be correct. Personal and family factors that may increase the challenging behavior include abuse, neglect, poverty, poor nutrition, divorce, loss of work for parents, health

Functional Behavior Assessment

Student:	Grade:	Date:

A. FBA TEAM MEMBERS

Please provide your name and title.

_____

_____

_____

_____

_____

_____

_____

_____

B. SOURCES OF INFORMATION

Please select the sources used:
- ❏ Anecdotal information provided by parents
- ❏ Diagnostic evaluation(s) completed by:
    - ❏ School district
    - ❏ Outside agency
- ❏ Interviews completed by:
    - ❏ Parent
    - ❏ Student
    - ❏ Teacher
    - ❏ Other professional

- ❏ Classroom/school observation
- ❏ Attendance records
- ❏ Discipline records

- ❏ Behavior Rating Scales
    - ❏ IEP(s)
    - ❏ Other: _____
    - ❏ Other: _____

C. STUDENT INFORMATION

1. Describe the student's behavioral strengths (i.e., positive interactions with staff and peers, accepts responsibility, ignores inappropriate behavior of peers, etc.).

2. Describe the things the student enjoys. For example, what makes him or her happy? What might someone do or provide that makes the child happy?

3. What has been tried in the past to change the problem behaviors?

D. DESCRIBE THE BEHAVIOR(S)

1. Describe the behaviors of concern. For each, define how it is performed; how often it occurs per day, week, or month; how long it lasts when it occurs; and the intensity at which it occurs (low, medium, high).

FIGURE 5.2. Adapted functional assessment interview form.

Note. Adapted from O'Neill et al. (1997)

Figure 5.2, Continued

	Behavior	How is it performed?	How often?	How long?	Intensity?
1.					
2.					
3.					
4.					

2. Which of the behaviors described above occur together (i.e., occur at the same time, occur in a predictable chain, occur in response to the same situation)?

3. Prioritize the top two behavioral concerns listed above. These are the targeted behaviors you will refer to throughout this form.

	Behavior
1.	
2.	

E. EVENTS THAT MAY AFFECT THE BEHAVIOR

1. What medications does the child take and how do you believe these may affect his or her behavior?

2. List medical complications the child experiences that may affect his or her behavior (i.e., asthma, allergies, seizures).

3. Describe the sleep cycles of the child and the extent to which these may affect his or her behavior.

4. Describe the eating routines and diet of the child and the extent to which these routines may affect his or her behavior.

5. Briefly list the child's typical daily schedule of activities and how well he or she does within each activity.

Time	Activity	Child's Reaction

F. DEFINE EVENTS AND SITUATIONS THAT MAY TRIGGER THE BEHAVIOR(S)

1. **Time of Day:** *When* are the behaviors most and least likely to occur?
Most likely:
Least likely:

Figure 5.2, Continued

2. **Settings:** *Where* are the behaviors most and least likely to occur?
   Most likely:
   Least likely:

3. **Social:** *With whom* are the behaviors most and least likely to occur?
   Most likely:
   Least likely:

4. **Activities:** *What* activities are most and least likely to produce the behaviors?
   Most likely:
   Least likely:

5. **Antecedents:** Describe the relevant events that precede the target behavior.

6. **Consequences:** Describe the result of the target behavior (i.e., what is the payoff for the student?).

7. How much of a delay is there between the time the child engages in the behavior and when he or she gets the "payoff"? Is it immediate, a few seconds, or longer?

8. What one thing could you do that would most likely make the problem behavior occur?

9. What one thing could you do to make sure the problem behavior did not occur?

G. IDENTIFY THE FUNCTION OF THE TARGET BEHAVIOR

Using the prioritized behaviors from section D, define the function(s) you believe the behaviors serve for the child (i.e., what does he or she get and/or avoid by doing the behavior?). Think SEAT: sensory, escape, attention, tangible.

Behavior	Function (What does he or she get? OR What exactly does he or she avoid?)
1.	
2.	
3.	

H. SUMMARY STATEMENTS

Setting Event	Antecedent	Behavior	Consequence	Function

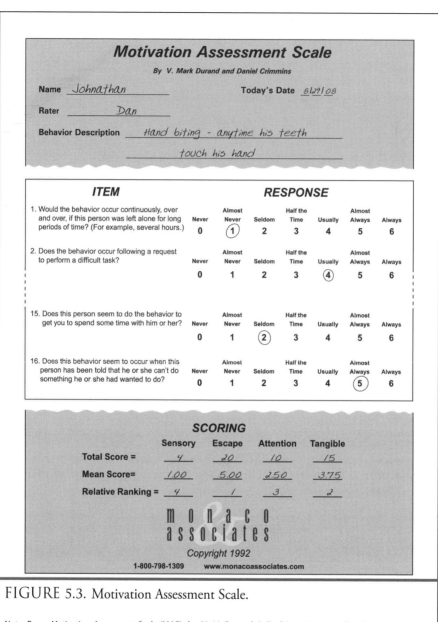

FIGURE 5.3. Motivation Assessment Scale.

conditions, and lack of sleep. School-related environmental factors that may be influencing a child include factors such as the size of the classroom, number of people in the environment, temperature, lighting, noise level, distractions, unclear directions, lack of organization, and unclear expectations. These indirect methods are useful tools for a team when attempting to identify patterns that may help predict the function of the student's behavior.

Step Three: Develop a Hypothesis

Children engage in challenging behavior because it works for them. Behavior can serve a number of functions for a student. There are four categories of functions of behavior that have been empirically validated: sensory, escape/avoidance, attention, and tangible. When behavior serves a sensory function, the behavior feels good or meets a sensory need through the auditory, visual, tactile, gustatory, olfactory, proprioceptive, or vestibular sensory channels. Everyone engages in behaviors to regulate an internal state; some individuals twirl their hair while other people shake their leg. Individuals with autism often lack the ability to regulate or filter sensory information. Their nervous systems seem to be overreactive or underactive. Some behaviors that are performed for sensory input can include behaviors such as rocking, spinning, mouthing objects, and hand flapping. When designing interventions for replacing sensory behaviors, the sensory channel that is used for the sensory input is the channel that needs to be addressed in the intervention. For example, if a child is chewing on the sleeve of her shirt, then the intervention should address the oral sensory channel.

When a child engages in behaviors because she wants to get away from something unpleasant, she may be trying to escape or avoid a particular activity, task, person, item, or environment. Escape or avoidance behaviors can take any shape or form. However, a child or adolescent often will choose a behavior such as aggression because it almost always leads to the consequence of being removed from the activity or the environment. Therefore, the behavior is reinforced. A natural intervention for escape/avoidance behaviors would be to alter antecedents to the behavior or teach the child an appropriate way to request a break.

When thinking about the function of attention, the child may be seeking attention from peers, staff, parents, or anyone in the environment. This may include both positive and negative attention; although it may be hard to imagine, negative attention is still attention. Usually when the function is attention, the behavior occurs when a specific individual is present in the environment. If the child or adolescent is seeking peer attention, the behavior will likely occur frequently. An intervention for a child who seeks attention might focus on teaching the child an appropriate way to gain attention or to give the child more attention and then slowly fade the amount of attention over time.

When a child behaves inappropriately to get a specific item, object, task, person, activity, or privilege, the function is thought to be for a tangible. Behaviors for tangible purposes often are exhibited after a child has lost a desired item or is denied access to a certain item. Interventions for children or adolescents who are exhibiting behavior to gain a tangible should be taught to ask for the item or they should be given a schedule and shown when they can have access to the desired item. Try to avoid removing tangibles for extended periods of time, unless they are deemed inappropriate tangibles.

Forming the hypothesis is one of the most crucial tasks of the FBA process. The hypothesis guides the intervention selection and formation of the behavior support plan. It is of the upmost importance that the hypothesis or the function of the behavior matches the intervention selected to replace the behavior. The child or adolescent still needs to have a way to have his or her needs met. If the replacement behavior matches the communicative intent or the function of the behavior, then the likelihood of a successful intervention dramatically increases.

It's important to know that some behaviors may serve more than one function. For example, a child could be hitting for multiple reasons including attention or to escape a situation. It's also true that different behaviors may serve the same function. A student may throw a pencil, tantrum, talk-out, or refuse something—all for attention. Gathering as much information about when, where, and why the behavior occurs helps to clarify why the negative behavior occurs and helps to identify the primary function or communicative message of the challenging behavior.

Step Four: Collect Observational Information

Observing the student in his or her environment is a direct method of gathering information. Direct measurement provides the most accurate representation of the student's behavior. It involves directly observing the student's behavior in his or her natural environment and analyzing the behavior's antecedents (environmental events that immediately precede the problem behavior) and consequences (environmental events that immediately follow the problem behavior). There are several methods for gathering direct observational information. These methods include, but are not limited to, the use of a scatter plot, the ABC collection, and observation collected on different dimensions of the challenging behavior.

Scatter plot charts can be used to record whether or not a child's behavior occurred across specific activities, routines, or time periods (see Figure 5.4). The scatter plot collection and analysis provides the observer with patterns that may be associated with the behavior. For instance, a scatter plot analysis could provide information that shows that the behavior occurred more often in tasks that involved independent work. With that information, the teacher could add supports, modify assignments, or specifically work on reinforcing the child for successful completion of independent work. The scatter plot is relatively easy to record and interpret and serves to narrow the field of analysis for the Antecendent-Behavior-Consequence assessment (Lennox & Miltenberger, 1989).

Antecedent-Behavior-Consequence (ABC) data help organize the information in a format that lends to identifying the function. The ABC format focuses the observation on the behavior and what occurs right before and after the challenging behavior. The ABC determines the extent to which specific environmental events are related to the behavior (Lennox & Miltenberger, 1989). If we look at the things that happen right before and right after the behavior we can begin to predict when

Student: _____

Observer: _____

Behavior: _____

Time	Monday	Tuesday	Wednesday	Thursday	Friday
8:00–8:30					
8:30–9:00					
9:00–9:30					
9:30–10:00					
10:00–10:30					
10:30–11:00					
11:00–11:30					
11:30–12:00					
12:00–12:30					
12:30–1:00					
1:00–1:30					
1:30–2:00					
2:00–2:30					
2:30–3:00					

FIGURE 5.4. Scatter plot chart.

the behavior will occur, why it is occurring, or its function. Figure 5.5 contains an example of a basic ABC data collection form.

Observational recording systems that include different dimensions of the challenging behavior include event recording, duration recording, latency recording, time sampling, and interval recording. Event, duration, and latency recording are easy to collect in the classroom setting and can provide meaningful information for the FBA process. Event recording is simply counting the number of times a behavior occurs. A tally mark is made each time the student engages in the target behavior. Event data is collected within a specified period of time, such as a 30-minute class period. To use event recording, the behavior must have a clear beginning and clear ending. It should not be used when the behavior is occurring at such a high rate that an accurate count is impossible such as tapping a pencil, flapping hands, or flicking fingers, or when the behavior occurs for an extended period of time such as out of seat behavior or staring out a window. Event recording is the easiest observation data to record and many different types of behaviors can be collected using it (see Figure 5.6 for an event recording form).

When the primary concern is the length of time the student engages in the behavior, duration data should be collected. For instance, tantrumming behavior

Student: _____

Observer: _____

Behavior: _____

_____

Date	Time	Antecedent	Behavior	Consequence

FIGURE 5.5. Basic ABC data collection form.

Student: _____

Observer: _____

Behavior: _____

_____

Date	Start Time	Stop Time	Number of Occurrences	Total Occurrences

FIGURE 5.6. Event recording data form.

might be better described using duration instead of event recording. Event recording could tell a teacher that the child had four tantrums during a week's period of time. That doesn't sound too bad. However, duration recording could tell a teacher that the child or adolescent tantrummed for a total of 320 minutes during that same week, or an average of 80 minutes per tantrum. Does that provide a more accurate picture of the tantrumming behavior? A stopwatch is a convenient way to measure the duration of a behavior by starting the stopwatch when the student begins the behavior, stopping the watch when the behavior has ended, and recording the duration. Another option is recording the actual start and stop times of the target behavior. This also could provide information about specific times or

Student: _____

Observer: _____

Behavior: _____

_____

Initiation _____

Termination _____

Date	Start Time	Stop Time	Total Duration	Average Duration

FIGURE 5.7. Duration recording data form.

activities during the day when the behavior is more likely to occur. An example of a duration recording form can be found in Figure 5.7.

Latency recording also focuses on time rather than the frequency or event. Latency recording is used to determine how long a student takes to begin performing a particular behavior once a directive or instruction has been given. For example, latency recording would be an appropriate measurement system for monitoring how long it takes a student to begin working once the teacher has provided a direction, how long it takes a student to begin to eat once lunch is given, or how long it takes a student to select a toy when he is taken to the play area. To record latency data, note when the student is given a directive and when the student begins the response. Total latency and average latency can be calculated from this type of recording (see Figure 5.8).

Identify times to collect data throughout the day or week. These times will vary depending on the target behaviors that have been selected and how frequently they occur. For example, if you are collecting data on a student's social behavior, you may choose to collect data during unstructured times such as lunch, recess, or during a break. Data should be collected on a consistent basis over time. It is extremely important to conduct as many observations as possible so that the child's team can be reasonably confident that the data obtained is both accurate and reflective of the child's or adolescent's behavior.

Step Five: Graphing Behavioral Data

To be useful, information gathered through data collection must be readable. Tallies or other forms of raw data can be difficult to interpret. Therefore, graphs should be used because they communicate information visually. Graphing data

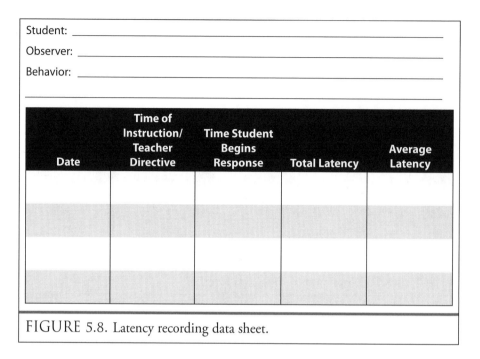

Student: _____

Observer: _____

Behavior: _____

Date	Time of Instruction/ Teacher Directive	Time Student Begins Response	Total Latency	Average Latency

FIGURE 5.8. Latency recording data sheet.

provides an easy, systematic way of displaying information about the target behavior. Data often are graphed because it makes it easier to review the data and to see changes in the student behavior or performance. Graphing is a two-step process. First, the raw data must be converted to a usable form, such as percentage, length of time, or average length of time. Second, the converted data should be entered into a graphic display.

There are several types of graphic displays. The most frequently used tool for displaying behavioral data is the line graph. The line graph contains two axes, the horizontal axis or x-axis, and the vertical axis or y-axis. The x-axis is labeled with the time element such as minutes, days, dates, or sessions. The vertical axis is labeled with the occurrence, percentage, or duration of the target behavior. Each data point is placed at the intersection of the session in which it occurred and the percentage or level of behavior. The basic elements of a line graph can be found in Figure 5.9.

Data collection must be a continuous, ongoing process. Baseline data is the original level of the target behavior before any intervention has taken place. Baseline data usually is collected for 3 to 5 days to provide the best description of the child's behavior. However, in the classroom setting, collecting baseline data for 3 to 5 days may be an unreasonable expectation, especially if the child or adolescent is exhibiting a behavior that is aggressive or harmful in nature.

To determine if a program has been effective, it helps to evaluate trends and patterns of the data. Trends are defined as three or more data points in the same direction. Trends in data indicate the effectiveness of programs and assist the team in determining the need for program changes, revising interventions, and making

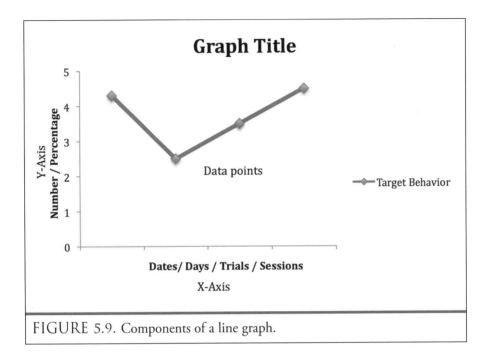

FIGURE 5.9. Components of a line graph.

instructional decisions. Graphs must regularly and frequently be examined to determine if progress is being made on the behavior targeted for change. If the data indicate progress is being made, then the intervention and collection procedures should continue. If the data indicate a lack of progress or that the behavior is not changing, modifications to or a complete change to the intervention should be considered while continuing to monitor the target behavior.

Oftentimes a change in behavior can seem unnoticeable. Sometimes change cannot be determined unless observation, data collection, and graphing are employed. Even the tiniest steps are progress. If a tantrum is shorter by only 1 minute every day, it is 30 minutes shorter by the end of a month.

DEVELOPING BEHAVIOR SUPPORT PLANS

The FBA process culminates with the development of a behavior support or intervention plan. This plan is a multicomponent plan that is focused on instruction and prevention, and is environmentally based (Sugai et al., 2000). Through a behavior support plan, the team develops an action plan that details the specific steps to be used with the student to teach a replacement behavior (Knoster, 2000; Lennox & Miltenberger, 1989; Scheuermann & Hall, 2008; Sugai et al., 2000). The strategies used for replacing the challenging behavior should directly reflect the results of the FBA process (Scheuermann & Hall, 2008). Behavior support plans include a description about the behavior, antecedents and setting events most often associated with the behavior, maintaining consequences, and the perceived function or purpose of the behavior. Student strengths and abilities are a focus of the plan so the interventions can build off of those strengths. Also included in the support plan are all previously implemented interventions so that the team has an idea of what has and has not worked in the past and the new skill or replacement behavior that will be taught and reinforced by the team.

The behavior support plan is a carefully developed plan (see Figure 5.10). According to Scheuermann and Hall (2008), there is a six-step process that the team should follow when developing the plan. First, the team is given 5 to 10 minutes to brainstorm a list of possible interventions. Second, any questions about the interventions on the list are clarified by the team member recommending the intervention. Third, the team discusses the feasibility of the interventions and their relationship to the hypothesis. Fourth, the interventions are prioritized by the team to determine the order in which the interventions will be tried. Fifth, the list is finalized and the types of support that team members will need to implement the strategies are identified. Last, the intervention strategies are documented in the behavior support plan, which is attached to the IEP.

In some cases, if the behavior is deemed dangerous for the child or other individuals in the environment, restrictive interventions may be needed. If restrictive interventions or crisis interventions are deemed necessary, then the exact plan for implementation also must be included in the behavior support plan. Methods for evaluation and measurement criteria should be agreed upon by all team members. Probably one of the most important factors to ensure success for the child, is the communication of the support plan between all environments in which the child interacts.

The Individualized Education Program (IEP) is the centerpiece of instructional and educational programming for a student with a disability. Beyond the inclusion of the behavior support plan, there are several ways in which behavior can be incorporated into an IEP. Information from an FBA may be included in the present level of performance. The data can be used to describe the student's current level of functioning including situations or settings in which the student's behavior is most or least appropriate and consequences that may positively or negatively influence the behavior. Annual goals and short-term objectives or benchmarks also can be written for a behavior by identifying the replacement behaviors the student will learn. The overall plan for and progress of the behavior should be well documented within the IEP.

Behavior Support Plan		
Student:	**Grade:**	**Date:**

A. TARGET BEHAVIOR

1. List the target behavior identified from the FBA.

2. This behavior is a: ❏ Skill Deficit or ❏ Performance Deficit
Skill Deficit: The student does not know how to perform the desired behavior.
Performance Deficit: The student knows how to perform the desired behavior, but does not consistently do so.

B. PURPOSE/FUNCTION OF THE TARGET BEHAVIOR

1. Describe the purpose of the behavior.

C. SUMMARY OF PREVIOUS INTERVENTIONS

1. Describe any environmental changes made, evaluations conducted, instructional strategies or curriculum changes made, or replacement behaviors taught.

D. REPLACEMENT BEHAVIORS

1. Describe which new behaviors or skills will be taught to meet the identified function of the target behavior. Include a description of how these behaviors will be taught.

E. BEHAVIORAL INTERVENTION STRATEGIES AND SUPPORTS

1. Environment: How can the environment or circumstances that trigger the target behavior be adjusted?

2. Instruction and/or curriculum: What changes in instructional strategies or curriculum would be helpful?

F. MOTIVATORS AND/OR REWARDS

1. Describe how the student will be reinforced to ensure that replacement behaviors are more motivating than the target behavior.

G. RESTRICTIVE DISCIPLINARY MEASURES

1. Describe any restrictive disciplinary measures that may be used with the student and the conditions under which such measures may be used (include necessary documentation and timeline for evaluation).

2. Crisis plan: Describe how an emergency situation or behavior crisis will be handled.

H. DATA COLLECTION PROCEDURES AND METHODS

1. Describe expected outcomes of the interventions, how data will be collected and measured, and timelines for and criteria to determine success or lack of success of the interventions.

I. PROVISIONS FOR COORDINATION WITH CAREGIVERS

1. Describe how the school will work with the caregivers to share information, provide training to caregivers if needed, and how often this communication will take place.

FIGURE 5.10. Behavior support plan.

Note. Adapted from O'Neill et al. (1997)

CASE STUDY

Mrs. Jones collapsed at the end of the day; the only thought in her head was that it was finally over! There must be a full moon tonight, as the children were all restless and rambunctious. Today seemed to be an especially difficult day for Kyle. Kyle is 8 years old and has a diagnosis of autism. He receives most of his services in Mrs. Jones' self-contained classroom and joins his first-grade general education class for art, music, PE, lunch, recess, computer time, library time, science, and all other activities that are social in nature.

This morning, Kyle arrived at school more agitated than usual. He rushed off the bus threatening, "I'm going to kill you!" while pointing a finger gun at the bus driver. In the note written in his communication book, Kyle's mother informed Mrs. Jones that their electricity had gone out the night before and Kyle was unable to watch his videos before bedtime. He tantrummed most of the evening, caused a considerable amount of damage to his bedroom, and didn't sleep much throughout the night. From previous conversations with Kyle's mom, Mrs. Jones knew that Kyle had difficulties falling asleep at night. He usually fell asleep on the couch around 9 or 9:30 p.m. and was carried to bed. He sleeps very restlessly and moves all over his bed.

This particular morning, Kyle also was unable to watch his videos before leaving for school. Kyle's mom wrote that she was looking forward to their meeting later in the day and wished Mrs. Jones good luck. That morning, Mrs. Jones tried engaging Kyle in the typical class routine, but he kept running to the TV in the room and screaming, "I want *Star Wars*! Put in *Star Wars*!" Mrs. Jones decided to remove the TV/VCR from the room. As she wheeled it out, Kyle became violent and began to hit and kick Mrs. Jones, leaving one large bruise on her leg and several tender spots. In an effort to calm Kyle down, she quickly brought back the TV. She knew that if she allowed him time to watch a movie, he would relax and be able to focus on his work. Kyle watched 15 minutes of *Star Wars* before it was time for art. Mrs. Jones knew that Kyle really enjoyed art class, so she didn't think the transition to art would be difficult. During art, Kyle needed minimal assistance getting his supplies out and proceeded to draw an amazing picture of a scene from *Star Wars*. Kyle's artistic abilities are one of his strengths.

Kyle usually does not transition well; he says "no" or "just a minute," so Mrs. Jones was delighted that Kyle wanted to go to art class with his first-grade peers. Transitions are exceptionally difficult for Kyle when he is engaged in a preferred activity and has to stop with short notice. If Kyle is transitioning to a work task he perceives as difficult, he will engage in physical and verbally aggressive behaviors. Kyle will negotiate more time, give reasons why he needs to continue with the preferred activity, and tell you he is not finished. To help with transitions, Mrs. Jones has implemented an individualized visual schedule for Kyle. Kyle follows his daily schedule but needs prompting for the first task. However, after the prompt he can complete a task, bring the icon back and put it in his "All Done" envelope, pull the next icon in the sequence, and get his materials. This has helped structure Kyle's day and has made the day at school more predictable.

Upon returning to Mrs. Jones' class, it was time for centers. Happy that art class was a success for Kyle, Mrs. Jones let Kyle choose his center. At school, Kyle is provided the opportunity for choice during activities outside and during centers and snack, and he gets to select his play partners. When there is free time during the day, Kyle often chooses to play on the computer.

Kyle chose to go to the math center, which is one of his favorites. The math-based center includes manipulatives such as blocks that allow for counting or sorting and paper materials that encourage patterning. Kyle began playing with the blocks independently, until another student was sent to the center. This peer began building a tower within close proximity to Kyle. Kyle immediately wanted the blocks the other child was using. He again became aggressive and hit his peer in the head, took the blocks from her hands, and rammed her tower over with a toy he held in his hand. Mrs. Jones immediately interceded, pulling Kyle out of the center and removing him to another area within the classroom. Kyle did not move willingly and again Mrs. Jones was kicked and hit while Kyle screamed, "Get away!" and growled. For a small boy, Kyle was strong, very physical, and very quick. Mrs. Jones disliked having to physically move Kyle but felt there weren't other immediate options, as the safety of the other students was at risk. Kyle was removed to an area within the classroom to "cool down." He banged the toy that was still in his hand and threw it against the wall. Situations like this had occurred before, but they were beginning to be more frequent. When he has been aggressive in the past, the children gave in to him by giving him the toy or by giving Kyle a duplicate toy. During play-based activities when Kyle interacts with a peer, he needs to be closely monitored because he will become aggressive. If an activity is lead by Kyle and what he is doing is not challenged or altered, there typically is not a problem.

Reflecting over the events of the day, Mrs. Jones pulled out notes she had taken on other days Kyle engaged in challenging behaviors. She hadn't realized how frequently the behaviors were occurring. Mrs. Jones talked with Kyle's mother who shared that Kyle exhibits physical aggression, verbal aggression, and destruction of property at home as well. Both Mrs. Jones and Kyle's mom decided to begin collecting data on what happened immediately prior to the problem behavior, what the challenging behavior looked like, whom it occurred with, and what happened immediately following the behavior in all environments in which Kyle interacted. After communicating with Kyle's mom, Mrs. Jones sent notification to Kyle's team to perform a functional behavior assessment and develop a behavior support plan to teach Kyle more socially acceptable behaviors.

After a few weeks of monitoring Kyle's behavior, Mrs. Jones began noticing that there were patterns. Challenging behaviors seemed to occur during unstructured periods of the day. It seemed as though issues occurred during center time when Kyle played with blocks and during recess on the playground when Kyle interacted with other children on the trains or bikes. When a highly preferred item, activity, or a novel activity occurred, Mrs. Jones noted that mornings seemed to be smoother for Kyle. Changes in the daily schedule or routine also seemed to increase Kyle's engagement in challenging behaviors. Mornings are very structured and filled with preferred activities such as circle time, story time, wiggle-time, small group, and snack time. Mrs. Jones also noticed that the behaviors occurred more frequently with her and with others who didn't know him well, for instance, with a substitute teacher. Interestingly, the behaviors seldom occurred with the general education teacher. If Kyle was playing and doing what he wanted, behaviors occurred very infrequently. Taking a toy away or removing him from the computer always resulted in Kyle becoming angry and aggressive. Mrs. Jones was beginning to feel like the only thing that worked was to let Kyle do whatever he wanted or to give him constant one-on-one attention at all times. Mrs. Jones looked forward to the team meeting to develop strategies to help support Kyle.

The team identified strategies that Mrs. Jones and Kyle's mom were comfortable implementing at both school and home. One of the first things Mrs. Jones intended to do was complete a reinforcer preference assessment to identify novel reinforcers. Kyle's mom provided the team with new rewards for Kyle including three new books and time on the computer. The team decided to teach Kyle play skills, social interaction skills, and communication repair strategies. Mrs. Jones looked forward to teaching Kyle how to use these new behaviors in place of the challenging behaviors he had exhibited previously. Data were to be taken daily on the number of occurrences of problem behaviors and the duration of each episode. The team decided to meet in 2 weeks to review progress, evaluate the effectiveness of the interventions, and tweak the strategies, if warranted. Refer to Figures 5.11 and 5.12 for Kyle's completed Functional Assessment Interview and Positive Behavior Support Plan.

Conclusion

Changes in the number of children and youth identified with ASD over the past decade and changes in education law have prompted schools to develop plans to effectively include children with challenging behaviors into the general education setting. Inherent characteristics associated with ASD, including impaired communication, socialization, and behavior, often leave children on the spectrum with no choice but to use their behavior as a way to get their wants and needs

Functional Behavior Assessment

Student:	Grade:	Date:
Kyle	First, Mrs. Jones	September 21, 2007

A. FBA TEAM MEMBERS

Please provide your name and title.

Lyn Phillip—Parent	Penelope Bartels—classroom aide
Mrs. Jones—Teacher	Mrs. Long—SLP
Mr. Rossi—Principal	Mrs. Overton—OT

B. SOURCES OF INFORMATION

Please select the sources used:
- ☒ Anecdotal information provided by parents
- ☐ Diagnostic evaluation(s) completed by:
    - ☐ School district
    - ☐ Outside agency
- ☒ Interviews completed by:
    - ☒ Parent
    - ☐ Student
    - ☒ Teacher
    - ☐ Other professional
- ☒ Classroom/school observation
- ☒ Attendance records
- ☒ Discipline records
- ☐ Behavior Rating Scales
    - ☒ IEP(s)
    - ☐ Other: _____
    - ☐ Other: _____

C. STUDENT INFORMATION

1. Describe the student's behavioral strengths (i.e., positive interactions with staff and peers, accepts responsibility, ignores inappropriate behavior of peers, etc.).

   Kyle likes playing and has many peers whom he interacts with positively. Kyle is integrated into the general education setting multiple times a day and behaves very appropriately in this setting.

2. Describe the things the student enjoys. For example, what makes him or her happy? What might someone do or provide that makes the child happy?

   Kyle likes playing with toys, especially blocks and the computer. Kyle loves Star Wars.

3. What has been tried in the past to change the problem behaviors?

   Rules, losing rewards, warnings with transitions, visual daily schedule. Choice is embedded throughout his day.

D. DESCRIBE THE BEHAVIOR(S)

1. Describe the behaviors of concern. For each, define how it is performed; how often it occurs per day, week, or month; how long it lasts when it occurs; and the intensity at which it occurs (low, medium, high).

FIGURE 5.11. Kyle's completed Functional Assessment Interview Form.

Note. Adapted from O'Neill et al. (1997).

Figure 5.11, Continued

	Behavior	How is it performed?	How often?	How long?	Intensity?
1.	Verbal aggression	Threatens by verbalizing "I'm going to kill you" while pointing a finger gun, "Get away," growls . . .	2–5 times/day	5 seconds–1 minute	Low–high
2.	Physical aggression	Hits, pushes, kicks, punches, rams with toy	2–3 times/week	5 seconds–30 seconds	High
3.	Property destruction	Throwing or banging toys	2–5 times/week	5 seconds–30 seconds	High

2. Which of the behaviors described above occur together (i.e., occur at the same time, occur in a predictable chain, occur in response to the same situation)?

At this point, it seems unpredictable. At times he will verbally aggress, then engage in either physical aggression or property destruction or they happen independent of each other. Other times, he will begin with property destruction and/or physical aggression and intersperse verbal aggression.

3. Prioritize the top two behavioral concerns listed above. These are the targeted behaviors you will refer to throughout this form.

	Behavior
1.	Physical aggression
2.	Verbal aggression

E. EVENTS THAT MAY AFFECT THE BEHAVIOR

1. What medications does the child take and how do you believe these may affect his or her behavior?

None

2. List medical complications the child experiences that may affect his or her behavior (i.e., asthma, allergies, seizures).

None

3. Describe the sleep cycles of the child and the extent to which these may affect his or her behavior.

His mother reports that he has frequent sleeping issues. Often, he will fall asleep on the couch around 9 or 9:30 and is carried to bed. He sleeps very restlessly and moves all over his bed.

4. Describe the eating routines and diet of the child and the extent to which these routines may affect his or her behavior.

Eats independently at school for snack and lunch.

Figure 5.11, Continued

5. Briefly list the child's typical daily schedule of activities and how well he or she does within each activity.

Time	Activity	Child's Reaction
8:45 a.m.	Arrives to school	Gets off bus shooting finger gun, sometimes yells, "I'm going to kill you," sometimes wants a hug
Until 9:30 a.m.	Playground	Verbal and physical aggression, property destruction
9:30 a.m.	Story Time	Sits and attends nicely
9:45 a.m.	Small Group	Sits and attends nicely
10:00 a.m.	Wiggle Time	Follows directions and enjoys movement and dancing
10:15 a.m.	Specials	Very attentive in art class, dislikes PE, enjoys music
10:30 a.m.	Centers/Snack	Eats snack and plays with computer nicely, once in centers (especially blocks) engages in verbal and physical aggression
11:30 a.m.	Circle	Sits and attends nicely
11:45 a.m.	Playground	Verbal and physical aggression
12:30 p.m.	Lunch	Eats nicely
1:00 p.m.	Science	Sits attentively
2:15 p.m.	Snack	Eats nicely
2:35 p.m.	Good-bye	Sits, attends
3:00 p.m.	Leaves	Picked up by his mother, no issues leaving

F. DEFINE EVENTS AND SITUATIONS THAT MAY TRIGGER THE BEHAVIOR(S)

1. **Time of Day:** *When* are the behaviors most and least likely to occur?
   Most likely: During centers and during recess on the playground
   Least likely: During circle and story time, small group, and other structured activities

2. **Settings:** *Where* are the behaviors most and least likely to occur?
   Most likely: Playground and in the blocks center
   Least likely: Story time, wiggle time, small group, and snack time

3. **Social:** *With whom* are the behaviors most and least likely to occur?
   Most likely: Mrs. Jones, Mom, and with someone who doesn't know him like a substitute teacher
   Least likely: General education teacher

4. **Activities:** *What* activities are most and least likely to produce the behaviors?
   Most likely: With a highly preferred item or activity or a novel activity, blocks/cars/magnetic people, with family and during a change in routine
   Least likely: Quiet time, story time, and when he is doing something he wants

5. **Antecedents:** Describe the relevant events that precede the target behavior.
   When an instruction or demand is given
   Other children enter in center where Kyle is playing

Figure 5.11, Continued

6. **Consequences:** Describe the result of the target behavior (i.e., what is the payoff for the student?).

Escape, immediate removal from situation, attention, and sometimes access to a tangible

7. How much of a delay is there between the time the child engages in the behavior and when he or she gets the "payoff"? Is it immediate, a few seconds, or longer?

Usually immediate

8. What one thing could you do that would most likely make the problem behavior occur?

Take a preferred toy away or remove him from the computer

9. What one thing could you do to make sure the problem behavior did not occur?

In a perfect world, there would be no boundaries and Kyle would have access to whatever he wants. Providing him with one-on-one attention and constantly talking to him would ensure no behavioral outbursts.

G. IDENTIFY THE FUNCTION OF THE TARGET BEHAVIOR

Using the prioritized behaviors from section D, define the function(s) you believe the behaviors serve for the child (i.e., what does he or she get and/or avoid by doing the behavior?). Think SEAT: sensory, escape, attention, tangible.

	Behavior	Function (What does he or she get? OR What exactly does he or she avoid?)
1.	Verbal aggression	Children react and then leave him alone Gains adult attention
2.	Physical aggression	Gets a specific toy or activity Avoids group play Avoids transitions Gains adult attention
3.	Property destruction	Gets a toy or activity Children run away Gains adult attention

H. SUMMARY STATEMENTS

Setting Event	Antecedent	Behavior	Consequence	Function
Little sleep night before	Peer attempts to play at same center as Kyle	Physical aggression	Teacher removes Kyle from Center	Avoids group play Gains adult attention

Positive Behavior Support Plan

Student:	Grade:	Date:
Kyle	First, Mrs. Jones	September 21, 2007

A. TARGET BEHAVIOR

1. List the target behavior identified from the FBA.

   Verbal aggression: Threatens by verbalizing "I'm going to kill you" while pointing a finger gun, verbalizes "Get away" and growls
   Physical aggression: Hits, pushes, kicks, punches, rams w/toy

2. This behavior is a: ☒ Skill Deficit or ❑ Performance Deficit
   Skill Deficit: The student does not know how to perform the desired behavior.
   Performance Deficit: The student knows how to perform the desired behavior, but does not consistently do so.

B. PURPOSE/FUNCTION OF THE TARGET BEHAVIOR

1. Describe the purpose of the behavior.

   In group-play situations (outside on the playground and inside during center time), Kyle uses verbal aggression (threatens by verbalizing "I'm going to kill you" while pointing a finger gun and/or verbalizes "get away" and may growl) and physical aggression (hits, pushes, kicks, punches, rams with toy) to obtain toys and/or join play. When this occurs, peers usually give up the desired object (toy) and leave the area. Usually the teacher intervenes and provides Kyle with an abundance of attention.
   Kyle will grab toys, scream, and use physical aggression to obtain toys when peers suggest that they play with toys in a new way, propose a different play theme, or join in his play. When this occurs, the peer gives into Kyle's ideas, gives up the toy, and asks the teacher for help.

C. SUMMARY OF PREVIOUS INTERVENTIONS

1. Describe any environmental changes made, evaluations conducted, instructional strategies or curriculum changes made, or replacement behaviors taught.

   In the past we have implemented rules with Kyle. We have setup a behavior management system where he loses rewards. Transitions warnings are used consistently. Kyle currently uses a visual daily schedule. Choice is embedded throughout his day.

D. REPLACEMENT BEHAVIORS

1. Describe which new behaviors or skills will be taught to replace the use of the challenging behavior. Include a description of how these behaviors will be taught.

   Social interaction/play skills: Skills including: Asking to play, turn-taking, flexibility, space boundaries, and asking for help will be taught one at a time to Kyle in one-on-one setting. A social story on appropriate play will be written and shared with Kyle. The story will include clear expectations for Kyle's behavior, the perspective of others, perspective of Kyle, and the communicative intent of Kyle's behavior. Before situations in which the challenging behavior occurs

FIGURE 5.12. Kyle's completed Positive Behavior Support Plan.

Note. Adapted from O'Neill et al. (1997).

Figure 5.12, Continued

(i.e., centers and playground), the story will be read. Each time Kyle engages in the inappropriate behavior the story also will be reviewed. To aid in teaching the newly identified play skills, visual cue cards (1. Do you want to play?; 2. Take-turns; 3. I need help, please; and 4. I'm finished) will be provided to Kyle. The cue cards will be available during all play interactions with peers and will be practiced during small group. First, Kyle will be shown the cue card paired with a verbal prompt (if needed). Kyle will be provided the opportunity for adult-directed play sessions to practice these new skills. Setting up play activities and engaging Kyle in new play activities will help teach Kyle how to play appropriately and engage in new play routines. All behavior needs to be interpreted as communicative. Adults in Kyle's environment should facilitate and model appropriate interactions. When Kyle fails to use his language and begins to show early signs of verbal or physical aggression, provide Kyle with scripted phrases that he can use.

Break card: An "I need a break" visual break card will be available for Kyle. At first, an adult in the environment will need to help determine when a break may be needed. Pair the picture card with the verbal prompt, "I need a break."

Token system: Kyle can earn time to watch movies for not engaging in challenging behavior. Anytime Kyle engages in appropriate social-play interactions, reinforce him immediately with social praise. Also, Kyle can earn 5 minutes of movie time at the end of each school day.

E. BEHAVIORAL INTERVENTION STRATEGIES AND SUPPORTS

1. Environment: How can the environment or circumstances that trigger the target behavior be adjusted?

   Visual strategies and environmental supports listed above will be used. Rules for each center time will be posted in the centers area.

2. Instruction and/or curriculum: What changes in instructional strategies or curriculum would be helpful?

   During small group, social and play interactions will be practiced. Communication repair strategies will be practiced during this time.

F. MOTIVATORS AND/OR REWARDS

1. Describe how the student will be reinforced to ensure that replacement behaviors are more motivating than the target behavior.

   Star Wars movies, computer

   Mrs. Jones will conduct a reinforcer preference assessment. Kyle's mom will complete a reinforcer menu. This was provided to her on 7/21/08 and she will return by next week. Results of both will be available at the next team meeting.

G. RESTRICTIVE DISCIPLINARY MEASURES

1. Describe any restrictive disciplinary measures that may be used with the student and the conditions under which such measures may be used (include necessary documentation and timeline for evaluation).

Time out: only to be used if Kyle engages in physical aggression. Kyle will remain in a designated quiet area of the room. Data on the occurrence of TO will be collected to confirm that TO is not reinforcing Kyle's inappropriate behavior.

Figure 5.12, Continued

2. Crisis plan: Describe how an emergency situation or behavior crisis will be handled.

At this time, the team does not feel a crisis plan for Kyle is needed.

H. DATA COLLECTION PROCEDURES AND METHODS [°]

1. Describe expected outcomes of the interventions, how data will be collected and measured, and timelines for and criteria to determine success or lack of success of the interventions.

Expected outcomes include Kyle learning to negotiate difficult social situations. Kyle will identify social cues, become more flexible in play routines, and use skills necessary for social play (asking to play, turn-taking, learning space boundaries, and asking for help).

Staff will monitor the frequency of Kyle's inappropriate behavior by tallying occurrences.

Self-monitor: Kyle will use self-monitoring to monitor progress toward social skill goals during center-time and recess on the playground. Goals will be identified during small group with Kyle and the teacher. Goals will be introduced one at a time. Kyle will use a form to indicate if he was successful in meeting his goals. If Kyle is not successful in meeting his goals, both Kyle and the teacher will brainstorm ideas to be successful in the future.

I. PROVISIONS FOR COORDINATION WITH CAREGIVERS

1. Describe how the school will work with the caregivers to share information, provide training to caregivers if needed, and how often this communication will take place.

Information between home and school will continue to be collected on the Home-School Communication form. This form will be modified to include a section on the newly added interventions listed above. This will be sent home daily and will contain a place for home to communicate how the behaviors are changing in the home and community environments. Team meetings will continue to occur biweekly. We will meet to evaluate the effectiveness of the strategies developed today on 7/29/2008.

BIP information, including information collected on rewards from the reinforcer preference assessment will be updated at the next team meeting scheduled for 7/29/2008.

met. The FBA is a necessary process in order to teach children and adolescents more appropriate ways to communicate with others in their environment. If the function of the challenging behavior is identified, then the team can identify and teach socially appropriate ways for the individual to communicate. It is unethical to extinguish or get rid of a socially inappropriate behavior without replacing it because it is serving a function for that individual.

Together, PBS and FBA make up a holistic approach that considers all of the factors that impact a child or youth, his or her family, and the learning community. The PBS and FBA framework provide schools with a process and plan for providing comprehensive support for children and youth with challenging behavior.

References

Alberto, P. A., & Troutman, A. C. (2006). *Applied behavior analysis for teachers.* Upper Saddle River, NJ: Pearson Education.

American Psychiatric Association. (2000). *Diagnostic and statistical manual of mental disorders* (4th ed., Text revision). Washington, DC: Author.

Centers for Disease Control and Prevention. (2007). *Autism and developmental disabilities monitoring network (ADDM).* Retrieved on August 1, 2008, from http://www.cdc.gov/ncbddd/autism/addm.htm

Conroy, M. A., Asmus, J. M., Sellers, J. A., & Ladwig, C. N. (2005). The use of antecedent-based intervention to decrease stereotypic behavior in a general education classroom: A case study. *Focus on Autism and Other Developmental Disabilities, 20,* 223–230.

Cooper, J. O., Heron, T. E., & Heward, W. L. (2007). *Applied behavior analysis* (2nd ed.). Upper Saddle River, NJ: Pearson Education.

Durand, M. V., & Carr, E. G. (1985). Self-injurious behavior: Motivating conditions and guidelines for treatment. *School Psychology Review, 14,* 171–176.

Durand, M. V., & Crimmins, D. (1992). *Motivation Assessment Scale (MAS).* Topeka, KS: Monaco & Associates.

Fouse, B., & Wheeler, M. (2005). *A treasure chest of behavioral strategies for individuals with autism.* Arlington, TX: Future Horizons.

Heflin, L. J., & Alaimo, D. F. (2007). *Students with autism spectrum disorders: Effective instructional practices.* Upper Saddle River, NJ: Pearson Education.

Horner, R. H., Dunlap, G., Koegel, R. L., Carr, E. G., Sailor, W., Anderson, J., et al. (1990). Toward a technology of nonaversive behavioral support. *Journal of the Association for Persons with Severe Handicaps, 15,* 125–132.

Hundert, J. P. (2007). Training classroom and resource preschool teachers to develop inclusive class interventions for children with disabilities: Generalization for new intervention target. *Journal of Positive Behavior Interventions, 9,* 159–173.

Johnston, S., & O'Neill, R. E. (2001). Searching for effectiveness and efficiency in conducting functional assessments: A review and proposed process for teachers and other practitioners. *Focus on Autism and Developmental Disabilities, 16,* 205–214.

Kluth, P. (2003). *"You're going to love this kid!" Teaching students with autism in the inclusive classroom.* Baltimore: Paul H. Brookes.

Knoster, T. P. (2000). Practical application of functional behavioral assessment in schools. *Journal for the Association of Persons with Severe Handicaps, 25,* 201–211.

Lecavalier, L. (2006). Behavioral and emotional problems in young people with pervasive developmental disorders: Relative prevalence, effects of subject characteristics, and empirical classification. *Journal of Autism and Developmental Disorders, 36,* 1101–1114.

Lennox, D. B., & Miltenberger, R. G. (1989). Conducting a functional assessment of problem behavior in applied settings. *Journal of the Association for Persons with Severe Handicaps, 14,* 304–311.

O'Neill, R. E., Horner, R. H., Albin, R. W., Sprague, J. R. Storey, K., & Newton, J. S. (1997). *Functional assessment and program development for problem behavior.* Pacific Grove, CA: Brooks/Cole Publishing.

Scheuermann, B. K., & Hall, J. A. (2008). *Positive behavioral supports for the classroom.* Upper Saddle River, NJ: Pearson Education.

Scott, T. M., & Nelson, C. M. (1999). Using functional behavioral assessment to develop effective intervention plans: Practical classroom applications. *Journal of Positive Behavior Interventions, 1*, 242–251.

Simpson, R. L., de Boer-Ott, S. R., & Smith-Myles, B. (2003). Inclusion of learners with autism spectrum disorders in general education settings. *Topics in Language Disorders, 23*, 116–133.

Simpson, R. L., Smith-Myles, B., & LaCava, P. (2008). Understanding and responding to the needs of children and youth with autism spectrum disorders. In R. Simpson & B. Smith-Myles (Eds.), *Educating children and youth with autism* (pp. 1–59). Austin, TX: Pro-Ed.

Smith-Myles, B., Simpson, R. L., & de Boer-Ott, S. R. (2008). Inclusion of students with autism spectrum disorders in general education settings. In R. Simpson & B. Smith-Myles (Eds.), *Educating children and youth with autism* (pp. 357–381). Austin, TX: Pro-Ed.

Sparrow, S., Balla, D., & Cicchetti, D. (1984). *The Vineland Adaptive Behavior Scales: Interview edition, survey form manual.* Circle Pines, MN: American Guidance Service.

Sugai, G., Horner, R. H., Dunlap, G., Heineman, M., Lewis, T. J., Nelson, C. M., et al. (2000). Applying positive behavior support and functional behavioral assessment in schools. *Journal of Positive Behavior Interventions, 2*, 131–143.

Webber, J., & Scheuermann, B. (2008). *Educating students with autism: A quick start manual.* Austin, TX: Pro-Ed.

CHAPTER 6

USING INSTRUCTIONAL TECHNOLOGY IN THE CLASSROOM

Marci Kinas Jerome

DEFINING ASSISTIVE TECHNOLOGY

DOES a student with autism supported in the general education classroom need assistive technology (AT) devices and services? Many teachers, both general and special education, struggle with this question as they plan for instruction for students with disabilities. The term *assistive technology* was first defined in the Technology-Related Assistance for Individuals with Disabilities Act of 1988. This act, known as the "Tech Act," provided funding to support statewide planning and support for the delivery of assistive technology (AT) services and was the first major legislation solely directed toward AT (Blackhurst & Edyburn, 2000). Since its initial enactment, the Tech Act of 1988 was repealed and replaced with the Assistive Technology Act of 1998 and was later amended in 2004. Although the Tech Act still supports statewide technology-related assistance for individuals with disabilities of all ages, it was the Individuals with Disabilities Education Improvement Act (IDEA) of 1997 that changed the role of AT for students with disabilities in schools (Dell, Newton, & Petroff, 2008). IDEA 1997 (and its later reauthorization in 2004) requires that each Individualized Education Program (IEP) team "consider whether the child *needs* assistive technology devices and services" for all students eligible for special education services (IDEA, 2004, Sec. 602[1]]).

Although IDEA 2004 requires IEP teams to consider whether students need AT devices and services as part of their individualized educational programs, the law does not provide explicit guidance on how to address this consideration. Research shows that many educators are unfamiliar with the exact definition of AT and feel they lack the necessary training to make informed AT decisions (Marino, Marino, & Shaw, 2006). Also, educators may tend to overlook AT for students with mild disabilities as their needs are not as "obvious" as those of students with physical or sensory disabilities (Puckett, 2005).

Assistive technology is a broad term that encompasses a range of devices and strategies, and can benefit students with a wide range of disabilities in various classroom settings, including students with autism supported in the general education class (Alper & Raharinirina, 2006; Okolo & Bauck, 2007). The intent of this chapter is to provide an overview of the definition of AT and the assessment process as well as an in-depth discussion of specific AT tools to support students with autism in the general education classroom.

IDEA 2004 defined an AT device as "any item, piece of equipment, or product system, whether acquired commercially off the shelf, modified, or customized, that is used to increase, maintain, or improve functional capabilities of a child with a disability" (Sec. 602[1]). This definition may be confusing because it is broad and the terms are not clearly defined. In the definition, an AT device is defined as "any item." This definition is intended to be broad, as to include a range of devices from inexpensive dollar store items such as pencil grips, to complex and expensive devices such as voice output communication systems. However, the definition does not suggest that any device can be considered AT.

The AT device must increase, maintain, or improve functional capabilities of a child with a disability, as stated in the second part of the definition. For students with autism, these functional capabilities include interpersonal skills, communication, motor aspects of writing, composing written materials, reading, study skills, and activities of daily living (Castellani, Nunn, & Warger, 2005). Therefore, teachers can define AT devices as any tools that enable students with disabilities to be successful in the general education classroom, without which the student would not have access to the curriculum and/or whose disability otherwise would interfere with the student's ability to learn.

Because the range of AT tools is so broad, teachers and therapists often discuss AT as a continuum from no technology (no tech), to low technology (low tech), to medium technology (mid tech), to high technology (high tech) tools. Generally, low-tech tools are simple devices/strategies that do not use electronics. For students with mild disabilities, this can include using highlighters to emphasize important words, using a reading guide to help with visual tracking, or using graph

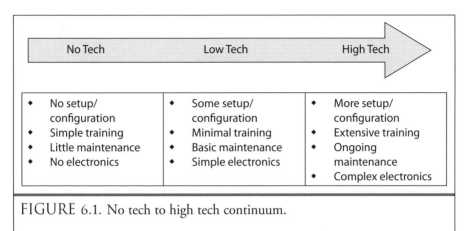

FIGURE 6.1. No tech to high tech continuum.

Note. Adapted from Castellani et al. (2005).

paper to help students line up numbers in a math equation. Electronic devices such as talking calculators, electronic dictionaries, voice recorders, and simple voice output communication devices are considered mid-tech tools. High-tech tools would include computer programs such as a talking word processor, book scanning and reading software, electronic graphic organizers, and software used to create visual supports.

It is important for teachers to conceptualize the AT continuum as more than just a way to classify AT tools based on electronics. As illustrated in Figure 6.1, AT also ranges in its simplicity of implementation, training, and maintenance. For teachers who implement AT tools in their general education classroom, they need tools that are easy to use and fit seamlessly into their daily classroom routines and activities. Many times a simple low-tech tool is the solution. However, teachers should not be intimidated by the complexity of high-tech tools. With the right support from a person trained in AT devices, teachers can implement such tools seamlessly into their classroom routines.

ASSISTIVE TECHNOLOGY ASSESSMENT

Teachers often are overwhelmed by the scope of available technology and may not know how to select appropriate tools for their students. Teachers also believe that they are not informed enough to make AT decisions, and that those decisions should be left to the therapists and AT specialists in their school district (Copley & Ziviani, 2004; Marino et al., 2006). However, teachers are an integral part of the process because they know the strengths and needs of their students and ultimately will be the ones implementing AT in their daily classroom routines. Thus, they should have a vested stake in the devices and tools that are selected.

As with any educational assessment, an AT assessment is a time-intensive, team-based approach. The AT team usually includes members of the IEP team, with one or more members having knowledge of AT devices and assessment. The AT specialist may be someone with formal educational training in AT and/or someone who has on-the-job experience. As a decision-making team, there are several commercial protocols available to help guide the team through the assessment and device selection process. These protocols include *Assessing Students' Needs for Assistive Technology* (Reed & Lahm, 2004), *Education Tech Points* (Bowser & Reed, 1998), and *Functional Evaluation for Assistive Technology* (FEAT; Raskind & Bryant, 2002).

Furthermore, there are several free resources that are available to IEP teams. The SETT Framework (Zabala, 2002) is an organizational tool that provides IEP teams with a set of questions to collaboratively discuss when considering AT tools for students; the framework considers the *student*, the *environment*, the *tasks*, and the *tools*. Also, the Wisconsin Assistive Technology Initiative (WATI) provides a series of free checklists and assessment forms on its Web site to guide IEP teams through the AT assessment process (see http://www.wati.org). The focus of this chapter is to help general education teachers understand the rationale and thought process behind an AT assessment, to look at and discuss the important questions in considering AT for their students, and to present appropriate technology options for students with autism supported in the general education classroom.

Teachers and therapists often start with the AT tool itself and omit the assessment process. They may have learned about a new tool from a colleague or at a conference and decide that this is the best AT device for the student, or they find a device in their classroom that is not being used and decide to use it with their student. Although this eagerness is greatly supported and appreciated, it is important to stress to teachers that the selection of AT starts first with the student. The AT selection process is a needs match process beginning with an examination of the learning expectations in the classroom, including academic, social, and behavioral.

First of all, identify what tasks (academic, interpersonal, behavioral) the student can do well and where he or she tends to struggle. Then, in areas in which the student struggles, identify what supports have already been tried. These supports include any curricular adaptations, strategies, and/or resources that are used to help students in areas in which they struggle. Once the supports have been identified, determine why these current supports are not working or may not be the most efficient way for the student to meet his or her goals. The assessment should identify the student's specific needs. Once those needs have been identified, choose AT tools that target those needs. Table 6.1 identifies a method for assessing student needs and determining supports.

TABLE 6.1

AT ASSESSMENT QUESTIONS

- What task(s) is the student required to complete?
- What are the student's strengths and needs?
- What strategies does the child currently use?
- What obstacles keep the student from being successful?
- What technology might be appropriate?

CASE STUDIES

Jack is a fourth grader. He is expected to write throughout the day in his classroom. Although Jack is very creative and likes to illustrate his work, he really struggles with writing. His handwriting is illegible and it seems to take him forever to get a few sentences written. He needs something to increase his legibility and speed of writing. The teacher has worked with the occupational therapist (OT) to try several pencil grips and other tools to improve the legibility, and the teacher has tried a positive reward system to try to motivate Jack to get his work done at the same pace as the rest of the class. However, Jack is frustrated because writing is still hard, and the teacher is frustrated because it takes Jack so long to complete his work. The teacher and the OT discuss using the computer as a way to alleviate the graphomotor difficulties Jack displays with handwriting. They still need to investigate whether a desktop computer or a portable word processing system would work best for Jack in his classroom.

The teacher and OT decided to have Jack try to use the computer to write in his morning journal. The first day he was really excited to try the computer. The teacher showed him all of the features and he liked it. Over the course of the week, Jack seemed less excited about using the computer. Although it was easier and faster for him to use, he did not like being separated from the other students in the back of the room. Plus, the teacher's computer was back there and while students worked on their morning journals, the teacher worked on her computer. The other students quickly started to make fun of Jack for being the teacher's pet because he sat next to her every morning on the computer. The teacher, in collaboration with the OT, decided to have Jack work on a portable word processing device at his desk. Although both Jack and his teacher needed some training on how to get the device to save and print his work, Jack was much happier because he could still sit with his friends at his desk and his friends thought his device was cool. His teacher was pleased because Jack was handing in his work on time and it was easy to read.

Emma is a fifth-grade student with autism, and she has a difficult time transitioning from homeroom to her first period class. Although Emma likes the teacher and the students, the "buzz" of morning energy is difficult for her to handle. She often does not want to enter the classroom because of the increased noise and activity level of the first period class. The teacher has tried a token system and a peer buddy system, but Emma still seems very fidgety and anxious in the class. The teacher and OT decide a sensory tool may help Emma remain calm during class. The OT worked with Emma to select a sensory tool that she likes from the OT's sensory toolbox. This toolbox included of a variety of fidgets, weighted objects, textured objects, and vibrating objects. Classroom fidgets generally are small bendable or squeezeable objects that can easily and discretely be hidden in desks or used in the student's lap. It also may be a vibrating pen, an art style eraser that is pliable, or a pencil topper that is safe to chew on. Emma had an opportunity to explore the options and test them out in class to see which one she liked best.

Once possible AT tools have been identified for students like Jack and Emma, the teacher often will work in conjunction with therapists or AT specialists. The teacher and the student will need to allow a trial period to see how effective or ineffective the tool is in meeting the student's goals. Sometimes, additional training and support may be needed for the student and/or the teacher. Use of the device needs to fit well into the daily routine of the general education classroom. However, it could take several adjustments to the device before the student and teacher are both comfortable with its use.

ASSISTIVE TECHNOLOGY TOOLS FOR STUDENTS WITH AUTISM

Identifying AT tools for students with autism can be challenging because the range of support needs for students with autism is very broad. Many students with autism with more intense support needs often require technology to support communication and sensory needs. Although these technologies are important, they are beyond the scope of this chapter. The technology tools discussed in this chapter represent tools most often used in general education classrooms for students with autism accessing the general education curriculum.

Written Language

Many students with autism have motor planning difficulties that may affect their ability to write (Dennis, Edelman, & Prelock, 2006). Many students with learning disabilities (LD) also struggle with writing mechanics and the writing process, and research shows that for students with LD, writing can be a frustrating and often laborious task. Although students may differ in their areas of writing need, they most often struggle with skills such as organization, spelling, grammar, revising, handwriting, and motivation (Behrmann & Jerome, 2002). The available technology tools for writing are similar for both students with autism and LD. This is important information to note because teachers and therapists may be more familiar with AT for students with LD than those for autism, as many AT products are marketed as tools to support learning disabilities.

Writing Mechanics

Many students with autism struggle with handwriting for different reasons. Some students with autism may perseverate on writing. They "draw" their letters, paying very close attention to the detail of each and every letter, thus taking an inordinate amount of time to complete a written assignment. Teachers may describe this as obsessive-compulsive behavior. Like students with LD, students with autism may have dysgraphia and struggle to produce legible writing. Finally, some students struggle with the sensory process of writing. They may not like the feel or color of the pencil, pen, or paper they are using, and this keeps them from wanting to engage in the writing activity.

There are several low-tech solutions that may help students with writing mechanics. Occupational therapists usually can recommend a variety of pencil grips and writing guides to help students. These tools may give students more control over the physical manipulation of their pencil, resulting in more legible handwriting. For students with sensory needs, it may take some trial and error to find a writing tool that meets their needs. Students may prefer a pencil or pen that has a certain feel, grip, thickness, or color.

Research pertaining to writing difficulties for students with autism supported in the general education classroom is limited (Delano, 2007). However, a look at the research related to writing difficulties and students with LD provides some insight into this topic. Research shows that students with LD who have difficulty with writing may overly concentrate on such mechanical concerns and lose track of their overall writing plans and thoughts (Baker, Gersten, & Graham, 2003; Gersten & Baker, 2001). Also, several errors may distract readers from the message that the writer is trying to convey (MacArthur, 2000). Finally, students may become frustrated with the writing process and "shut down," producing a limited amount of writing in both quantity and quality (Baker et al., 2003).

As with students with LD, working on the computer often alleviates the handwriting struggle and allows students with autism to write more freely. For other students, using the computer serves as a motivational tool, as they associate the computer with being cool and easy for them to use. For students struggling with writing, having the opportunity to work on the computer is motivating enough for them to engage in writing tasks. As students get older, they may become increasingly embarrassed by their poor handwriting. They often want to find ways to improve their written work in order to avoid negative comments made by their peers. Thus, there are two high-tech choices for providing writing support for students—using the desktop computer or a portable word processor.

Desktop computer. Computers are available in most general education classrooms and many come preloaded with a standard word processing program. The benefits of using a desktop computer in the classroom are that they are readily available, most students are familiar with their general operation, and there are standard word processing file formats so files can be moved across computers with ease. In addition, they support any secondary technology that may be needed, such as screen magnification software for the student with vision impairment. As with the example of Jack introduced earlier in this chapter, classroom computers often are placed away from the main classroom learning activities. Students may feel conscientious or embarrassed about standing out from their peers, and therefore, may be uncomfortable using the computer for daily assignments.

Portable word processing. Students' feelings of alienation from their peers and standing out can be minimized by using a laptop computer for writing instead of a desktop computer. A laptop has all of the same capabilities as a desktop computer, but is portable. Laptops may be a good option for some students, but their size, weight, and price may deter from their appeal. Another solution is a portable word processor. A portable word processor is similar to a laptop in that it is smaller than a computer and runs on a battery, so there are no attached wires or plugs to keep the student restricted to a certain area of the room. However, a portable word processor varies significantly from a laptop because its functionality is severely limited, allowing students in most models to only use a basic word processor. Some newer models have additional applets for enhanced writing tools and organizational tools, but they are not designed to surf the Internet and play multimedia files. Portable word processors also have smaller screen sizes, usually only displaying 5–7 lines of text at a time. The main appeal of portable word processors is their portability, durability, and price as compared to a standard laptop.

The advantage of using a portable word processing device for a student with autism is its simplicity of use. The devices generally have few keyboard options and simpler processes to save files. There are fewer visual distractions as the screen only shows letters and words, and there is no graphic support on the devices. Students also are free to move around the room with these devices. At the same time, students may dislike the device because of the small screen size and the lack of color on the screen. Of course, if a student or teacher wants to engage in more dynamic and creative activities such as developing brochures or multimedia presentations, they will need to either transfer the text from the portable word processor to a computer and then further manipulate it, or complete the entire activity on a desktop or laptop computer.

For students with autism, it may come down to personal choice over whether they want to use a laptop or a portable word processing device. As with selecting a specific pen or pencil because of its texture, they may like the feel of one device over another. Young students may select to use a portable word processor because they think it is cool and their peers like it. However, as they get older and their peers are using laptops, they may decide that they prefer to use a laptop.

Organization tools. Students with writing difficulties often struggle with organizing their thoughts to write efficiently. "Planning and organizing tools can encourage activities such as concept mapping, story webbing, brainstorming, visual graphing, and/or outlining. These tools help students organize their ideas and investigate relationships during the writing process" (Blair, Ormsbee, & Brandes, 2002, p. 3). Research has shown that using computer-generated graphic organizers (e.g., Inspiration software) reduced students' reluctance to write, thus increasing their motivation and attitude toward writing (Blair et al., 2002; Sturm & Rankin-Erickson, 2002).

There are several ways to integrate graphic organizers into classroom writing instruction to support students with autism. First, teachers can use a computer program such as Inspiration™ to create print-based graphic organizers for students to use to take notes on during class lectures or to organize their thoughts at the beginning of a writing assignment. Using the computer, teachers easily can customize the size, font, and color of the graphic organizer for each student, as well as additional supports such a picture symbols or additional directions. The advantage of a print-based graphic organizer is that it easily integrates into the classroom routine; students can remain at their desks to complete them and also can easily take them along for group work or other class activities. Students also may develop their own graphic organizers on the computer using a variety of software programs. Teachers are able to develop and save custom templates for students or students can use the program to brainstorm writing ideas and create their own maps.

There are several advantages for students to use the graphic organization software to develop their own organizers and maps. As with word processing, students with autism may benefit from typing their thoughts instead of writing them on a print-based web for sensory, motivation, or graphomotor reasons. Furthermore, programs such as Inspiration™ and Kidspiration™ enable students to manipulate the visual elements on the screen either with a mouse or using a touch sensitive screen (such as a SMART Board™). Students with autism may seek this type of visual and kinesthetic approach, while occupational therapists may support its use to reinforce motor planning and visual tracking skills. Also, when used in a group setting with a projector, graphic organization software fosters communication and socialization opportunities for students with autism.

Editing. Students with writing difficulties often struggle with editing their written work. In particular, when asked to review their written work either by reading it silently or out loud, many students will read what they think they wrote as opposed to what is actually written on the paper. Although this problem is not specific only to students with writing difficulties, it may be more pronounced in this population. One AT tool that can help is a software program that reads aloud the text typed on the screen. These programs may be referred to as *speech synthesis software* or as *text readers*.

Although students may not identify mistakes when they read something they have written, they may recognize the errors when the text is read back to them in a different voice, thus providing them with the opportunity to correct their mistakes. There are a variety of programs available that vary in price, voice quality, and additional features such as built-in spell checkers and homophone checkers. Some students with autism may identify better with certain reading voices, while others may prefer not to have their text read at all. It is an individual preference.

General Education Software

Computers have become standard teaching and learning tools in the general education classroom. As discussed previously, computers are efficient tools for many students with autism to enable them to be successful writers. Students with autism also may benefit from using an educational software program as a learning tool.

The terms *educational software* or *academic software* are general terms that broadly represent a range of programs. When discussing academic software there are two distinct types of software programs. The first group is productivity software; these programs usually are teacher tools, or sometimes student tools, that enable teachers to create materials to use in the classroom. Productivity programs include graphic organization software (Inspiration™, Kidspiration™), worksheet development software (Math Companion™), and picture symbol/activity programs (Boardmaker™, Picture It™).

The second category includes activity-based programs; these programs present educational content to students and may include drill and practice activities, simulation and problem-solving activities, information presentations, and tutorials on various educational concepts. There is an abundance of educational software on the market and these include popular programs found in many schools and homes such as the Jump Start Series™, the Reader Rabbit Series™, and the Math Blaster Series™. This section of the chapter focuses on selecting activity-based educational software programs for students with autism.

The task of selecting software involves trying to find a program that is both visually interesting and engaging to the student while providing the support features that students with disabilities need (see Table 6.2). Also, the program should provide the teacher with control options as well as the flexibility to expand the program by adding his or her own content and also differentiating the content

---

Table 6.2

Features to Consider in Selecting Software for Students With Autism

Teacher Features	• Adjust the initial skill level for each student • Control auditory and visual feedback/reinforcement • Adjust criteria for mastery level • Adjust response times to answer questions • Modify content • Generate student progress and data reports
Student Features	• Consistency • Ease of navigation • Self-paced instruction • Built-in access methods • Auditory and visual cues • Auditory and visual feedback • Online help (can a question or directions be repeated any time?)

Note. Adapted from Hurley and Shumway (1997).

---

for different learners (i.e., adjusting the difficulty level). Some programs will even monitor progress and generate student data reports.

The most supportive programs are ones that provide scaffolding. For example, the program will prompt the student in some way when he or she chooses a wrong answer. Each time the wrong answer is selected, the student will continue to receive prompts until they are only left with the correct answer. The most important thing teachers should do when they are evaluating software programs is to deliberately get the same answer wrong at least three times to see how the program responds.

For students with autism, educational software is a valuable teaching tool in the general education classroom. Many students with autism respond well to the steady presentation of information and consistent reinforcement provided by drill and practice activities. Research shows that computer assisted instruction increased student motivation and reduced behavior problems for students with autism (Higgins & Boone, 1993; Mirenda, 2001). Furthermore, because most students are motivated by educational games, their use in the classroom increases social opportunities for students with autism through multiplayer or cooperative games and activities.

Many educational programs are not designed with students with disabilities in mind, and thus do not support their learning needs (Boone & Higgins, 2007; Kimball & Smith, 2007). Although educational programs that include animated graphics and sounds may seem visually appealing to general education students and teachers, these same programs may appear visually "cluttered" and overwhelming for some students with disabilities. Also, without consistent menus, tools, and navigational support, students may become lost within the software program, thus increasing their frustration level and limiting their ability to use the program independently.

With regards to reinforcement, programs often reward students for answering questions correctly with a sound and animation sequence such as an animation of hands applauding paired with an applause sound. When students answer incorrectly, programs also often respond with a sound and animation sequence. Some students may find the reinforcers provided for the wrong answer (such as an animation of a tomato splattering on the screen paired with a splat sound) more interesting than the correct answer, thereby increasing reinforcement of incorrect responses (Kimball & Smith, 2007). Finally, many educational software programs do not provide enough flexibility to support students with autism. The inability to adjust elements such as the content learned, number of questions, and type of feedback and reinforcement provided may increase student frustration and aversion to a program, thus eliminating it as a possible teacher tool.

For example, Miguel is an 11-year-old student with autism. He loves to use the computer. The general education teacher often rewards Miguel with free time on the computer for following classroom rules and completing his work on time. During free time, Miguel's favorite program is Amazing Animals™ by DK Software because he likes anything to do with animals. Every day Miguel would read the information related to his favorite animals, watch the animal videos, and play included games. Because of his love for the computer, the general education teacher thought he would be motivated to complete written work on the computer as well as play other educational games to reinforce concepts he was currently learning in class. Miguel liked typing in Microsoft Word. However, he became very upset anytime he misspelled a word and the red line would appear under his misspelled word. His first response was to shut down the entire program, losing all of his written work. Miguel exhibited the same response when he used the typing program, Type to Learn™, that other students were using in his computer class to practice and reinforce keyboarding skills. In the typing exercises, when a student completes the activity without making a certain amount of typing errors the student is rewarded with a fun typing game. If the student scores below the criterion, then the student needs to repeat the typing exercise and is not rewarded with a game.

Miguel would become extremely agitated if he did not score well enough to earn the game. He would shut down the program, bang his fists, and scream out "It's too hard, it's too hard!" disrupting the entire class. The general education teacher was concerned and spoke with her district's educational technology support specialist. The technology specialist showed the general education teacher settings in Microsoft Word to both remove the red line from misspelled words and also how to increase the number of times a file is auto-saved when writing a Word document. The auto-save features would minimize the amount of work lost. For the Type to

Learn™ program, the technology specialist showed the general education teacher how to access the teacher options in the program. Along with the ability to set the starting level of difficulty and how often students should receive a game break, the teacher options menu allows teachers to set the criterion level needed for "mastery" of the typing exercise. The general education teacher was able to lower the mastery level, so Miguel could earn the reward game. Over time, the teacher could slowly increase the level of mastery required as Miguel improved his typing skills.

Time Management/Organization

Many students with autism and Asperger's syndrome have poor organizational skills (Myles, Ferguson, & Hagiwara, 2007; Myles & Simpson, 2002). Students may have trouble completing homework assignments because they have left the required materials at school, forgotten to write down their homework assignments, or left completed homework at home.

There are several technology tools to support students with organization of daily schedules, homework assignments, and classroom routines. Many general education teachers already implement a wide range of low-tech AT solutions to help students stay better organized that include providing students with calendars, planners, visual timers, and checklists that outline daily schedules, routines, assignments, and expectations. Classrooms often have daily schedules posted in a place that is accessible to all of the students, and teachers may review those schedules each morning with the class. For homework, teachers may post daily homework assignments and ask students to write down those homework assignments in their daily planner. At the end of the day, teachers may ask students to review their daily planner when packing up their backpacks to ensure they take home the necessary work. For some students with autism, these strategies may not be enough to stay on track, and additional support strategies such as personal digital assistants (PDAs) may need to be implemented.

Personal Digital Assistants

For students with autism, using a daily planner to write down homework assignments and class schedules may be difficult for several reasons. First, typical homework planners often are small and allow only a few words or lines to be written. Students with fine motor difficulties may struggle to write legibly in small spaces. Second, the prompts/directions that are written in the daily planner may not be enough for the student to understand what is expected of him when he is working on the assignment independently. Students may need assistance in understanding what they need to take home when discussing homework or what the expectations are in regards to completion of assignments both in the classroom and at home.

Personal Digital Assistants (PDAs) are small, portable electronic devices that enable individuals to use, manipulate, save, and transfer a wide range of applications and data. PDAs range in size, price, screen color and resolution, memory storage, and availability of additional software and hardware features. Simple PDAs afford users portable personal organization tools such as an address book, calendar, task lists, and a notepad. More advanced PDAs act as mini computers and allow users to record and play multimedia components (audio, images, and videos), to store and manipulate word processing documents and spreadsheets, play games, and surf the Internet. Users add information to the PDA through a variety of methods. Students can type in the information using a stylus pen with an onscreen keyboard or they can use the stylus pen to write directly on the PDA in what is known as "graffiti." They also can use a thumb pad keyboard built into the PDA or use an external full-size keyboard that attaches to the PDA. Furthermore, most PDAs synchronize with a desktop computer to backup information and to transfer additional files.

Research (Myles et al., 2007) shows that students with autism may benefit from using a PDA because it provides structure as well as auditory/visual cues, matching the learning needs of students with autism. For students with dysgraphia, using a PDA to type in information may be easier than writing it down on paper. Furthermore, PDAs allow students to write more information in less time because most calendar and organizational tools accept an unlimited amount of text. An important feature of the PDA is the ability to backup entered data so if a student accidently erases something, his or her data is saved and can be restored. Because many PDAs support audio notes, students and teachers can easily record important assignment information as well as detailed instructions when needed. Using a PDA with multimedia capabilities, teachers can develop visual supports and cues for students. For instance, using the built-in camera, teachers can help students take a picture of each of their textbooks. The teacher can organize the books into class folders. When the student is packing his backpack, he can refer to his pictures as a visual cue to pack the correct books for his class. Finally, because students with autism may have difficulty completing work in a timely manner, students and teachers can use the alarm capability available in many PDAs to help them work within the allotted time.

Research conducted by Myles et al. (2007) discusses a high school student with Asperger's syndrome and his use of a PDA as an AT tool to improve his organizational skills. Joseph was expected to enter his homework assignment daily into his homework planner for each class as was required of all general education students in the high school. However, Joseph was inconsistent in recording his homework assignments. When he did, he left out important information such as the due date, the class the assignment was for, or details about the assignment. Joseph was given a PDA and he and his resource teacher were trained on how to use it. Joseph was asked to use the PDA to record his homework assignment in three classes over 25 class sessions. Joseph was scored not only for entering an assignment into the PDA, but for providing the salient information for the assignment, including the due date and assignment details.

The study showed that Joseph made significant improvements in using his planner. He used it 75% of the time compared to an average of 30% of the time when he used the paper planner. The researchers contributed the success to (a) difference in handwriting demands, (b) ease of PDA use, and (c) motivation. Also, the PDA was appealing to Joseph, which may have increased his motivation to use it. Finally, because PDAs are common technology tools among high school and college students, Joseph would not feel out of place using one in his general education classroom.

There are several considerations in using PDAs for students with autism. First, because PDAs are very small, they are easy to lose or break. Unlike a paper homework planner, there can be a considerable cost associated with the continual replacement of electronic equipment. Also, the size limits both how large content appears on the screen and the fine motor skills required to manipulate the device itself. Because some individuals with autism have fine motor problems, it is important to test out several devices to see which one is the best fit. There are some larger PDAs available, however the larger the device, the less portable it becomes. Also, both students and teachers need to be provided with adequate training and support in selecting and using software for the PDA. There are several software options available to use as "planners" or "task lists," and it is important that easy-to-use programs are selected that also support students' learning needs.

CONCLUSION

This chapter provided a brief overview of how assistive technology tools can support students with autism in the general education classroom. Although IDEA 2004 requires IEP teams to consider whether a student with autism needs assistive technology, the law does not provide specific guidance for selecting, integrating, and troubleshooting using assistive technology in the classroom. AT devices include no-tech, low-tech, mid-tech, and high-tech devices that enable students with disabilities to be successful in the general education classroom, without which the student would not have access to the curriculum and/or otherwise would interfere with his or her ability to learn.

General education teachers, in collaboration with special education, related services therapists, and education technology specialists, can implement a range of technology tools to best meet their students' needs. The team should identify and recommend AT tools through a needs match process. The AT selection process begins with an examination of the learning expectations in the classroom, including academic, social, and behavioral, and ends with the pairing of assistive technology that targets the specific needs of each student. There are many resources available to help educators with the AT consideration process.

For students with autism, assistive technology can help them stay engaged in the academic content while supporting their distinct learning needs. Furthermore, AT can help students with autism be engaged in the social dynamics of the general education classroom. As discussed, many students with autism struggle with writing, specifically handwriting, organization, and editing. A range of tools are available including using adapted writing instruments that feel comfortable, typing using a desktop computer or portable word processor to alleviate handwriting difficulties, using graphic organizers to aid in brainstorming and organization of ideas, and using text-to-speech software to assist students with the editing process. Students with autism also may benefit from using educational software programs as a learning tool that include specific features that support their learning needs. Consistent navigation, reinforcement, and scaffolding along with other student and teacher features engage and support students in the academic content while reducing problem behavior. Finally, personal digital assistants can support students with organization of daily schedules, homework assignments, and classroom routines.

REFERENCES

Alper, S., & Raharinirina, S. (2006). Assistive technology for individuals with disabilities: A review and synthesis of the literature. *Journal of Special Education Technology, 21*, 47–64.

Assistive Technology Act of 1998, 29 U.S.C. §3001 et seq. Retrieved October 21, 2008, from http://frwebgate6.access.gpo.gov/cgi-bin/TEXTgate.cgi?WAISdocID=675836 104933+45+1+0&WAISaction=retrieve

Baker, S., Gersten, R., & Graham, S. (2003). Teaching expressive writing to students with learning disabilities: Research-based applications and examples. *Journal of Learning Disabilities, 36*, 109–123.

Behrmann, M., & Jerome, M. K. (2002). *Assistive technology for students with mild disabilities: Update 2002.* Arlington, VA: ERIC Clearinghouse on Disabilities and Gifted Education. (ERIC Document Reproduction Service No. ED463595)

Blackhurst, A. E., & Edyburn, D. L. (2000). A brief history of special education technology. *Special Education Technology Practice, 2*, 21–36.

Blair, R. B., Ormsbee, C., & Brandes, J. (2002). *Using writing strategies and visual teaching software to enhance the written performance of students with mild disabilities* (Report No. RC 023 427). Reno, NV: Annual National Conference Proceedings of the American Council on Rural Education. (ERIC Document Reproduction Service No. ED463125)

Boone, R., & Higgins, K. (2007, Nov). The software √-List: Evaluating educational software for use by students with disabilities. *Technology in Action, 3*, 1–16.

Bowser, G., & Reed, P. (1998). *Education tech points: A framework for assistive technology planning.* Winchester, OR: Coalition for Assistive Technology in Oregon.

Castellani, J., Nunn, J. A., & Warger, C. L. (Eds). (2005). *Considering the need for assistive technology within the individualized education program* [Monograph]. Columbia, MD: Johns Hopkins University, Center for Technology in Education.

Copley, J., & Ziviani, J. (2004). Barriers to the use of assistive technology for children with multiple disabilities. *Occupational Therapy International, 11*, 229–243.

Dennis, R., Edelman, S., & Prelock, P. (2006) Sensory and motor considerations in the assessment of children with ASD. In P. Prelock (Ed.), *Autism spectrum disorders: Issues in assessment and intervention* (pp. 303–343). Austin, TX: Pro-Ed.

Delano, M. E. (2007). Use of strategy instruction to improve the story writing skills of a student with Asperger syndrome. *Focus on Autism and Other Developmental Disabilities, 22,* 252–258.

Dell, A. G., Newton, D. A., & Petroff, J. G. (2008). *Assistive technology in the classroom: Enhancing the school experiences of students with disabilitie*s. Upper Saddle River, NJ: Pearson.

Gersten, R., & Baker, S. (2001). Teaching expressive writing to students with learning disabilities: A meta-analysis. *The Elementary School Journal, 101*, 251–272.

Higgins, K., & Boone, R. (1993). Creating individualized computer-assisted instruction for students with autism using multimedia authoring software. *Focus on Autism and Other Developmental Disabilities, 11,* 69–78.

Hurley, K., & Shumway, P. (1997). Features of award winning software for special needs students. *Closing the Gap, 16,* 6, 30, 46.

Individuals with Disabilities Education Improvement Act, PL 108-446, 118 Stat. 2647 (2004).

Kimball, J. W., & Smith, K. (2007). Crossing the bridge: From best practices to software packages. *Focus on Autism and Other Developmental Disabilities, 22,* 131–134.

Marino, M. T., Marino, E. C., & Shaw, S. F. (2006). Making informed assistive technology decisions for students with high incidence disabilities. *Teaching Exceptional Children, 38*(6), 18–25.

MacArthur, C. A. (2000). New tools for writing: Assistive technology for students with writing difficulties. *Topics in Language Disorders, 20*(4), 85–100.

Mirenda, P. (2001). Autism, augmentative communication, and assistive technology: What do we really know? *Focus on Autism and Other Developmental Disabilities, 16,* 141–151.

Myles, B. S., Ferguson, H., & Hagiwara, T. (2007). Using a personal digital assistant to improve the recording of homework assignments by an adolescent with Asperger syndrome. *Focus on Autism and Other Developmental Disabilities, 22,* 96–99.

Myles, B. S., & Simpson, R. L. (2002). Asperger syndrome: An overview of characteristics. *Focus on Autism and Other Developmental Disabilities, 17,* 132–137.

Okolo, C. M., & Bauck, E. C. (2007). Research about assistive technology: 2000–2006. What have we learned? *Journal of Special Education Technology, 22,* 19–33.

Puckett, K. (2005). An assistive technology toolkit: Type II applications for students with mild disabilities. *Computers in the Schools, 22,* 107–117.

Raskind, M. H., & Bryant, B. R. (2002). *Functional evaluation for assistive technology (FEAT)*. Austin, TX: Psycho-Educational Services.

Reed, P., & Lahm, E. (Eds.). (2004). *Assessing students' needs for assistive technology*. Oshkosh: Wisconsin Assistive Technology Initiative.

Sturm, J. M., & Rankin-Erickson, J. L. (2002). Effects of hand-drawn and computer-generated concept mapping on the expository writing of middle school students with learning disabilities. *Learning Disabilities Research and Practice, 17,* 124–139.

Zabala, J. S. (2002). *Update of SETT framework, 2002*. Retrieved October 21, 2008, from http://sweb.uky.edu/~jszaba0/SETTupdate2002.html

CHAPTER 7

SUPPORTING PARENTS OF CHILDREN DIAGNOSED WITH AUTISM

An Acceptance and Commitment Therapy Approach

JOHN T. BLACKLEDGE, DANIEL J. MORAN, & THANE DYKSTRA

MELISSA and Michael have been married for 17 years, and are the parents of three children: Carl, Denise, and Tim. Carl and Denise are both in their early teens and in junior high school. Tim is 4 years old and has been diagnosed with autism. Tim exhibits poorly developed verbal skills, engages in self-stimulation behaviors (such as flapping his hands and repeatedly rocking back and forth), and is not socially interactive with his family. Tim can occasionally vocalize when he wants to eat, but cannot otherwise make his needs known. Since Tim was 30 months old he sleeps very little (approximately 4 hours per night), screams and cries when frightened, and is not easily soothed by his parents. Melissa and Brian have chosen to hire a board certified behavior analyst (BCBA) to develop a home-based curriculum to improve his social skills, activities of daily living, and verbal skills. Starting the curriculum was an arduous task, but also has been very rewarding because Tim began to acquire important verbal skills. When friends ask about Tim's progress with the Applied Behavior Analysis (ABA) program, the parents report being very pleased. Family members who only see Tim every few months remark on how well his skills are improving between each visit. Most importantly, when the BCBA consultant summarized a year's worth of data, it was obvious that Tim, at 5 years old, had improved in noteworthy domains.

When family members ask Melissa and Michael for an honest appraisal about their life situation, they report high levels of stress, frequent marital conflicts, and lingering feelings of depression and anxiety about Tim's future. In response, their family suggested that they each seek individual counseling. During the first meeting with her individual therapist, Melissa said,

> I'm proud of how far Tim's come since beginning treatment. But let's face it . . . I'm never going to be able to leave him home alone. Sure he's doing great, but he's not going to be able to live independently or hold a job. He's asking for things and mellowing out a bit, but he's a 24/7 kid. And the treatment is expensive. Michael is working more than ever because insurance isn't covering the treatment. Managing and training the college kids who work with Tim on his daily program is a tough task. Some experts say Tim needs 40 hours of treatment. I can barely handle the 20 hours we give him! That makes me feel guilty. And I'm confused by all the conflicting reports about the types of treatments. Plus, Mike's absence makes me feel angry and isolated; it leads to fights. And our financial situation makes me feel helpless. I was so involved in my older kids' lives, and I'm not anymore, so I feel ashamed of myself. I had high expectations for Tim, you know? But when I'm honest with myself, I'm scared . . . scared and sad about his life . . . about him.

After the session, the therapist session notes summarized Melissa's situation with words all too familiar to many parents of children diagnosed with autism: "despair, fatigue, financial stress, organizational challenges, guilt, confusion, anger, isolation, marital conflict, helplessness, shame, fear." We'll revisit Melissa, Michael and their son, Tim, later in the chapter. But first, we'll discuss in detail the multitude of psychological stressors parents with children like Tim face. Educators and administrators should understand that supporting parents can help provide for better education and support systems for their students with autism.

STRESSORS FACED BY PARENTS OF CHILDREN DIAGNOSED WITH AUTISM

In recent years, autism has received more attention than ever in the research literature, at professional conferences, and in the popular media (Tager-Flusberg, Joseph, & Folstein, 2001). This can be attributed to a variety of factors, including the potentially extreme behavior of children diagnosed with autism, the controversy over which treatment is best, the potential for some children diagnosed with autism to recover completely, the rise of empirically supported treatments, judicial interventions mandating quality care, and the emotional impact of the situation faced by these children and their families.

In the context of this greatly increased attention to children with autism and their problems, it is surprising how little attention has been paid in the literature to the myriad difficulties faced by the parents of children diagnosed with autism. Even less attention has been paid to the development and implementation of treatments designed to help these parents cope with some very overwhelming problems. Little research exists regarding the treatment of parents of children diagnosed with autism. Teachers of children diagnosed with autism will be better prepared to provide services when they understand the context of the child's family life. Familial stress and strain in the household environment can diminish a child's capacity to learn and develop appropriately. It is in the best interests of the child for educators to be aware of these factors and to understand that there are supportive services to assist with these challenges. Educators are part of the interdisciplinary team treating children with autism, so being sensitive to these stressors, and being able to make appropriate referrals for the families to seek professional assistance are critical to providing excellent educational care.

The defining characteristics of autism directly describe the difficulties and distress parents can expect to face. A core characteristic of autism spectrum disorder is "the presence of markedly abnormal or impaired development in social interaction and communication and a markedly restricted repertoire of activity and interests" (American Psychological Association [APA], 1994, p. 66). Although autism characteristics vary greatly, they often include features such as a relative lack of communication skills, various types of repetitive self-stimulation (Lovaas, Litrownik, & Mann, 1971), self-injurious behavior, aggression, low tolerance for changes in the environment, and a preoccupation with various objects (Koegel & Koegel, 1995).

The number of treatments for children diagnosed with autism stands in stark contrast to treatments available for the parents affected by the disorder's repercussions. A variety of interventions have been developed and implemented in the treatment of autism, including pharmacotherapy, treatments such as TEACCH (Treatment and Education of Autistic and Related Communication-Handicapped Children) that attempt to build on existing child strengths, standard public school special education classes, sensory motor therapy, facilitated communication, and even dietary/vitamin treatments (Maurice, Green, & Luce, 1996). The most intensively tested and effective treatments incorporate behavior analysis (Koegel & Koegel, 1995; Lovaas, 1977; Maurice et al., 1996). Behavior analytic treatments of autism are time and labor-intensive. They can involve five 8-hour days per week of therapy by skilled behavior analysts. Parents or caretakers of the child with autism are required to continue this kind of training during the hours when the child is at home. Doing so requires consistency and willingness to tolerate aversive interactions with the child, and to respond to the child's behavior (often during difficult circumstances) in ways that often may differ from what the parent may strongly feel like doing. Such treatments also can impose a significant financial drain on parents, costing tens of thousands of dollars per year. All of this is in addition to the inherent emotional and practical difficulties of the disorder itself. As might be expected, such emotional, physical, and financial demands can be a source of extreme stress on the caregivers of children diagnosed with autism. However, in many instances, if delivered early enough, well enough, and long enough such treatments usually lead to marked improvement and have the potential to make some treated children virtually indistinguishable from nondisabled children.

CHARACTERISTICS OF PARENTS OF CHILDREN DIAGNOSED WITH AUTISM

The often extreme challenges discussed in the last section hint at the toll that rearing a child with autism can take on a parent. The following research review describes the specific forms this toll can take. Because there is a relative lack of empirical work focused specifically on the parents of children diagnosed with autism, this literature review has been expanded to include studies on the impact of developmentally disabled children in general on their parents. This is a reasonable research strategy given the similarities in the amount of time and degree of effort required to take care of both groups of individuals, as well as autism's status as a specific example of a developmental disability.

General Distress

A number of studies have provided evidence for a high degree of distress in parents of children diagnosed with autism and parents of developmentally disabled children in general. Parents of children diagnosed with autism tend to experience a great deal of stress (DeMyer, 1979; Holroyd, Brown, Wikler, & Simmons, 1975), even more than parents of children with Down syndrome and psychiatrically diagnosed children (Holroyd & McArthur, 1976; Wolf, Noh, Fisman, & Speechley, 1989). Mothers of children diagnosed with autism, given that mothers are generally the primary caregivers for children diagnosed with autism, tend to have unusually stressful concerns about their children's current dependencies, future occupational prospects, and the restrictions placed on other family members by the child with autism (DeMyer, 1979; Holroyd & McArthur, 1976).

Other studies have found that daycare and treatment needs for children with autism and other developmental disabilities significantly contribute to parental stress. Challenges in finding and maintaining supportive services and the limited understanding of the disorder by many childcare and health professionals also are significant stressors (Cutler & Kozloff, 1987; Unger & Powell, 1980).

Maintaining consistent contact with school and treatment facility personnel, once treatment is finally provided, often continues to elevate stress levels (McCubbin, Cauble, & Patterson, 1982).

The severity of the child's problematic behaviors and the fact that they continue to occur throughout much of the child's life are major stressors. In general, the more severe the symptoms are, the more distressed the parents (Konstantareas, 1991). Level of dependency of the child and the problematic nature of the behaviors are significant stressors (Bristol & Schopler, 1984). Families of developmentally delayed children tend to experience increasing stress when transitioning between childhood and adolescence and from adolescence to adulthood (Wikler, 1986). In families with children who are developmentally disabled children, factors associated with the child's dependency on the parents and related caretaking responsibilities, family disharmony, and a relative lack of personal rewards were related to higher degrees of stress (Minnes, 1988). Mothers of children diagnosed with autism reported having more disrupted plans and higher levels of caretaker and family burden than matched mothers of children with Down syndrome and children who were not disabled (Rodrigue, Morgan, & Geffken, 1990).

At least some of the distress associated with parenting a child diagnosed with autism comes with the demands on time and finances created by the child. Mothers in particular have been subjected to severe time demands in caring for their children diagnosed with autism, often not being able to pursue desired careers (Howard, 1978). Emotional and lifestyle difficulties arise from severe impositions on finances and available time, and limited access to appropriate services if the child is misdiagnosed as not having autism (Konstantareas, 1990). Both financial difficulties and serious changes in the nature of family activities constitute sources of stress in families of children who are not disabled in general (McCubbin et al., 1982). Often, extreme limits on time and finances may severely compromise the quality of these parents' lives.

Concerns about competency and adaptability also add to parent distress. At least a third of mothers were uncertain if they had the ability to competently rear their children with autism (DeMyer, 1979; Tavormina, Boll, Dunn, Luscomb, & Taylor, 1981). Mothers of children diagnosed with autism felt less competent as parents and perceived their families as less adaptable than mothers of children who were not disabled and even other children with developmental disabilities (Rodrigue et al., 1990).

Frey, Greenberg, and Fewell (1989) investigated the effects of several predictor variables on stress—the child's characteristics, adequacy of social network, personal beliefs, and coping styles—and wanted to see how these variables affected the parenting stress, family adjustment, and psychological distress in parents of children with disabilities such as Down syndrome, cerebral palsy, and other nonautism related disabilities. Collectively, the predictor variables cited above accounted for between 37% and 51% of parenting stress, 43% and 50% of family adjustment difficulties, and 30% and 57% of reported psychological distress. Parents who made negative comparisons about the difficulties in their families compared to other families tended to experience the most stress. Additionally, out of fathers who perceived a low degree of control over family well-being and mothers who blamed themselves more frequently for family problems, both tended to report more distress than their counterparts.

These findings point to a troublesome reality often experienced by the parents of children with developmental disabilities. Negative appraisals of the difficulties in raising these children, and beliefs in diminished personal control over one's well-being (and the well-being of the family) may be logically accurate. It usually will be true that more time and effort is required to raise a disabled child than a nondisabled one and that the presence of such a child in the household constitutes a more disruptive influence than the presence of a child without disabilities. With these increased difficulties, it also may be likely that these parents have less control over their well-being than parents of children without disabilities. Given the logical basis of such beliefs and their sizable correlations with stress, distress, and lack of adaptability, relatively high levels of these negative outcomes may be inevitable for these parents. Although all people must learn to cope with adversities, parents of children with autism and other developmental disabilities must learn to live with these adversities nearly every day.

Specific Emotions Commonly Encountered

A range of feelings more specific than general distress often are experienced by parents of children diagnosed with autism, according to several researchers. Parents of children diagnosed with autism experience a variety of emotions upon learning their child's conditions, including "alarm, ambivalence, denial, guilt, grief, shame, self pity, sorrow, depression, and a wish for their child's death" (Price-Bonham & Addison, 1978, p. 223). Mothers of children diagnosed with autism feel frustrated, anxious, and tense more often than mothers of children without disabilities and children with Down syndrome (Rodrigue et al., 1990). In addition, two thirds of these mothers reported feeling guilty about their child's conditions (DeMyer, 1979). Parents of children diagnosed with autism strongly tend to feel responsible and blamed for their child's conditions, feel guilty and ashamed, and even feel hatred, anger, and blame toward their partners for their perceived responsibility (Konstantareas, 1990). Frustration and anger deriving from all-too-common delayed diagnoses or experiences with ineffective treatments can occur (Konstantareas, 1990). Such parents also tend to feel more exhausted and pessimistic about the future than parents of children without disabilities (DeMyer, 1979; DeMyer & Goldberg, 1983). Parents of children with developmental disabilities often feel grief over the imagined child without disabilities their child could have been (McCubbin et al., 1982). All of these feelings, when present, could have a seriously compromising effect on the ability of these parents to effectively care for their children and to live more fulfilling lives.

DIAGNOSTIC ISSUES

Certain mental health diagnoses seem to be more prevalent amongst the parents of children diagnosed with autism. Parents of children diagnosed with autism have about five times greater incidence of bipolar disorder than the general population (DeLong & Dwyer, 1988). Whether this condition exists in parents before the arrival of the child with autism or whether such symptoms arise in response to the demands of raising the child is unknown. Parents of disabled children in general were more frequently diagnosed with depressive and anxiety disorders than parents of nondisabled children (Breslau & Davis, 1986). In one study, 16 out of 35 parents of children diagnosed with autism were described as having schizoid traits such as "social gaucheness and a tendency towards the single-minded pursuit of special, often intellectual, interests" (Narayan, Moyes, & Wolff, 1990, p. 528; also see Wolff, Narayan, & Moyes, 1988). Eight of these subjects were specifically described as schizoid by clinicians in the study. However, the diagnosis of schizoid personality disorder was never actually made in the study, and it should be noted that no recognized diagnostic instrument of acceptable validity or reliability was used in the study.

Autism appears to be more prevalent in families with an identified history of psychological disorders, including depressive, bipolar, and obsessive-compulsive disorders (DeLong, 1999; DeLong & Nohria 1994). A review of research conducted in the United States and Great Britain concluding that parents of children diagnosed with autism had higher rates of psychopathology than parents of nondisabled children found that instances of such pathology, when present, have never been causally linked to the onset of autism (Sanua, 1986a, 1986b). Thus, it is plausible that the behaviors described by such disorders could occur *in response to the demands* of raising a child diagnosed with autism. As Konstantareas (1990) stated, "Although family or parental pathology may also be present, such pathology may be secondary or reactive to the stress and special non-normative adaptations members of the child's family may have to make [to the autistic child]" (p. 60).

Regardless of whether psychological disorders contribute to autism or arise in response to autism, the relatively high rates of diagnosis in parents of children diagnosed with autism is alarming. The presence of clinically significant levels of depression, anxiety, manic, hypomanic, and obsessive-compulsive behavior is observed in a disproportionate number of these parents, representing the presence of pervasive and long-term stressors, and points to the need for a treatment that is broadly applicable.

Marital and Interpersonal Difficulties

Parents of children diagnosed with autism often find that issues surrounding the child cause marked strain on interpersonal relationships. This is particularly true with marital and intrafamilial relationships. Most mothers of children diagnosed with autism are less satisfied with their marriages than mothers of nondisabled children, in part because of the pressures and difficulties of raising their children diagnosed with autism (DeMyer, 1979; DeMyer & Goldberg, 1983). Mothers of children diagnosed with autism tend to feel less satisfied in their marriages than mothers of nondisabled and other developmentally delayed children (Rodrigue et al., 1990). These findings take on special significance because marital satisfaction appears to be a predictor of a mother's coping ability with respect to her child's condition (Friedrich, 1979; Friedrich & Friedrich, 1981). Even couples with solid relationships may be challenged by the demands of parenting children diagnosed with autism, as opportunities for intimacy, companionship, and privacy are limited (Sabbeth & Leventhal, 1984). Family members of disabled children in general tend to have strained relationships (McCubbin et al., 1982). It is plausible that distress, when not effectively managed, seeps into interactions with spouses and family. Beliefs about the role family members play in contributing to the child's diagnosis and disruptions also may play a role in this distress.

Social relationships between parents of children diagnosed with autism and people outside the family also tend to suffer. There typically are marked reductions in time available for socializing, negative reactions from friends, embarrassment over the autistic child's behavior, and subsequent social isolation (McCubbin et al., 1982). Parents of children diagnosed with autism often feel rejected by and isolated from their communities (Davidson & Dosser, 1982; Intagliata & Doyle, 1984; Kazak & Wilcox, 1984; Trute & Hauch, 1988). Although time constraints undoubtedly play a role in these changes, sometimes embarrassment and shame regarding the child's behavior can lead a parent to avoid others as well.

Understanding and Expectation

Parents of children diagnosed with autism also tend to have difficulties making sense of their child's disorder and struggle with expectations about their child's future. Such parents generally have problems with understanding the nature and causes of the child's disorder, including their child's prognosis. They also are often confused about which treatments are most effective and unclear about what types of problems the child will face when he or she is older (Konstantareas, 1990). A great deal of stress can arise from the realization that treatment for their children might always be necessary (Mesibov, 1983). Another difficulty in having children diagnosed with autism involves the development of reasonable expectations about them, as they usually look normal and even attractive (Bristol & Schopler, 1984). Apparently bleak and uncertain futures can be anxiety-provoking, especially when made persistently obvious.

Life Satisfaction and Coping

Several indicators of more adaptive functioning by parents of autistic and developmentally disabled children have been reported in the literature. Higher marital satisfaction appears to enhance a mother's ability to cope with her child's condition (Friedrich, 1979; Friedrich & Friedrich, 1981). Harmony and quality of parenting (Nihira, Meyers & Mink, 1980), the presence of both parents at home (Beckman, 1983), and acceptance and understanding of the child's condition (Darling, 1979; Denhoff & Holden, 1971) also are correlated with more successful coping and adjustment.

The following characteristics in mothers of children diagnosed with autism have been exhibited by those with higher degrees of life satisfaction:

- less emphasis on career success;
- more leisure time with extended family;
- less emphasis on others' opinions regarding their child;
- more emphasis on spousal support and parental role;
- more difficulty understanding their child's behavior; and
- greater tolerance for ambiguity.

These same characteristics were not associated with greater life satisfaction in mothers of nondisabled children (Tunali & Power, 1993). Social support also may play an important role in helping parents of children diagnosed with autism cope because parental satisfaction is related to the level of perceived support (Bristol & Schopler, 1984; Potasznik & Nelson, 1984). These findings generally point to the importance of maintaining intra- and extrafamilial support and of maintaining flexible ways of thinking about one's circumstances.

Certain coping strategies commonly used by parents of children diagnosed with autism have been found to be ineffective or counterproductive. Relatively ineffective parents tend to be overly permissive with their child with autism, perhaps because it can be difficult to maintain discipline with these children (Konstantareas, 1990). Mothers of children diagnosed with autism used self-blame as a coping strategy more frequently than mothers of nondisabled children (Rodrigue et al., 1990). Parents who blame themselves for their child's condition also cope less successfully than parents who do not blame themselves (Frey et al., 1989). Parents of children diagnosed with autism have a tendency to deny, downplay, or otherwise avoid the severity or even the existence of their coping difficulties (Konstantareas & Homatidis, 1989). Parents using specific coping strategies such as active problem solving, help-seeking, and utilization of available resources tend to cope better with the demands of raising a child diagnosed with autism, while parents using strategies described as avoidance tend to cope less effectively (Darling, 1979; Denhoff & Holden, 1971; Frey et al., 1989). Use of psychological treatments designed to enhance the use of effective coping strategies, such as active problem solving, full use of available resources, and elimination of ineffective strategies like avoidance, self-blame, and excessive permissiveness, would be directly applicable to such parents.

TREATMENTS FOR PARENTS OF CHILDREN DIAGNOSED WITH AUTISM

Given the prevalence and severity of the diagnosis of autism, and the well-established findings regarding the degree of stress parents of children diagnosed with autism encounter, it is surprising how little attention has been paid in the literature to the support and treatment of such parents. In fact, prior to the application of Acceptance and Commitment Therapy (ACT) to address the stress of these parents, only three attempts at addressing needs beyond parenting skills for this population have been reported in the literature (Davidson & Dosser, 1982; Micheli, 1999; Samit, 1996). Two of these approaches imparted little more than parenting skills training (Micheli, 1999; Samit, 1996), and all three were methodologically weak. Prior to the application of ACT, the state of treatments for parents of children diagnosed with autism now differs little from what was offered more than 15 years ago: "The common thread that ties most of these intervention strategies together is that their focus is . . . either directly or indirectly on the developmentally disabled child" (Intagliata & Doyle, 1984, p. 4). Acceptance and Commitment Therapy, discussed later in this chapter, offers an approach directed toward the caregiver.

Micheli (1999) offered a treatment consisting of a didactic training group for parents of children diagnosed with autism designed

> . . . to broaden the scope of parent training, to go beyond the current needs of the child and the application of behavioral techniques and enable parents to foresee future difficulties, cope with changes in family needs, and gain knowledge of techniques involved in more general "parenting skills." (p. 100)

The group treatment lasted six sessions. Although the parents reported that the group was beneficial, no standardized measures were used to assess the effectiveness of the treatment. It should be noted that most of this training program provided information typical to standard parent training programs for children diagnosed with autism.

Samit (1996) aimed to teach behavioral management techniques to parents as an intervention for parental stress. However, parents also were educated about the nature and etiology of autism, partially in an effort to diffuse blame, confusion, and other problematic reactions, and were provided "a forum for the sharing of concerns and experiences with other parents of children diagnosed with autism and for open discussion with the professional staff" (p. 24). This forum was provided in hopes that parents would learn "acceptance of the child as he or she was" (p. 27). The group met weekly and consisted of parents and sometimes extended family and support staff. Different issues were discussed in each meeting, picked by therapists in response to parental concerns. Unfortunately, no objective assessments of parent functioning or distress were made, allowing no firm conclusions to be drawn about the treatment's effectiveness.

The third intervention (Davidson & Dosser, 1982) consisted of the creation of a support group for families of infants with developmental disabilities. Unfortunately, no objective assessment of the group's effects was made, although parents reported finding it helpful.

TREATMENTS FOR PARENTS OF CHILDREN WITH DISABILITIES

The literature on treatment for parents of children with development disabilities also is very limited. One of the first attempts to develop a treatment for parents of children with developmental disabilities involved interpersonal skills training (Intagliata & Doyle, 1984). Although the practitioners speculated that this treatment was helpful, the research on the treatment is inconclusive due to problems in the design of the research study.

A training program for parents of children who were mentally retarded and developmentally disabled resulted in significant improvement on several self-report measures (Baker, Landen, & Kashima, 1991). Although the intervention was designed simply to teach parents how to respond to their children's behaviors in a manner similar to the way they were responded to in their day treatment programs, the intervention is notable because the outcome measures used included assessments of parental coping. The parents who completed the study reported high degrees of satisfaction with the program, and showed small but statistically significant decreases in reports of depressive symptoms, parent and family problems, overall family stress, and dissatisfaction regarding family adaptability. Unfortunately, no control group was used, and the statistical analyses used only examined families who completed the training. The study also noted that certain family characteristics were highly correlated with ineffective use of the skills taught in the training program: these factors included lower levels of marital adjustment, a higher degree of dissatisfaction regarding family adaptability and cohesion, and perceptions that one's family is relatively unable to adapt to changes.

The effects of a comprehensive treatment program for parents having difficulty coping with their children who were moderately and severely disabled were reported by Singer, Irvine, and Irvin (1989). The treatment package included coping skills training, stress management training, parental support groups, individual therapy for depression, marital therapy, and parent training. Although systematic evaluations of each of the treatment components alone were not made, results indicated that parents participating in all components of the treatment were significantly less distressed after treatment than a group that received case management and weekly respite care services, and these differences were maintained at a 1-year follow-up.

In addition, the effects of a specific treatment component were evaluated. Stress management classes, including relaxation training, coping self-statements, self-monitoring, and identification of environmental stressors, were combined with a 2-hour child behavior management class. Thirty-six parents of children who were moderately and severely disabled were randomly assigned to a treatment and wait-list control group, with the treatment group receiving stress management training delivered in seven 2-hour group sessions and child behavior management training delivered in the eight 2-hour group session. Significant decreases in the Beck Depression Inventory and State-Trait Anxiety Scale scores relative to the control group were found (Hawkins & Singer, 1989), and were maintained at a 1-year follow-up. In addition, parents reported significant improvements in child behavior following participation in the parent-training module compared to a control group that received no parent training. Although direct observations found no significant differences in problematic child behaviors, such observations did find significant, positive differences in parent behavior with respect to their children. These significant differences were maintained at a 1-year follow-up.

What Treatment Is Most Appropriate for Parents of Children Diagnosed With Autism?

Comprehensive treatment approaches like the one described by Singer et al. (1989) would seem to be desirable for virtually all problems, including those faced by parents of children diagnosed with autism. Such approaches, however, pose practical problems. The most obvious of these problems involves the resources required to implement such broad and intensive avenues of treatment. Simply put, few, if any, agencies would have the resources to implement a multitiered program without substantial funding. A second problem involves the time that would be required to participate in such a variety of intensive treatments. Drop-out rates of 40% to 80% have been observed, for example, in parent training programs designed for parents of children who were disabled and developmentally disabled (Dangel & Polster, 1984). This may be due to a variety of reasons, but time limitations would seem to be one. Parents of children diagnosed with autism may experience even more limitations on time than parents of other disabled children, in part because of their child's potential to recover. Because this depends on consistently sound parenting on the weeknights and weekends when the child with autism is not in day treatment, parents may be unwilling or too exhausted to commit the amount of time to treatment that would maximally benefit their child. Third, although the Singer et al. (1989) approach is impressive in its breadth, convincing evidence of clinically significant or meaningful change resulting from the intervention has not been established.

Given the well-documented incidences of stress in parents of children diagnosed with autism, stress-management training would seem to be a logical first choice for an intervention. Particularly, a package like that of Singer et al. (1989), containing components such as coping skills and relaxation training (perhaps with communication and conflict resolution training provided as well), might have a significant impact on parents lacking such skills. However, skills training approaches in general tend to pose a number of problems. To begin with, individuals must have deficits in a particular skill in order to benefit from such training. This requires a level of assessment and subsequent treatment matching that usually does not occur in skills training to assure that clients are being taught something they don't already know. Second, skills training has been criticized by many as often being "too simple to deal adequately with many of life's complexities" (O'Donohue & Krasner, 1995, p. 8). It is one thing to learn rules about how to behave in given situations, and another to behave in accordance with those rules in contexts often very different from where the skills were taught and practiced. Third, in many cases, apparent skill deficits exhibited by individuals actually have involved skills that are part of their behavioral repertoires, but are not used because other factors block their use (e.g., Ammerman & Hersen, 1986; Ammerman, Van Hasselt, Hersen, & Moore, 1989; Fingeret, Monti, & Paxson, 1985). These individuals would likely benefit if the factors interfering with effective skill use (such as anxiety or a lack of self-confidence) were identified and targeted, but not if they were simply taught skills they already knew.

Cognitive restructuring and psychoeducation also might be helpful in alleviating some of the suffering experienced by parents. On the one hand, thoughts of personal responsibility and blame for the child's condition, about the unfairness of their plight, the near-hopelessness of the child's future, and the overwhelming nature of current levels of effort and stress, might be usefully construed as irrational and treatable with cognitive disputation and restructuring strategies that are a cornerstone of conventional forms of cognitive behavior therapy. On the other hand, one could argue that such thoughts, to a large extent, are rationally accurate. The "reality" that parents of children diagnosed with autism are faced with *could* be rationally described as unfair, near-hopeless, and a function of their genetic makeup, and the remarkable effort (and subsequent distress) required to parent such children could be rationally described as overwhelming, especially at times. Cognitive restructuring might be helpful, but it might be pitted against some evidence-based thoughts that are correspondingly resistant to rational change attempts. Such attempts might even be construed by these parents as invalidating or lacking empathy. In fact, Singer (1993), in addressing the efficacy of cognitive restructuring with parents of disabled children, stated that many of these parents "are unimpressed with these methods and find them either irrelevant, or, in some cases, somewhat offensive" (p. 213).

An alternative to skills training and cognitive restructuring that seems to address the persistent problems of parenting children diagnosed with autism is found in Acceptance and Commitment Therapy (ACT; Hayes, Strosahl, & Wilson, 1999). Briefly, ACT was created in part to treat those with chronic levels of distress that have debilitating effects on functioning in multiple life domains. ACT attempts to cut across conventional psychiatric diagnostic categories to minimize client use of potentially problematic processes called *cognitive fusion* and *experiential avoidance* that influence diagnosable conditions. ACT brings a different set of assumptions to human suffering than typical psychosocial treatments, and uses a relatively unique constellation of techniques to effect change. The nature of ACT is described in the next section.

Acceptance and Commitment Therapy

Acceptance and Commitment Therapy (Hayes, 1994; Hayes et al., 1999) was designed as an alternative to more conventional methods of psychotherapy that are designed *to decrease* the intensity and frequency of aversive affect and cognitions. Rather than direct attempts to decrease such levels, ACT aims to *increase* behavioral effectiveness, regardless of the presence of unpleasant thoughts and emotions of varying degrees of intensity. More specifically, the goals of ACT are: (1) clarification of the client's personally held values and corresponding goals, and (2) enhancement of the client's effectiveness in moving toward those values and goals. ACT may be appropriate for stressed parents due to the necessity for parents of children diagnosed with autism to weather chronically high levels of aversive emotions and thoughts and still effectively pursue a variety of courses of action.

The Foundations of ACT

ACT was developed in response to several factors. In a general sense, it arose as a response to the failure of more conventional forms of psychotherapy to achieve significant changes in more than 30% to 35% of clients. Of course, some treatments have achieved more than a 35% success rate with certain circumscribed disorders, including enuresis (bed-wetting), specific phobias, panic disorder, and others. Most of these traditional treatments subscribe to the very logical assumption that minimizing or eliminating the occurrence and intensity of negative affect and negative or maladaptive cognitions is the path to psychological wellness. Hayes and his colleagues (Hayes, 1994; Hayes et al., 1999) have argued that one main reason for the failure of such treatments to achieve decisive success may actually come from this assumption. They questioned whether reductions in the levels and frequencies of aversive thoughts and emotions are necessary to achieve psychological well-being. The assumption behind ACT is that such reductions are not necessary, and that psychological wellness can be thought of as an enhanced ability to effectively pursue personally held values and goals, whether or not there are negative thoughts and emotions.

ACT also remained highly responsive to the growing body of literature detailing the effects of thought and emotional suppression. This literature (briefly detailed below) repeatedly demonstrates that attempts to suppress or distract oneself from specific thoughts and emotions result in a paradoxical increase in the frequency of these thoughts and emotions. In concordance with these data, ACT makes no attempts to suppress or otherwise avoid thoughts or emotions of any kind, instead employing a variety of techniques designed to enhance client *acceptance* of such stimuli.

Finally, ACT was influenced by the relative success of behaviorally based exposure treatments, such as systematic desensitization (Wolpe, 1990) and cognitive-behavioral treatment for panic disorder (e.g., Barlow, 1988). Exposure techniques are logically applicable to a variety of problems from an ACT perspective.

The Essential Components of ACT

ACT uses mindfulness and acceptance strategies to help clients effectively cope with the distress they encounter when pursuing personally important values and goals. Symptom reduction is not the primary aim in ACT, but symptoms may and often do decrease. The aim is increased psychological flexibility, which is described as a person's ability to persevere or change his or her behavior in the service of attaining valued goals and outcomes.

According to ACT, one core clinical issue influencing people is experiential avoidance, which is described as the avoidance of one's own difficult and unwanted emotions, thoughts, bodily sensations, and other private events. Avoidance in general is not problematic. It is important to avoid life-threatening events and physical danger, but emotions and thoughts do not cause actual physical danger (except, perhaps, in extreme circumstances, such as when high anxiety helps trigger a heart attack in someone at high risk). Further, attempts to avoid unwanted private experiences actually can increase objectionable thoughts and feelings. Plus, the types of things people do to try to eliminate their own feelings and thoughts

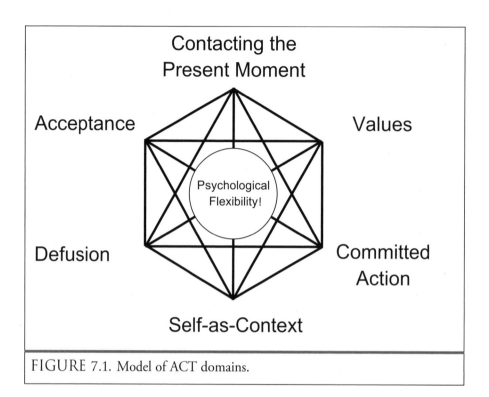

FIGURE 7.1. Model of ACT domains.

can cause even more problems. Imagine the types of behaviors a person needs to emit to no longer think about his or her own parenting difficulties. He or she might turn to alcohol or drugs, or perhaps neglect his or her responsibilities because the responsibilities are a constant reminder of his or her life circumstance. With ACT, clients are taught that attempting to control thoughts and feelings can be seen as the person's problem and not the solution. In other words, attempts to alter private experiences can create more problems than they solve.

The Core ACT Intervention Strategies

ACT frequently is described as being comprised of six interrelated therapy strategies aimed at treating a person's clinical issues: self as context, acceptance, defusion, values clarification, contact with the present moment, and committed action (Hayes, Strosahl, Bunting, Twohig, & Wilson, 2004). These component strategies interrelate and none of the six should be thought of as a distinct intervention. The six parts work together as a whole.

The six ACT domains have been set to a hexagon model for a visual aid (see Figure 7.1). In the center of the six domains is the aim of ACT: psychological flexibility. Conceptually, if all six of the ACT processes are enacted, the person is likely to be behaving in a psychologically flexible manner, meaning that he is moving creatively and effectively toward what is important to him even in the presence of difficult thoughts and emotions. The ACT community has dubbed this model the "Hexaflex," because it is a *hexa*gon model aimed at increasing *flex*ibility.

In order to highlight each of the six processes on the Hexaflex, we'll revisit Melissa and Michael and how they struggle while parenting their son, Tim.

SELF-AS-CONTEXT

Adopting a sense of *self-as-context* requires consideration of different senses of self and self-knowledge. According to the ACT literature, there are three ways of looking at "the self." *Self-as-content* includes one's personal verbal descriptions and evaluations (e.g., that one is a man, is 35 years old, is an accountant, likes dogs, has a social phobia, is bad at relationships, etc). *Self-as-process* is the ongoing self-awareness or the sense of self where one notices ongoing processes, such as thoughts, feelings, and bodily sensations such as "Now I am feeling anxious," or "Now I have a headache." *Self-as-context*, which also is called *self-as-perspective*, and the observing self, is a transcendent sense of self. Self-as-context is not an object of verbal evaluations; instead, it is the locus from which a person's experience unfolds. Self-as-context is transcendent in that it has no form or verbal content. Instead, it can be thought of as the place from which observations are made. As such, it is the least talked about sense of self, and it is a sense of self that has no boundaries (Barnes-Holmes, Hayes, & Dymond, 2001). Increased contact with or awareness of one's experience of self-as-context can be a benefit for increasing willingness and acceptance as well as a positively evaluated experience in its own right. ACT provides experiential opportunities to become present with the self-as-context.

ACCEPTANCE

According to ACT parlance, acceptance means willingness to experience what one is experiencing "fully and without defense" (Hayes, 1994). It does not mean *wanting* one's experience and current conditions. In acceptance work, the therapist clarifies with the client that life for all people includes struggle and turmoil. Certain events, such as frustration and sadness are likely, if not inevitable. The ACT therapist invites the client to be willing to notice the inevitable feelings as they are (just feelings) and not as something to be avoided. It is sometimes misconstrued that ACT attempts to have people "just accept" their life situation as a whole. On the contrary, ACT therapists encourage people to change the events that they can change (even in the midst of painful feelings and thoughts). If a person were on the second story of a burning building, the ACT therapist doesn't yell up to the person and say "Accept your situation." The therapist would say "Jump out of the window!" However, when the person says "I'm too afraid to jump," the ACT therapist would encourage the person to *notice* the fear, but not wait around trying to get rid of the fear first before saving his or her own life. The therapist might yell "Of course you are scared. That's natural. Feel the fear, and jump anyway!" Acceptance work aims to show that emotions and thoughts don't have to be obstacles to living one's life fully and abundantly.

Let's revisit Tim's parents, Melissa and Michael. Melissa had many thoughts and feelings that she tried to avoid. Melissa often was unwilling to have angry feelings. In an attempt to get rid of her anger, she would yell at all of her children and her husband. She reasoned that her anger would subside if everyone would just listen to her and make things go her way all the time. After a bout of yelling, she usually felt less angry, but that only lasted a little while. Moreover, the long-term results of the yelling started to deteriorate the fabric of the family relations, which in turn led to a greater lack of communication, eventually leading to more things for her to be angry about. Thus Melissa's "solution" to her problem became another, more insidious problem; she yelled so she would get rid of her "bottled up" anger, and then the yelling created a family environment to be angry about.

Michael often was unwilling to have his thoughts of despair. He would sometimes say to himself, "This situation with Tim is horrible." In order to control these thoughts, he would avoid interacting with Tim because any interaction with him would inevitably lead to such thoughts. He also began to avoid talking with Melissa because the conversations eventually would turn to talking about Tim and his treatment, or having to pay the consultant, or the problems they had with finding good behavior therapists and respite care workers. He was unwilling to be burdened with these thoughts. He started coming home later and later. After some time, Michael realized he was having the thoughts about his son and his life situation even without being home, so he turned to drinking alcohol because he believed it numbed his thought processes. These "solutions" to Michael's problems became problems of their own. His noncommunication, frequent absences from home, and increase in alcohol consumption became additional events for him to think despairingly about, which led to more drinking and avoiding.

Melissa's individual ACT therapist highlighted the futility of avoiding her feelings. During therapy, the clinician incorporated an exercise called "Feeding a Baby Tiger." Here is how their conversation surrounding this exercise went:

Therapist: I've been thinking about your anger issues. Let me know if it's something like this . . . It's like you have this little tiger here in your left hand. It growls every once in a while, and to shut it up, you feed it some chow. You don't like the growling, so you are quick to shut it up. But what happens when you feed this tiger?

Melissa: I assume it gets bigger.

Therapist: Right, much bigger. And, the growls are louder. And, by the way, this chow you're feeding it . . . well, that is the stuff that you eat too, so you're getting a bit shortchanged out of that chow too.

Melissa: OK?

Therapist: So, what do you propose to do in this situation?

Melissa: Well, I guess I'll stop feeding the thing. But, then what'll happen? It'll probably start growling more.

Therapist: Probably growl louder too.

Melissa: Hmm. (Long pause). So, you're saying that I'm feeding my own anger problems . . . making them bigger myself. And, if I just learn to accept the "anger growls," if I just let them happen without feeding into it, the growls might stop.

Therapist: They might stop. They might not. I would imagine in this scenario that a hungry tiger might growl a lot, but if you stop feeding it, it'll go somewhere else looking for food. It still might come sniffing back around occasionally. But, here's the best part: If you stop feeding it, you get to have more of your own chow.

Melissa: That chow we're talking about represents my relationship with my family, doesn't it?

Therapist: It represents all the precious moments of your life that you give away so that you don't feel feelings of anger. If you let it growl . . . just let it growl . . . notice the anger as it is, then you get to act effectively. You aren't throwing away all that chow to silence a growl . . . you aren't yelling and tossing away your relationships just to silence your feelings of anger.

ACT does not primarily aim at symptom reduction. The therapist in this exchange is not primarily aiming at making the anger go away (the tiger to stop growling), but rather helping Melissa spend more time doing what she cares about (consuming her own "life chow" instead of using it to silence the tiger). ACT typically uses metaphors to get points across. If you were to tell Melissa directly, "Accept your feelings and your life would be better," it isn't likely to have the same effect. Such a statement would be just another rule to rigidly try to follow. Metaphors help people discover the treatment principles in their own way, by relating the ideas to other personally relevant ideas.

Acceptance interventions attempt to engender clients with a willingness to have their own private experiences. When a person is more willing to have and notice their emotions and thoughts, and isn't distracted by futile attempts to get rid of them, the client can move more flexibly in valued directions with their life. Acceptance facilitates the other five domains of the Hexaflex, and also is aided by the other five dimensions.

DEFUSION

Fusion is a word used to describe the process of putting two separate things together to make one single item. When two pieces of metal are fused together, it becomes one piece of metal. Cognitive fusion is when thoughts and the other parts of the person's environment become one. For instance, a client who thinks, "Everyone hates me" doesn't see that as a mere thought. Instead of noticing those are just plain words that are cropping up in his mind, the person takes it as a literal truth, thereby approaching people he meets through the lens of "Everyone hates me." This can influence the person to avoid socializing even when the people around him might actually like him. Defusion exercises learned in therapy can assist clients to see thoughts as thoughts, rather than regarding thoughts as absolute truth. Defusion strategies are therapy techniques that aim to decrease unhelpful effects of language and cognition. Defusing from thoughts can free the client to act on the basis of what she really cares about and also come into contact with what is going on in her life.

Michael's therapist chose to work on acceptance and defusion at the same time. Michael was taught that thoughts can just be *noticed* as they are, without need for alteration or avoidance. He learned that trying to get rid of thoughts wasn't moving him toward the goals he really cared about. His therapist also taught him that such thoughts are not a cardinal reality: Just because a person thinks something is horrible does not make it horrible. Words do not have to carry the weight that we commonly give them. Put simply, the ACT therapist shows the client that the letters and/or sounds that are all combined to make our words and sentences, and thereby our thoughts, are really just symbols. A Zen parable suggests that if you use your finger to point at the moon, your finger pointing is very helpful at indicating the location of the moon, but your finger is *not* the moon. In the same way, if a person uses a word like *horrible* to indicate the state of a situation, it does not mean that the situation is objectively and irrefutably horrible. Clients learn that evaluating a situation as bad, horrible, or any other evaluation, are just private verbalizations, not the physical state of the event.

Sometimes ACT therapists use deliteralization exercises to highlight the arbitrariness of words, as seen in the following conversation between Michael and his therapist:

Therapist: What happens when you hear me say the word "lemon"?

Michael: Huh? Well . . . I see a lemon in my mind.

Therapist: What else? Give me a few reactions.

Michael: I see a lemon. I see a yellow lemon. I think of lemonade and how my grandma makes great lemonade. I can almost smell it. My mouth starts watering and puckering a bit.

Therapist: Wow. Lots of reactions. And you know what? There aren't any lemons in the office. You can almost smell them and you start salivating even though there's no lemons around. Now I can imagine you salivating if I put citric acid on your tongue, but there isn't even any lemon juice in the building!

Michael: Hmm . . .

Therapist: See the power of the words? Now let's see what we can do about that power. Repeat along with me, loud and fast: *lemon-lemon-lemon-lemon.* (They both repeat together for about 20 seconds.)

Therapist: We said "lemon" a lot. Did you have a lot of thoughts of yellow fruit? Are you salivating a lot more?

Michael: Uh . . . no. It kinda disappears. Wasn't even thinking of lemons after a while, and my mouth actually dried up a bit.

Therapist: See that? Words can at first bring up lots of stuff for you. At first you can see yellow fruits, think of your grandma, smell the lemons, and even salivate. Then after lots of presentations of the word, you react *less* to the words. The point here is that words *can be* powerful, but they don't *have to be.*

Michael: So, are you saying I should just repeat *horrible* over and over and things won't be as horrible?

Therapist: Absolutely not. I'm inviting you to take a new stance on words. Give yourself a new perspective. See if you can distance yourself from your evaluations about things. Notice that they are just words. If you can take this stance more often, it might give you some room to react differently to your own private verbalizations. You don't have to take all your thoughts as the literal fact.

Helping clients learn defusion allows them to experience words from a distance. ACT teaches that people do not have to robotically follow their own private evaluations or unhelpful rules for behavior. If Michael begins to see his evaluations of his life with Tim as simply words that do not have to be adhered to as if they were law, then he can make a choice to behave in a way that he truly values. This kind of distancing is aided when clients clarify their own personal values.

VALUES

ACT therapists often ask their clients "What do you want your life to be about?" The purpose of this line of questioning is to help the client clarify his or her values. Hayes et al. (1999) define values as "verbally construed global desired life consequences" (p. 206), but more generally, values are the ways people talk about their chosen life directions and what they truly care about. When a person takes the time to illuminate his or her own desires, it helps the person orient the direction of his or her life's journey.

A value is not the same as a goal, but accomplishing certain goals can be in the service of values. Goals are not here and now, but something to strive for, while values are lived in the present moment. Valuing is done here and now. Clarifying what one wants his or her life to stand for can help people be more willing to accept difficult events in their lives. Values help dignify the type of suffering that people go through. In addition, clarifying what one wants in life helps the person commit to important actions.

After Melissa and her therapist discussed the difference between values and goals, the following exchange occurred:

Therapist: If you only get to live one life, just one, and you could choose how to live that life, what would you want to do?

Melissa: Oh wow. I wanna do a lot of stuff.

Therapist: OK. How about in the parts of your life we're talking about . . . what you are struggling with?

Melissa: With Tim and stuff. (Therapist nods. Melissa becomes tearful.) I wanna be a good mom.

Therapist: Let's get a little deeper. What makes you care about being a good mom?

Melissa: (Long pause.) My kids are my heart, my love. I want my kids to have great lives. (Begins crying.) I choose to make my life about raising my children happy and healthy. I want to do the best parenting I can.

Therapist: Mmhmm. (Nods in appreciation for her sharing, and acknowledging her tears.) I hear you. Can you make *that* present for you in your times of despair? (Long pause.) When there are obstacles, like when you're tired or feeling guilty, can you contact that? Can you contact that direction of your life?

Melissa: But Tim . . . it seems he'll never recover. Tim can't be happy the way I want him to be happy.

Therapist: Hmm. You are rating yourself and your life on whether or not a certain goal is met. You said, "I choose to make my life about raising my children happy and healthy. I want to do the best parenting I can." That's value-directed living. I think you've got an admirable goal in aiming for Tim's recovery, and at the same time, his recovery is not entirely in your hands. However, how you bring vitality and meaning to *your* life is in how *you* live it, not whether your loftiest goals are attained. Helping him live well will help you live well. And, rating your life on whether or not he recovers seems to make you sad, feel despair. It makes you give up sometimes, doesn't it?

Melissa: Uh huh. (Crying.)

Therapist: But, what if you make life about the journey, not the destination? Make your moments about living a life you care about. Right now, in fact, any "right now" you have, you can make it about raising your children to be happy and healthy and doing the best parenting you can in that moment. What if you base what you do on doing what you care about rather than on being just dreadfully beholden to meeting a certain goal that might not be entirely in your power? You can live your values right now. They are always available in the current moment.

It seems Melissa is fused to a rule for her life—"I must work to have my son recover to be happy"—and that leads to inflexibility and frequent evaluations of whether she is doing the "right" thing for her future goal. She misses the vitality and "right-nowness" of her interactions with her son. Clarifying her values of wanting to be a committed parent might help her focus more on the process rather than the product. And frankly, it is likely that a more genuine relationship with her son that is firmly committed to the present moment interactions rather than the long-term outcomes in the treatment plan might actually help move the treatment plan along with greater integrity and dedication. That is because the treatment focus is on *now* rather than the *later* goal. Helping clients come into contact with the present moment more often assists in valued living.

Contacting the Present Moment

Oftentimes people think about time as having a past, a present, and a future. Yet, during our life, we really only experience the present. Time goes from now to now if we are talking about what we are experiencing in our life. Our way of describing our lives tends to give us a perspective that we can reexperience our past and react to a future that hasn't yet arrived. But, the only place and time we can do any behaving is here and now. Consider this passage by Bach and Moran (2008) about contacting the present moment:

> Words have a tendency to pull us away from the present moment. Have you ever noticed that the words you use while thinking are usually reminiscing about the past or planning the future? Even when you say to someone, "Come here right now," by the time they hear and respond to their perception of "now," your "now" is already in the past. When one learns to contact the present moment, he or she learns to embrace all that the moment affords, including private events (e.g., depressive or joyous thoughts, anxiety-provoking or laugh inducing images, etc.) and notices that the come and go are no more or less than private events. From this stance the person can act mindfully and on the basis of chosen values. (p. 9)

Mindfulness and meditation exercises can assist clients in coming into greater and more frequent contact with the present moment. ACT encourages clients to become more mindful or present-focused. Kabat-Zinn (1994) defines mindfulness as: "Paying attention in a particular way: on purpose, in the present moment, and nonjudgmentally" (p. 4). Although there is a vast literature on mindfulness available for the reader to consume, experiencing a few mindful moments can be even more instructive.

At the end of this paragraph, consider taking a few moments to undergo this mindfulness exercise. An introductory mindfulness exercise can begin by merely sitting down and letting go of any tension by relaxing your muscles. Then consider closing your eyes and begin paying attention to your breathing. Follow each breath as you inhale and exhale. See if you can notice any thoughts or evaluations that seem to arrive. Are you saying to yourself "My neck is stiff," or "This is boring," or "Am I doing this right?" See if you can simply notice those words without attaching to them. Bring your focus back to your breathing. As a bodily sensation comes up, notice it and come back to your breathing. Notice the feeling of your breath. Feel its coolness as you inhale, and how much warmer it is as you exhale. If an emotion or urge to stop arrives, acknowledge it, and bring your attention back to your breathing. Your breathing is your tether back to the present moment. Your breathing is something you always do *right now*. You can focus on it and notice the other events going on in your life. Breathe in and breathe out. When you open your eyes, notice that all of the behaviors you do for the next few minutes can be done purposefully and done with your new ability to focus on the present moment.

ACT encourages individuals to become more mindful and present focused. Melissa and Michael's therapists suggested that they experience in-session mindfulness exercises and then begin to practice mindfulness on a regular basis. Melissa became involved in a YMCA yoga class, which taught her how to contact her feelings and be present with those emotions and thoughts, and also, at the same time, remain connected to her commitments. She was able to learn to notice feelings of despair and run Tim's ABA program simultaneously. This mindfulness practice helped her defuse from her thoughts of "Tim's never gonna get better," accept feelings of fatigue as simply a "right now" feeling, and maintain her value directed behavior of working his plan and being his mom, even in the presence of those private experiences. Michael began listening to meditation CDs and podcasts. He practiced mindfulness as he took his afternoon walks, while he ate, and while he washed the dishes. He then began practicing it at the end of his workday, and began to notice the thoughts and urges he had to go to the bar for a drink instead of going home to his family. And, in contacting his present moment, he *chose* in that moment to go home, even while encumbered with feelings of dread and thoughts of "It'll be a fiasco at home." He learned to defuse and accept during these events, and because he clarified his values, began to make important choices for his life-directions in the current moment.

The mindfulness orientation can be helpful because human beings can only behave *now*. Being aware of present circumstances allows for greater behavioral flexibility. Engaging in mindfulness practice over time can assist in helping people just notice their thoughts and feelings (aiding the defusion and acceptance domains in ACT). Valued behavior is only executed in the present moment, and also can facilitate committed action.

COMMITTED ACTION

When an individual directly engages in personally important, clinically relevant overt behavior, he is executing committed action. Bach and Moran (2008) suggest that "committed action is where the 'rubber meets the road' in therapy" (p. 9). In encouraging psychological flexibility, ACT therapists encourage the development of broader behavioral repertoires. Clients who are reluctant to do certain important behaviors are assisted in making a commitment to move forward, even if it's just a small step, toward that direction. Clients who behave impulsively are assisted in slowing down their responses. In addition, psychological flexibility sometimes requires not changing a behavioral repertoire, even if the current living arrangement pulls the client to do so. Melissa and Michael provide a good example of that kind of commitment. They behaved as committed parents to their older two children, but became less so when given the challenges of Tim's behavior. Melissa's therapist once summarized the therapy process, highlighting committed action at the end:

> *Therapist:* Melissa, here is what we've been talking about. You've learned that you aren't a "failure" or a "bad mom." *You* aren't the content of your mind, and you can learn to observe the difference between you and the thoughts you have [*self-as-context*]. And, you've been able to have your feelings as they come up [*acceptance*], and simply *notice* the words that sometimes pull you away from what you care about [*defusion*]. You've learned that emotions and thoughts just come up automatically, especially when you are pursuing what you care about [*values*]. Parenting Tim can certainly be a challenge, and it's a challenge you deeply care about. And, you can live your life, in the service of these important things moment by moment [*contacting the present moment*], doing the stuff that you care about doing. What can you commit to doing this week, in the service of what you care about, even in the presence of your obstacles? [This is a question about *committed action*.]

Commitment to important actions can take on many forms. Sometimes it takes the form of making behavioral contracts or promising to schedule important events. Some clients commit to more comprehensive traditional behavior therapy treatment plans, such as contingency management programs to increase the frequency of important behaviors, exposure treatment for anxiety, or social skills training for anger or depression concerns. For Melissa and Michael, it included keeping regular treatment schedules for Tim, committing to a more reasonable budget, going to integrative behavioral couples therapy, and spending time with their other children. They committed to supporting each other's mindfulness practice, to communicating more frequently and amicably, and—even though it presents them with difficult thoughts and feelings—to their value directed behavior of being loving and engaged parents to Tim.

CONCLUSION

For more information about where and how to find an ACT therapist, or if you are just interested in ACT therapy and the science behind the therapy, more information is available from the Association for Contextual Behavioral Science Web site at http://www.contextualpsychology.org. Also see Blackledge and Hayes (2006) for further empirical research on the subject of implementing ACT to assist parents of children diagnosed with autism.

REFERENCES

American Psychiatric Association. (1994). *Diagnostic and statistical manual of mental disorders* (4th ed.). Washington, DC: Author.

Ammerman, R. T., & Hersen, M. (1986). Effects of scene manipulation on role-play test behavior. *Journal of Psychopathology & Behavioral Assessment, 8*, 55–67.

Ammerman, R. T., Van Hasselt, V. B., Hersen, M., & Moore, L. E. (1989). Assessment of social skills in visually impaired adolescents and their parents. *Behavioral Assessment, 11*, 327–351.

Bach, P. & Moran, D. J. (2008). *ACT in practice: Case conceptualization in acceptance and commitment therapy.* Oakland, CA: New Harbinger Press.

Baker, B. L., Landen, S. J., & Kashima, K. J. (1991). Effects of parent training on families of children with mental retardation: Increased burden or generalized benefit? *American Journal on Mental Retardation, 96*, 127–136.

Barlow, D. H. (1988). *Anxiety and its disorders: The nature and treatment of anxiety and panic.* New York: Guilford.

Barnes-Holmes, D., Hayes, S. C., & Dymond, S. (2001). Self and self-directed rules. In S. C. Hayes, D. Barnes-Holmes, & B. Roche (Eds.), *Relational frame theory: A post-Skinnerian account of human language and cognition* (pp. 119–139). New York: Plenum Press.

Beckman, P. J. (1983). Influence of selected child characteristics on stress in families of handicapped infants. *American Journal of Mental Deficiency, 88*, 150–156.

Blackledge, J. T., & Hayes, S. C. (2006). Using acceptance and commitment training in the support of parents of children diagnosed with autism. *Child & Family Behavior Therapy, 28*, 1–18.

Breslau, N., & Davis, G. C. (1986). Chronic stress and major depression. *Archives of General Psychiatry, 43*, 309–314.

Bristol, M. M., & Schopler, E. (1984). A developmental perspective on stress and coping in families of children diagnosed with autism. In J. Blacher (Ed.), *Severely disabled young children and their families* (pp. 91–141). New York: Academic Press.

Cutler, B. C., & Kozloff, M. A. (1987). Living with autism: Effects on families and family needs. In D. Cutler (Ed.), *Handbook of autism and pervasive developmental disorders* (pp. 513–527). New York: Wiley.

Dangel, R. F., & Polster, R. A. (1984). *Parent training: Foundations of research and practice.* New York: Guilford.

Darling, R. B. (1979). *Families against society.* Beverly Hills, CA: Sage.

Davidson, B., & Dosser, D. A. (1982). A support system for families with developmentally disabled infants. *Family Relations, 31,* 295–299.

DeLong, G. R. (1999). Autism: New data suggest a new hypothesis. *Neurology, 52,* 911–916.

DeLong, G. R., & Dwyer, J. T. (1988). Correlation of family history with specific autistic subgroups: Asperger's syndrome and bipolar affective disease. *Journal of Autism and Developmental Disorders, 18,* 593–600.

DeLong, G. R., & Nohria, C. (1994). Psychiatric family history and neurological disease in autistic spectrum disorders. *Developmental Medicine and Child Neurology, 36,* 441–448.

DeMyer, M. K. (1979). *Parents and children in autism.* Toronto: Wiley.

DeMyer, M. K., & Goldberg, P. (1983). Family needs of the autistic adolescent. In E. Mesibov (Ed.), *Autism in adolescents and adults* (pp. 225–250). New York: Plenum Press.

Denhoff, E., & Holden, R. H. (1971). *Counseling parents of the ill and the handicapped.* Springfield, IL: Charles C. Thomas.

Fingeret, A. L., Monti, P. M., & Paxson, M. A. (1985). Reliability of social skills and social anxiety ratings with different sets of raters. *Psychological Reports, 57,* 773–774.

Frey, K. S., Greenberg, M. T., & Fewell, R. R. (1989). Stress and coping among parents of handicapped children: A multidimensional approach. *American Journal on Mental Retardation, 94,* 240–249.

Friedrich, W. N. (1979). Predictors of the coping behaviors of mothers of handicapped children. *Journal of Consulting and Clinical Psychology, 47,* 1140–1141.

Friedrich, W. N., & Friedrich, W. L. (1981). Psychosocial assets of parents of handicapped and nonhandicapped children. *American Journal of Mental Deficiency, 85,* 551–553.

Hawkins, N. E., & Singer, G. H. (1989). A skills training approach for assisting parents to cope with stress. In G. Irvin (Ed.), *Support for caregiving families: Enabling positive adaptation to disability* (pp. 71–83). Baltimore: Paul H. Brookes.

Hayes, S. C. (1994). Content, context, and the types of psychological acceptance. In S. C. Hayes, N. Jacobson, V. Follette, & M. Dougher (Eds.), *Acceptance and change: Content and context in psychotherapy* (pp. 13–32). Reno, NV: Context Press.

Hayes, S. C., Strosahl, K. D., Bunting, K., Twohig, M., & Wilson, K. (2004). What is acceptance and commitment therapy? In S. C. Hayes & K. D. Strosahl (Eds.), *A practical guide to acceptance and commitment therapy* (pp. 3–29). New York: Springer.

Hayes, S. C., Strosahl, K., & Wilson, K. G. (1999). *Acceptance and commitment therapy: An experiential approach to behavior change.* New York: Guilford.

Holroyd, J., Brown, N., Wikler, L., & Simmons, J. Q. (1975). Stress in families of institutionalized and noninstitutionalized autistic children. *Journal of Community Psychology, 3,* 26–31.

Holroyd, J., & McArthur, D. (1976). Mental retardation and stress on the parents: A contrast between Down's syndrome and childhood autism. *American Journal of Mental Deficiency, 80,* 431–436.

Howard, J. (1978). The influence of children's developmental dysfunction on marital quality and family interaction. In R. Spanier (Ed.), *Child influences on marital and family interaction: A life-span perspective* (pp. 275–297). New York: Academic Press.

Intagliata, J., & Doyle, N. (1984). Enhancing social support for parents of developmentally disabled children: Training in interpersonal problem solving skills. *Mental Retardation, 22,* 4–11.

Kabat-Zinn, J. (1994). *Mindfulness meditation for everyday life.* London: Piatkus Books.

Kazak, A. E., & Wilcox, B. L. (1984). The structure and function of social support networks in families with handicapped children. *American Journal of Community Psychology, 12,* 645–661.

Koegel, R. L., & Koegel, L. K. (1995). *Teaching children with autism: Strategies for initiating positive interactions and improving learning opportunities.* Baltimore: Paul H. Brookes.

Konstantareas, M. M. (1990). A psychoeducational model for working with families of autistic children. *Journal of Marital and Family Therapy, 16,* 59–70.

Konstantareas, M. M. (1991). Autistic, learning disabled and delayed children's impact on their parents. *Canadian Journal of Behavioural Science, 23,* 358–375.

Konstantareas, M. M., & Homatidis, S. (1989). Assessing child symptom severity and stress in parents of autistic children. *Journal of Child Psychology and Psychiatry, 30,* 459–470.

Lovaas, O. I. (1977). *The autistic child: Language development through behavior modification.* New York: Irvington.

Lovaas, O. I., Litrownik, A., & Mann, R. (1971). Response latencies to auditory stimuli in autistic children engaged in self-stimulatory behavior. *Behaviour Research and Therapy, 9,* 39–49.

Maurice, C., Green, G., & Luce, S. C. (1996). *Behavioral intervention for young children with autism: A manual for parents and professionals.* Austin, TX: Pro-Ed.

McCubbin, H., Cauble, A. E., & Patterson, J. M. (1982). *Family stress, coping and social support.* Springfield, IL: Charles C. Thomas.

Mesibov, G. B. (1983). Current perspectives and issues in autism and adolescence. In E. Mesibov (Ed.), *Autism in adolescents and adults* (pp. 37–53). New York: Plenum Press.

Micheli, E. (1999). A training group for parents of autistic children. *International Journal of Mental Health, 28,* 100–105.

Minnes, P. M. (1988). Family resources and stress associated with having a mentally retarded child. *American Journal on Mental Retardation, 93,* 184–192.

Narayan, S., Moyes, B., & Wolff, S. (1990). Family characteristics of autistic children: A further report. *Journal of Autism and Developmental Disorders, 20,* 523–535.

Nihira, K., Meyers, C. E., & Mink, I. T. (1980). Home environment, family adjustment, and the development of mentally retarded children. *Applied Research in Mental Retardation, 1,* 5–24.

O'Donohue, W., & Krasner, L. (1995). Psychological skills training. In W. O'Donohue & L. Krasner (Eds.), *Handbook of psychological skills training: Clinical techniques and applications* (pp. 1–19). Boston: Allyn & Bacon.

Potasznik, H., & Nelson, G. (1984). Stress and social support: The burden experienced by the family of a mentally ill person. *American Journal of Community Psychology, 12,* 589–607.

Price-Bonham, S., & Addison, S. (1978). Families and mentally retarded children: Emphasis on the father. *The Family Coordinator, 27,* 221–230.

Rodrigue, J. R., Morgan, S. B., & Geffken, G. (1990). Families of autistic children: Psychological functioning of mothers. *Journal of Clinical Child Psychology, 19,* 371–379.

Sabbeth, B., & Leventhal, J. (1984). Marital adjustment to chronic childhood illness. *Pediatrics, 73*, 762–768.

Samit, C. J. (1996). A group for parents of autistic children. *Handbook of short-term therapy groups.* Northvale, NJ: Jason Aronson.

Sanua, V. D. (1986a). The personality and psychological adjustment of family members of autistic children: I. A critical review of the research in Britain. *International Journal of Family Psychiatry, 7*, 221–260.

Sanua, V. D. (1986b). The personality and psychological adjustment of family members of autistic children: I. A critical review of the research in the United States. *International Journal of Family Psychiatry, 7*, 331–358.

Singer, G. H. (1993). When it's not so easy to change your mind: Some reflections on cognitive interventions for parents of children with disabilities. In A. Turnbull & J. Patterson (Eds.), *Cognitive coping, families, and disability* (pp. 207–220). Baltimore: Paul H. Brookes.

Singer, G. H., Irvine, A. B., & Irvin, L. K. (1989). Expanding the focus of behavioral parent training. In G. Irvin (Ed.), *Support for caregiving families* (pp. 85–102). Baltimore: Paul H. Brookes.

Tager-Flusberg, H., Joseph, R., & Folstein, S. (2001). Current directions in research on autism. *Mental Retardation and Developmental Disabilities Research Reviews, 7*, 21–29.

Tavormina, J. B., Boll, T. J., Dunn, N. J., Luscomb, R. L., & Taylor, J. R. (1981). Psychosocial effects on parents of raising a physically handicapped child. *Journal of Abnormal Child Psychology, 9*, 121–131.

Trute, B., & Hauch, C. (1988). Social network attributes of families with positive adaptation to the birth of a developmentally disabled child. *Canadian Journal of Community Mental Health, 7*, 5–16.

Tunali, B., & Power, T. G. (1993). Creating satisfaction: A psychological perspective on stress and coping in families of handicapped children. *Journal of Child Psychology and Psychiatry, 34*, 945–957.

Unger, D. G., & Powell, D. R. (1980). Supporting families under stress: The role of social networks. *Family Relations, 29*, 566–574.

Wikler, L. M. (1986). Periodic stresses of families of older mentally retarded children: An exploratory study. *American Journal of Mental Deficiency, 90*, 703–706.

Wolf, L. C., Noh, S., Fisman, S. N., & Speechley, M. (1989). Brief report: Psychological effects of parenting stress on parents of autistic children. *Journal of Autism & Developmental Disorders, 19*, 157–166.

Wolff, S., Narayan, S., & Moyes, B. (1988). Personality characteristics of parents of autistic children: A controlled study. *Journal of Child Psychology and Psychiatry, 29*, 143–153.

Wolpe, J. (1990). *The practice of behavior therapy* (4th ed.). New York: Pergamon Press.

CHAPTER 8

BUILDING LEARNER-FOCUSED COLLABORATIVE RELATIONSHIPS

JOHN LLOYD LOWDERMILK III, CHERYL FIELDING, & CAREY LOWDERMILK

INTRODUCTION

THROUGHOUT the typical school day, the special education teacher is the member of the individual education program (IEP) team most frequently relied upon to monitor progress and ensure that the child's IEP is implemented as agreed. This requires the special education teacher to assume the role of a "case manager" and adds to the already long list of tasks for which he or she is responsible. Parents and each professional involved in the provision of services to a child with autism must regularly be apprised of important events and occurrences. This responsibility requires the effective special education teacher to develop expertise in the areas of collaboration and communication. Table 8.1 provides a visual look at the differences between collaboration and communication.

This chapter will focus on three types of learners: the emerging learner, the intermediate learner, and the independent learner.

Collaboration	Communication
TABLE 8.1	
COLLABORATION VS. COMMUNICATION	
The process of interaction between two or more people actively working toward a common goal. Each person must bring knowledge, skills, and/or abilities that are unique within the group.	The process of effectively sending and receiving relevant information.

Emerging Learner

An emerging learner is a child with autism whose social interaction and communication skills are in the prelearning, emerging, or acquisition phase. They may display high rates of repetitive or stereotypical behaviors and/or perseverate on highly specific and restricted areas of interest. Characteristics of emerging learners include:

- The emerging learner does not use words or displays very limited use of words to communicate.
- The emerging learner displays little reciprocal social interaction such as:
    - looking toward an individual when his name is called;
    - smiling in response to being smiled at;
    - following the point (as a prompt) of another individual to look at an object or pointing toward an object to prompt another person to attend to that object; and
    - following the eye gaze (as a prompt) of another individual to look at an object.

- The emerging learner heavily depends on parents, teachers, paraeducators, and related services personnel for guidance through daily activities.

Intermediate Learner

An intermediate learner is a child with autism who has developed some social interaction and communication skills, however, these skills require repeated practice with prompting and guidance. Fluency in communication and social interactions has not been reached. An intermediate learner also may display some repetitive or stereotypical behaviors and/or perseverate on highly specific and restricted areas of interest. Characteristics of intermediate learners include:

- The intermediate learner uses speech in the form of multiple word sentences to communicate desires but has difficulty engaging in a to-and-from conversation that includes more than two or three exchanges for the purpose of sharing information.

- The intermediate learner displays some reciprocal social interaction such as:
  - responding to basic social overtures (e.g., looking toward an individual or responding verbally when his or her name is called);
  - shaking hands during a greeting;
  - reflecting facial expressions for a variety of emotions; and
  - initiating social interaction for the purpose of directing the attention of another to an object.

- The intermediate learner needs high levels of prompting from parents, teachers, paraeducators, and related services personnel for completion of daily activities.

Independent Learner

An independent learner is a child with autism who has relatively well-developed social interaction and communication skills in comparison to typical learners. Additionally, an independent learner's social interaction and communication skills may appear qualitatively different from that of typical children. An independent learner also may display some repetitive or stereotypical behaviors and/or perseverate on highly specific and restricted areas of interest. However, the independent learner has learned to self-monitor and moderate these behaviors and interests so that they do not interfere with routine daily activities.

Characteristics of independent learners include:

- The independent learner uses speech fluently to communicate desires and also engages in to-and-from conversations for the purpose of exchanging information.
- The independent learner engages in reciprocal social interaction such as:
  - initiating social overtures;
  - using a variety of nonverbal gestures interspersed with verbal conversation;
  - understanding and reflecting a variety of emotions by using facial expressions as cues; and
  - displaying an interest in the interests of others.

- The independent learner needs little prompting from parents, teachers, paraeducators, and related services personnel for completion of daily activities.

Goal of Collaboration

In any collaborative process, the members of the collaboration need to have the same goal in mind. In this case, the goal is to facilitate the provision of appropriate special education and related services to the child with autism. The four main categories or groups of individuals with whom the special education teacher is responsible for collaborating with are (a) parents, (b) general education personnel, (c) paraeducators, and (d) related service providers. A *parent* may be someone other than a biological mother or father. For the purposes of this chapter, a parent also may be a grandparent, aunt, uncle, older brother or sister, other family members, friend of the family, or a person appointed by the state. General education personnel includes professionals in the following areas:

- *General education teachers* have knowledge in specific content areas and oversee curriculum and instructional goals. They are responsible for developing content and the sequence of activities to meet the goals of a particular course (Burggraf & Sotomayor, 2005).

- *School administrators* are the leaders of the school responsible for a wide variety of duties that keep the school operating on a daily basis. Administration officials set the pace for academic achievement, help shape policy and oversee its implementation, and represent the school to the public at large (American Association of School Administrators, 2008).

- A *paraeducator* performs tasks under the direction of a fully licensed special education professional. He or she delivers services to children with autism in a wide variety of settings from the general education classroom to community-based learning sites. Paraeducators perform a variety of activities from one-on-one instruction to personal care assistance (Council for Exceptional Children, 2004).

- *Related service providers* are those who provide support beyond or outside of what a parent, educator, or paraeducator might provide. Figure 8.1 presents the definition of related services under the Individuals with Disabilities Education Improvement Act (IDEA; 2004).

Figure 8.2 illustrates how the special education teacher facilitates this process as the coordinator or "case manager." Notice that the child, represented by the image of the human figure, always remains at the center of the process.

DIVERSE EXPERTISE AND COLLABORATION MODELS

Expertise is needed in so many areas that it is impossible for one or even two teachers to provide it (Smith, 2007). This is where collaboration becomes an indispensable tool in the teacher's tool-bag. Collaboration can be considered in terms of (a) effective communication among professionals, (b) working with knowledgeable professionals in the school setting, and (c) working with knowledgeable professionals outside of the school setting.

Related services under IDEA are defined as:

(a) General. Related services means transportation and such developmental, corrective, and other supportive services as are required to assist a child with a disability to benefit from special education, and includes speech-language pathology and audiology services, interpreting services, psychological services, physical and occupational therapy, recreation, including therapeutic recreation, early identification and assessment of disabilities in children, counseling services, including rehabilitation counseling, orientation and mobility services, and medical services for diagnostic or evaluation purposes. Related services also include school health services and school nurse services, social work services in schools, and parent counseling and training.

(b) Exception: services that apply to children with surgically implanted devices, including cochlear implants.

> (1) Related services do not include a medical device that is surgically implanted, the optimization of that device's functioning (e.g., mapping), maintenance of that device, or the replacement of that device.
>
> (2) Nothing in paragraph (b)(1) of this section—
>
>> (i) Limits the right of a child with a surgically implanted device (e.g., cochlear implant) to receive related services (as listed in paragraph (a) of this section) that are determined by the IEP Team to be necessary for the child to receive FAPE.
>>
>> (ii) Limits the responsibility of a public agency to appropriately monitor and maintain medical devices that are needed to maintain the health and safety of the child, including breathing, nutrition, or operation of other bodily functions, while the child is transported to and from school or is at school; or
>>
>> (iii) Prevents the routine checking of an external component of a surgically implanted device to make sure it is functioning properly, as required in Sec. 300.113(b). (IDEA, 2004, Section 602)

In addition, IDEA defines the following as related services:

- audiology,
- counseling services,
- early identification and assessment of disabilities,
- interpreting services,
- medical services,
- occupational therapy,
- orientation and mobility services,
- parent counseling and training,
- physical therapy,
- psychological services,
- recreation services,
- rehabilitation counseling,
- school health services and school nurse services,
- social work services,
- speech-language pathology services,
- transportation assistance, and
- assistive technology devices and services.

FIGURE 8.1. Related services as defined by IDEA (2004).

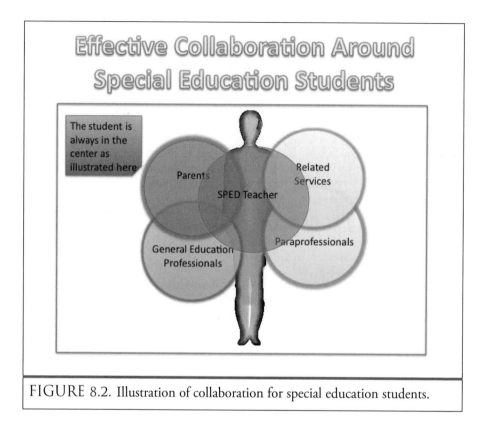

FIGURE 8.2. Illustration of collaboration for special education students.

In an interview, Dr. Marilyn Friend said, "At the broadest level, collaboration is important in schools because it has become a defining characteristic of society in the 21st century" (Brownell & Walther-Thomas, 2002, p. 223). Dr. Friend goes on to say that collaboration for schools is pragmatic because there simply is too much information for any one educator to know. To effectively meet the needs of all his or her students, teachers must collaborate with others (Brownell, Yeager, Rennells, & Riley, 1997).

Various models for collaboration often are demonstrated at workshops, professional development trainings, and in many textbooks. However, school days are filled with ever mounting paperwork, increased pressure to perform well on accountability tests, and the push to do more with less. Therefore, teachers are in need of efficient and effective models of collaboration.

First, it is important to understand when and how effective communication takes place. Researchers Claude Shannon and Warren Weaver first introduced the modern model of effective communication (see Figure 8.3). The Shannon-Weaver Communication Model (Shannon & Weaver, 1998) includes:

1. person sending the message (sender),
2. how the message is sent,
3. person receiving the message (receiver),

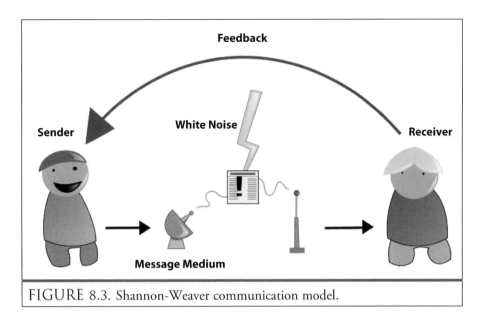

FIGURE 8.3. Shannon-Weaver communication model.

4. feedback, and

5. white noise (environment or perspective).

In Figure 8.3, there is a character on one side (the sender) and a character on the other side (the receiver). The communication should be done so that it reaches the intended audience in the most effective and efficient way. The most effective model might not be the most efficient, so a balance between the two must be reached. For example, going to the office of an administrator and having a face-to-face conversation is very effective, but not an efficient use of time or available technology. Additionally, there is white noise to consider. How StuffWorks.com described white noise as follows:

The adjective "white" is used to describe this type of noise because of the way white light works. White light is light that is made up of all of the different colors (frequencies) of light combined together (a prism or a rainbow separates white light back into its component colors). In the same way, white noise is a combination of all of the different frequencies of sound. You can think of white noise as 20,000 tones all playing at the same time.

Because white noise contains all frequencies, it is frequently used to mask other sounds. If you are in a hotel and voices from the room next-door are leaking into your room, you might turn on a fan to drown out the voices. The fan produces a good approximation of white noise. Why does that work? Why does white noise drown out voices? Here is one way to think about it. Let's say two people are talking at the same time. Your brain can normally "pick out" one of the two voices and actually listen to it and understand it. If three people are talking simultaneously, your brain can probably still pick out one voice. However, if 1,000 people are talking simultaneously, there is no way that your brain can pick out one voice. It turns out that 1,000 people talking together sounds a lot like white noise. So when you turn on a fan to create white noise, you are essentially creating a source of 1,000 voices. The voice next-door makes it 1,001 voices, and your brain can't pick it out any more. (How Stuff Works, 2008, para. 4)

The above example is one of environmental white noise that comes from an external source. White noise also can be internal. An example of internal white noise is a parent who reacts negatively when the teacher mentions a particular treatment model such as applied behavior analysis (ABA). The parent may immediately "jump" or respond to his or her own personal idea of what ABA is—in this case, his or her experience and knowledge based on someone who incorrectly implemented ABA. This is an example of internal white noise. The special education teacher is saying one thing and the parent is using his or her past experiences to "interpret" what the teacher is saying.

In a collaboration, everyone involved comes to the table with his or her own unique perspective of what is most important and environments change across settings and time. These factors are referred to as white noise because they may have the effect of moving the focus away from what is best for the child. In other words, individual perspectives and environments may "drown out" what should be the focus of the collaboration, which is the child.

It is the responsibility of the special education teacher to facilitate the collaboration process by making sure everyone is on the same page and that the focus on the child is not lost in white noise. It is crucial for everyone to understand the goal of the collaboration and the plan for reaching it.

Butler and Coleman (2003) created an extremely powerful model of collaboration based on the concept of community. They refer to this model of collaboration as the Community of Interest. The Community of Interest model has been modified here to specifically address collaboration related to children with autism. The model contains the following characteristics (Butler & Coleman, 2003):

- Collaborative communities have the common interest, affinity, and goal of providing appropriate services to children with autism.
- Collaborative communities seek to further their understanding of best practices for the child with autism.
- Collaborative communities seek to share information that will be beneficial to the child with autism.
- Collaborative communities encourage all members to provide new approaches and suggestions to help the child with autism.

♦ Collaborative communities encourage all members to understand that most interactions are asynchronous, utilizing technologies such as e-mail to communicate.

STEPS IN THE COLLABORATION PROCESS

According to Snell et al. (2000) and Smith (2007), six steps typically are followed during the collaborative process among professionals. We also feel that these are effective steps to utilize when working with parents:

1. Identify the problem: *Identify your concern*
2. Gather information: *Watch, think, and talk*
3. Generate potential solutions: *Think and throw out ideas*
4. Evaluate potential solutions: *That sounds good or that won't work*
5. Implementation: *Give it a shot*
6. Evaluation: *More watch, think, and talk*

When collaborating, an idea (e.g., message) may not always work out as planned. As Robert Burns wrote in the poem *To a Mouse* in 1785, "The best-laid plans of mice and men often go awry." In other words, plans don't always go as hoped, especially when several parties are involved. When this happens, going back and reassessing can help to clarify the situation and bring about a better outcome.

TECHNOLOGY FACILITATED COLLABORATION

Communication can be asynchronous. It is not always necessary to have a face-to-face meeting. You can use e-mails, checklists, post information on the school's secure Web server, or send information home with the child. Teachers can use a telephone service to record how the day went and what homework is assigned. In turn, parents call the same number to find out how well their child performed. For parents who do not have these resources, there is always the old-fashioned way: The teacher can send a note home and have parents sign it.

Key Features of Using E-Mail and the Internet for Effective Communication and Collaboration

Collaboration can take place in real-time or in virtual-time. For this chapter, virtual time is defined as any type of collaboration that is not face-to-face. The use of e-mail to facilitate collaboration can be very effective. As we stated earlier and as most teachers know, there is never enough time to do everything you need to do. Coordinating meetings with other people can be very difficult and e-mail is a good way of communicating without having to get everyone together. O'Conner and Kellerman (2002) offer some suggestions for e-mailing:

- Use your work e-mail instead of personal e-mail because it typically will end with the .edu or .org extension. This helps to distinguish your e-mail from junk mail.
- Always include a brief statement in the subject line that reflects the purpose of the e-mail.
- Remember that e-mails should not be multiple pages of text. Keep e-mails on topic and concise.
- Include your full name, contact information, and title in the e-mail. There may be more than one person with the same last name and similar e-mail addresses working at the same campus.
- Do not include confidential information on an unsecured e-mail. It also is a good idea to include a privacy statement in the signature of your e-mails. Here is an example of a privacy statement that anyone can use:

> CONFIDENTIALITY NOTICE: This e-mail transmission and any documents accompanying this transmission may contain personal information subject to such privacy regulations as the Health Insurance Portability and Accountability Act of 1996 (HIPAA). This information is intended only for the use of the authorized individual named above. Such authorized recipient of this information is prohibited from disclosing this information to any other party unless required to do so by law or regulation and is required to destroy the information after its stated need has been fulfilled. If you are not the intended recipient, you are hereby notified that any disclosures, copying, distribution, or action taken in reliance on the contents of these documents is strictly prohibited.

- Do not put anything in an e-mail that you would not want read by everyone in the school. This is not the time to complain about how the custodial staff always forgets to empty your trash.
- If you add attachments, make sure that the person you are e-mailing can open the attachment. Most computers have Microsoft Word or Adobe Acrobat Reader, so Word documents or pdfs usually work for all parties.
- Make sure your computer's virus detection software is up-to-date. You do not want to send someone a virus. Your school's technology department should monitor this also.

Using the Internet as a Resource

The Internet can provide you with a wealth of information, or at least a starting place. You can use the Internet and search engines such as Google, MSN, Ask, and Google Scholar to answer many questions and to find experts where you live or work. Some experts also donate their time to answer questions and can be found at sites such as http://www.allexperts.com and http://www.justanswer.com.

COLLABORATION AND LEARNER LEVEL: AN INVERSE RELATIONSHIP

Children with autism have difficulties with social interactions and communication and they also may display a variety of repetitive behaviors or they may have an area of interest that is very specific. When considering the needs of a child with autism and working collaboratively with other professionals and parents, it stands to reason that the level of the learner impacts the level of services provided and collaboration needed. Therefore, when considering the appropriate collaboration model it is necessary to address the intensity and frequency of collaborative efforts. Others have written about the importance of and different ways to approach collaboration. However, less has been written about factors influencing intensity and frequency. It is apparent that the *more* independent a child with autism is, the *less* intense and frequent collaboration efforts need to be.

In other words, there is an inverse relationship based around the learner's levels (i.e., emerging learner, intermediate learner, and independent learner; see the introductory section of this chapter) and the need for intensive and frequent collaboration. This is illustrated in Figure 8.4.

CONSIDERATIONS FOR BUILDING RELATIONSHIPS WITH PARENTS FOR STUDENT SUCCESS

There are many people who may be considered or called a *parent* who, in fact, are not biological parents of a child for whom they have taken responsibility. Because of a variety of circumstances that may occur, a grandmother, for example, might assume the role of mother. When biological parent(s) are unable to care for their child, a family friend, relative, or foster parent may assume the role of parent. It is important that the special education teacher be aware of relevant family situations and the roles that various individuals play in the life of a child. It can be difficult and even sometimes confusing to sort out which family member, family friend, or other person currently is assuming the role of parent. Additionally,

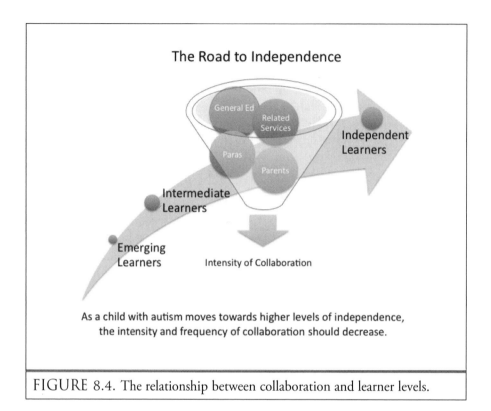

FIGURE 8.4. The relationship between collaboration and learner levels.

for some children this can be a process that changes over time. For the child with autism, this is of particular concern because children with autism typically do not adjust easily to changes in routine. In these types of situations, establishing and maintaining a good line of communication with the parent is very important.

Parents of children with autism at the emerging learner level often are parents who have recently received the diagnosis of autism for their child. These parents will go through a number of different emotions. Karten (2005) noted that it is important for the special education teacher to be aware of the emotions a parent experiences. Such emotions may include:

- *shock*: as in something that jars the mind or emotions as if with a violent unexpected blow,
- *denial*: as in refusal to accept or believe something,
- *guilt*: as in self-reproach for supposed inadequacy or wrongdoing,
- *shopping behavior*: as in looking around to find some explanation,
- *depression*: as in feeling sad or despondent,
- *hostility*: as in a feeling of deep and bitter anger, and
- *acceptance:* as in a recognized or acknowledged state of reality.

It is necessary for the special education teacher to be aware of and understand the different emotions the parent is experiencing (Prizant, Wetherby, Rubin,

Laurent, & Rydell, 2006). The special education teacher also needs to recognize and be sensitive to these emotional stages while realizing that they influence the interaction between the parent and professionals (Karten, 2005). Additionally, a parent can go through emotional stages multiple times. Regular parent communication can help the parent realize that the special education teacher is a collaborative partner with the parent. For example, sending home a daily note or card that emphasizes the child's strengths (however brief) can have a tremendous positive effect on the relationship between a parent and a special education teacher. Demonstrating that you want to keep the parent informed is an excellent way of fostering collaboration.

Marcus and Schopler (1987) offered the following principles to special education teachers of early learners:

- *Avoid judgmental attitudes.* Remember that you have not been in the shoes of the parent and your perspective may not be the same as the parent's.
- *Remember that raising a child with autism is complicated.* Early learners do not always regulate their behavior. The new parent is learning how to interact and guide the early learner and mistakes will happen.
- *Professionals are guides, not experts, in family dynamics.* Many times parents are struggling to find information and strategies, and develop an understanding of their child with autism. The parents do not want or need someone telling them what to do. Instead the parents need the special education teacher to be a source of good information and a partner in teaching the child appropriate behavior and social skills.
- *Promote fair and honest interactions between the special education teacher and the parent.* Effective communication must include the ability for all parties to be honest. It may be necessary for a special education teacher to tell the parent something painful. When this arises, the special education teacher needs to be honest, making sure that the parent understands what is being said. Additionally, the special education teacher has to be willing to listen to concerns of the parent, even if the teacher may not agree.

When a special education teacher communicates with the parent of a newly diagnosed child with autism, the special education teacher should be aware that there are things the parent may not understand. This type of parent differs from a parent whose child was diagnosed sometime in the past in the following ways:

- The parent of a newly diagnosed child with autism may not be as familiar with the buzzwords associated with autism or special education (e.g., "stimming" for self-stimulation behavior).
- The parent of a newly diagnosed child with autism may be uncomfortable being separated from his or her child.

- The parent of a newly diagnosed child with autism may be afraid to ask questions, incorrectly believing certain questions are "common knowledge" and he or she does not want to appear uninformed.
- The parent of a newly diagnosed child with autism typically does not know his or her rights as a parent of a child with autism.
- The parent of a newly diagnosed child with autism may not know what information about his or her child should be given to the school.
- The parent of a newly diagnosed child with autism may not know what school support is available for both the child with autism and the parent.
- Most parents typically have not been in a public school setting since they finished high school and if a parent comes from a private school background, he or she may never have attended a public school.

The role of the special education teacher is pivotal when it comes to communicating to the parent the intricacies associated with having a child with a disability in public school. It is important to remember that a parent may be in any one of several emotional stages when first bringing his or her child with autism to school. The special education teacher typically is the first and the main point-of-contact over time. To ensure a successful outcome for the student with autism, it is crucial for the parents and teacher to have meaningful collaboration. Effective collaboration can best be achieved by the teacher demonstrating interest in the child and creating a support system for the child and parents.

As time passes, parents of a child with autism typically will have gone through the issues discussed above and have a greater understanding of the child and the school system than when their child was newly diagnosed. At this level it is important for the special education teacher to continue to build on the knowledge and relationships that have been established. One caveat for the special education teacher to be aware of is that not all of the parents' previous experiences during the collaborative process with the public school have been positive. Some parents may focus on past negative events and misperceive present events. It is the responsibility of the special education teacher to help the parents stay focused on the outcome. One way to learn more about the parent and child's past schooling experiences is simply to talk with them to learn more. Use the following questions as your guide:

- What has your child's previous experiences been? What about your experiences?
- Is there anything that I can do to help make this a good school year?
- Is there anything that I should know about your child? (This question is asked to help you determine what [if any] behavioral, communication, or other problems exist of which you need to be aware.)
- How does your child play with other children?
- When meeting someone new, how does your child react?

- What types of toys does your child like to play with?
- What types of activities does your child like to engage in?
- What types of activities does your child *not* like to engage in?
- What are your child's favorite activities? (Try to learn at least 3 or 4 preferred activities but make sure you know which single activity is the child's absolute favorite.)
- Does your child have a nickname that he or she likes to be called?
- When your child is upset or mad, what do you do to calm him or her down?
- What are your expectations of the school year?
- Is there anything that you (the parent) can think of that I should be aware of? (This question is very important because it gives the parent an opportunity to introduce a topic that may not have been previously covered.)

Remember, the goals for the emerging, intermediate, and independent learners are different. The emerging learner is being introduced to new skills. The intermediate learner is maintaining skills, while learning to acquire new skills. The long-term goal is that, hopefully, the student with autism will advance to the independent learner stage where he will need minimal support.

The parent of an independent learner hopefully is seeing his or her child with autism demonstrating higher levels of independence. It is very important that the special education teacher is talking to both the student with autism and the parent about what is going to happen after high school. The student's chronological age is not as important as the child's ability to participate in activities independently.

Parents are a very important part of the collaboration process. They bring a point of view that is unique from all other members of the collaboration team. In fact, parents are the only members of the team who likely do not have formal training in providing services for students with autism. Because of this, the special education teacher must approach collaboration with parents by making them feel comfortable while reaching consensus about what is best for their child. This requires patience and understanding on the part of the special education teacher. Keep in mind that a parent who is made to feel like an equal partner on the collaboration team is likely to become a parent that will work with the teacher instead of against her. Many times this means the special education teacher must look at the situation from the point of view of the parent. We recommend remembering the American Indian Prayer that says, "Great Spirit, grant that I may not criticize my neighbor until I have walked a mile in his moccasins," (Fussell, 1992, p. 89).

CONSIDERATIONS FOR BUILDING RELATIONSHIPS WITH GENERAL EDUCATORS FOR STUDENT SUCCESS

Moll (2005) stated, "Twenty-three years of empirical evidence suggests that 99% of classroom learning challenges for students with disabilities can be identified as a mismatch between content and instructional planning and how the student best learns" (p. 47). To truly teach children with autism effectively, there are a number of issues that need to be considered and planned for in advance. With regard to the general education administration, teacher, and setting, first and foremost is the issue of differentiated instruction.

Differentiated Instruction

Instruction must be differentiated to meet the individual needs of children with autism. Whereas all children differ across a wide range of characteristics, there is a common saying among professionals who work with children who have autism: "If you've seen one child with autism, you've seen one child with autism." This means that although there is a common core set of features that all children with autism share, these children vary greatly in terms of behaviors, specific areas of interest, academic skills, preferences, ability to communicate, and capacity to interact socially. This also is the reason the term *autism spectrum* commonly is used. Regardless of where a child with autism is in terms of learner level (i.e., emerging learner, intermediate learner, or independent learner), he or she is going to have unique needs in terms of how instruction should be delivered.

The delivery of instruction is not the only area in which differentiation is required. Children with autism often display challenging behaviors that require teachers to differentiate the way in which they proactively plan for behaviors (to reduce the chances that the behavior will occur before it happens) and respond to behaviors after they have occurred. The number one rule of thumb to keep in mind when dealing with any child who has behavioral challenges is that if you want to change a child's behavior, the first thing you must do is change your own behavior (Alberto & Troutman, 2005). It has long been said that the definition of insanity is to do the same thing over and over again and to expect different results. This is especially true when dealing with challenging behaviors.

In contrast to the general education setting, the special education classroom typically has been the environment where more differentiation has occurred. Over the years, special educators have realized that students with disabilities, in general, have varying needs that require teachers to differentiate instruction and how they deal with challenging behaviors. This practice has not been as commonly seen within the general education setting due to the more homogeneous population served within this setting. Therefore differentiating instruction and dealing with problem behaviors may be particularly challenging for the teacher of the child with autism who is included in the general education setting.

Students are more involved, engaged, and have a higher sense of fulfillment within the classroom when they are involved in activities tailored to their learning needs and preferences (Heacox, 2002). They are even more successful when they are involved in goal setting and decision making about their learning (Tomlinson & Allan, 2000). Children with autism often need an extra push to become involved in the general education classroom, so it is key that the teachers in the classroom provide multiple opportunities and increase students' motivation for this to occur.

For differentiated instruction to become second nature for the general education teacher who teaches children with autism, it is crucial that administrators are well versed in how to differentiate instruction and deal with challenging behaviors. Additionally, administrators need to hold their teachers to a high standard of performance. Because the administrators are the instructional leaders of the campus, they can make or break how well this works within the classroom. A. Ahumada, an inclusion specialist for a school district, said an administrator needs to be, "open, fair, proactive, and show initiative" to ensure effective implementation of differentiated instruction in classrooms (personal communication, May 20, 2008). The inclusive classroom will be successful only if there are good leaders with the necessary qualities to effect change.

Effective educational leadership for differentiation comes from dogged, unremitting insistence on and support for the fact that expert teachers teach students the most important things in the most effective ways (Tomlinson & Allan, 2000). The administrator who presides over the special education department should periodically meet with the collaborating special education and general education teachers to ensure effective teaching of children with autism is taking place in the general education setting. In this meeting, a review of what has been working well and has been effective should take place. After the meeting, the administrator can use this information to make a tip sheet detailing ideas and successful strategies. This document, much like the classroom, will forever be evolving and progressing. On the flip side, both general and special education teachers need to make their administrators aware of what was not working well and what has been ineffective in the inclusive classroom. At this point in the collaboration, the administrator and teachers should give feedback and suggestions. For this to work effectively, the administrator needs to stay abreast of best practices in differentiated instruction and differentiated behavioral techniques. The administrator also should regularly facilitate professional development for faculty in these areas. Not only does the administrator need to be aware of and support differentiation, he also needs to be an advocate for it because it is truly the only way for children with autism to be successful in the general education environment.

Although there are many differentiation models available, teachers still face challenges in their implementation. There are the challenges of shifting away from traditional views of intelligence and traditional reliance on print media; the challenges of acquiring and mastering new technology; and the challenges of garnering support from the school system (CAST, n.d.). Because the implementation of differentiated instruction is a challenge, it is important for the administrator to help both the special and general education teachers reach their goal of student success.

Teachers in inclusive classrooms should have the opportunity to have someone with expertise in differentiating instruction and behavioral techniques observe their classroom and make suggestions on how best to group students and plan for differentiation based on specific students' needs and their abilities. Reading about differentiation in a textbook is informative, but in order to truly grasp the concept and be able to perform it well, both general and special education teachers need the concept to be modeled for them and they need to be able to ask follow-up questions. After the teachers have practiced differentiating for a period of time, a follow-up observation should be scheduled with the goal of giving positive feedback and constructive criticism regarding the effectiveness of the techniques used to differentiate instruction and behavioral techniques.

Education does not happen in a vacuum. It takes several people, ideas, trials, and strategies to do what is best for children with autism. Now both a rarity and a profound need, effective differentiated instruction stands a chance of proliferating where determined partnerships exist between teachers and administrative leaders with a vision of more effective classrooms, a plan to realize the vision, and a dogged will to persist (CAST, n.d.).

The chance for success is much more powerful when the special and general education teachers and administrators partner and collaborate together. The administrator and teachers also should partner together to help lay the groundwork for differentiating instruction in the IEP team meeting. The administrator presiding over the IEP team meeting should guide the team in how to design an IEP that details how the curriculum can be modified and how the instruction should be differentiated, whether it be through the content, the process, or the product (Tomlinson, 1997). Differentiation of content refers to a change in the material being learned by the student. Differentiation of process refers to the way in which the student accesses material. Differentiation of product refers to the way in which the student shows what he or she has learned. Additionally, the administrator should facilitate the development of a behavior intervention plan (BIP) if the child displays challenging behaviors that interfere with his or her learning or that of other students.

The ultimate determinant in whether this process is a success is in the hands of the special education and general education teachers during implementation. Both general and special education teachers are responsible for conducting ongoing classroom assessments to determine whether instruction is effective and also collecting data on the frequency of behaviors to determine if behavioral interventions are effective.

Collaboration and communication between the administrator, special education teacher, and general education teacher is crucial. The administrator should regularly check on the progress of the students for whom he or she helped create the IEP. Therefore, it is not only the teachers but also the administrator who has a vested interest in the success of the child with autism.

Co-teaching now occurs in the general education environment with greater frequency. General and special educators continue to work increasingly close together regarding the specific duties, roles, and responsibilities of each professional in the co-teaching arrangement. Burggraf and Sotomayor (2005) suggested that successful co-teaching requires that professionals be tolerant, reflective, nonterritorial, and display flexibility. They also indicate that co-teachers must equally share:

- students,
- planning,
- evaluation of all students,
- instructional decisions based on evidence of students' progress,
- grading duties,
- space,
- classroom management/procedures systems,
- expectations for all students,
- supplies,
- philosophy,
- communication with parents,
- record keeping,
- teaching responsibilities,
- blameworthiness for poor student performances, and
- credit for student successes.

Burggraf and Sotomayor further indicated that co-teaching is not:
- one person teaching, usually the regular educator, always taking the lead in instruction;
- the special educator standing on the side of the room waiting to help when the regular educator gives the signal;
- solely the special educator copying all of the material and passing out the papers;
- the regular educator planning all of the components of the lesson;
- the special educator working with just students with special needs;
- the regular educator owning the classroom and giving the special educator permission to work there; and
- the regular educator working only with students who do not struggle.

An important outcome of a successful collaboration between general and special education teachers is that each teacher gains a specific understanding of his or her roles and responsibilities with regard to issues such as grading student work, lesson planning, providing instruction, and managing the classroom.

Although several models of co-teaching have been demonstrated to be effective, Burggraf and Sotomayor (2005) described the following models of co-teaching as well as their benefits and disadvantages:

- Station/Center Teaching
- Assisted/Support Teaching
- Team Teaching
- Large Group/Small Group Teaching
- Parallel Teaching or Two Heterogeneous Groups

Teachers and administrators interested in these models are encouraged to consult Burggraf and Sotomayor (2005) for more information. In addition, The Access Center is a Web site that gives free access to training modules on the topic of co-teaching (see http://www.k8accesscenter.org/training_resources/Co-TeachingModule.asp). Regardless of which model of co-teaching is utilized, the crucial point is that the collaboration process includes open and honest communication on a regular basis to ensure success.

CONSIDERATIONS FOR BUILDING RELATIONSHIPS WITH PARAEDUCATORS FOR STUDENT SUCCESS

The special education paraeducator works under the supervision of the special education teacher or other professional staff and may be responsible for a very wide range of duties and activities. The National Resource Center for Paraprofessionals (n.d.) lists the following as possible duties for the paraeducator:

- instructing individual and small groups of learners following programs and lessons developed by teachers;
- assisting with supplementary work for learners and supervising independent study;
- reinforcing lessons with small groups of learners;
- assisting with the preparation of materials;
- performing informal/functional assessment activities, scoring objectives tests, and keep appropriate records;
- assisting teachers in collecting and maintaining data about learner behavior and performance;

- implementing behavioral management programs developed for individual learners;
- assisting teachers with crisis intervention and discipline;
- participating in the IEP and other program planning meetings at the request of a teacher or administrative personnel;
- performing bus duty;
- supervising playgrounds and lunchrooms;
- assisting students with personal and hygienic care;
- setting up and maintaining adaptive equipment and learning centers; and
- operating office or video equipment.

Because the special education teacher may be the direct supervisor of a paraeducator, it is vital that he or she possesses knowledge and skills related to effective supervision and management. First, it is important to get to know the paraeducator by establishing a friendly working rapport. This may be accomplished by visiting with the paraeducator to determine his or her previous work experience, skills, talents, and/or interests. You also may wish to visit with the paraeducator regarding his or her short- and long-term professional goals and also to discuss any initial concerns.

Once you begin to instruct the paraeducator as to his or her specific duties, keep in mind that the paraeducator is a facilitator to the teacher in the completion of job responsibilities. This makes the educational process for the child with autism more productive. Further, the special education teacher can help provide a positive and friendly work environment that will help motivate the paraeducator to complete his or her duties.

The special education teacher and paraeducator must consider these basic strategies for clear communication (Center for Advanced Study in Education, 1990):

- meet regularly to discuss problems and share concerns;
- work together to build an environment of trust, cooperation, loyalty, and respect;
- develop and share a common vocabulary;
- ensure all directions and expectations are understood clearly, including what is necessary to perform a particular task, what is needed to do the job (materials), who will complete the task, where it will be performed, when it will begin and end, how the task will be performed (methods, reinforcers, techniques), how the learner's progress will be monitored and assessed, and how the paraeducator's performance will be monitored and assessed;
- work together to ensure the paraeducator has the knowledge and skills required to perform the tasks assigned to him or her;
- ensure that each assignment is understood (paraeducators should be encouraged to ask for clarification or assistance when needed);

- ◆   maximize appropriate delivery of educational services by discussing what special interests, talents, or training the paraeducator has that will complement and enhance his or her performance;
- ◆   communicate to recognize, understand, and appreciate the feelings of each other that may be influenced by differing points of view regarding educational practices and strategies, value systems, cultural heritage, ages, and levels of education and experience; and
- ◆   communicate openly and honestly with each other

Although some school systems may have policies and procedures in place along with specific criteria to conduct evaluations of paraeducators, others may not. An evaluation process will proceed much more smoothly if the special education teacher remembers that the purpose of an evaluation is not to place blame or criticize. Rather, the purpose of an evaluation is to provide feedback that will improve the quality of the paraeducator's performance.

CONSIDERATIONS FOR BUILDING RELATIONSHIPS WITH RELATED SERVICES PROVIDERS FOR STUDENT SUCCESS

Up to this point, we have discussed collaborating with general education professionals, paraeducators, and parents. The special education teacher also collaborates with related services providers. Related service providers (RSP) come from a varied background. They provide specific services to the child with autism; however, these services typically are not specifically educational in nature. The RSP addresses areas of functioning that are necessary for effective learning to occur so that the child may benefit from the educational process (IDEA, 2004).

Earlier in this chapter we defined related services using the federal definition. This definition included a list of related services. It is important to remember that this list includes differing related services for all students in special education based on their needs. For example, although most children with autism may never have a need for orientation and mobility services, this service may be available for a child with autism who also has a visual impairment. Orientation and mobility provide children and adults with visual impairments the skills and services that enable them to move independently in familiar and unfamiliar environments.

Another point of importance to note is that while assistive technology (AT) devices and services are not defined in IDEA (2004) as a related service, many school personnel think of and include it as part of related services. AT instead is defined by the Assistive Technology Act of 1998. Assistive technology means any item, piece of equipment or product system, whether acquired commercially off the shelf, modified, or customized, that is used to increase, maintain, or improve the functional capabilities of children with disabilities (see Chapter 6 of this book for an in-depth discussion of assistive technology).

The federal regulations also include many different types of services that are considered part of the definition of AT. These AT services may include activities such as evaluation of a person's needs for assistive technology devices, purchasing or leasing assistive technology devices for people, designing and fabricating devices, coordinating services offered by those who provide assistive technology services, providing training or technical assistance to a person who uses assistive technology, and giving training and technical assistance to those who work with people who use assistive technology devices, such as teachers or employers (Bausch, Ault, & Hasselbring, 2006).

Assistive technologies can be divided into four different levels:

1. *No tech*: this is when an AT service is provided but not any equipment or devices (e.g., AT evaluation).
2. *Low tech*: this includes a device that has few or no moving parts (e.g., a walking cane).
3. *Medium tech*: this is a relatively complicated mechanical device (e.g., a manual wheelchair).
4. *High tech*: this is the most complicated type of AT (e.g., an augmentative or alternative communication device). Augmentative and alternative communication (AAC) includes all forms of communication (other than oral speech) that are used to express thoughts, needs, wants, and ideas. Special augmentative aids, such as electronic devices, are available to help people express themselves. This may increase social interaction, school performance, and feelings of self-worth (American Speech-Language-Hearing Association, n.d.).

The above level of services and technologies are used by students with disabilities to (a) assist them in learning, (b) make the environment more accessible, (c) enable them to compete in the workplace, (d) enhance their independence, or (e) otherwise improve their quality of life. These may include commercially available or *homemade* devices that are specially designed to meet the idiosyncratic needs of a particular individual (Blackhurst & Lahm, 2000; National Assistive Technology Research Institute, n.d.). Many times the child with autism will use AT for assisting with communication. In the area of communication, AT can be anything from simple pictures placed on cardboard to very advanced alternative communication devices such as the Tango, an electronic speech-generating device.

Because many RSPs are educated outside of colleges of education they may not have the in-depth knowledge of public schools of the special education teacher. It is the responsibility of the special education teacher to keep everyone focused on the educational needs of the child with autism. Related services providers are many times educated in allied health programs at universities, where working in school systems typically is not the main focus. Although professionals such as speech-language pathologists (SLP) do work in schools, they also can work in many other environments such as hospitals, physician offices, rehabilitation clinics, and corporations. This also is true of other RSPs. An assistive technology practitioner may have been trained as a rehabilitation engineer, taking all of his or her classes in engineering programs, never having a course in education. This does not mean that the RSP is not qualified to work in a school system; instead, it means that the special education teacher needs to understand that the RSP's focus may be something other than strictly education. For example, the transportation specialist is primarily concerned with ensuring the child with autism arrives to and from school safely. When collaborating with the RSP, he needs to know that you value his contribution to the child while keeping the primary focus on the education of the child.

Related service providers bring an indispensable service to the collaboration table. They help the child with autism achieve to the maximum extent possible within the seven areas of human functioning. Most of these are outside of the educational purview. See the Seven Areas of Human Functioning description in Table 8.2.

As Table 8.2 delineates, AT practitioners and RSPs provide services that are beyond the responsibilities of the special education teacher. Because human functioning areas occur across the environments of community, home, and school (Bausch et al., 2006), a responsibility of the special education teacher is to assure that the collaboration stays focused on educationally related topics.

CASE STUDY

Bruce is 12 years old and has been diagnosed with moderate to severe autism. He is considered an early learner. Bruce currently is attending sixth grade at a middle school. Recently his teacher of 3 months left the classroom and was replaced with Ms. Gordon. Ms. Gordon has been a special education teacher for 6 years, however, her experiences have been as an inclusion teacher for children with specific learning disabilities (SLD). Bruce is able to use fewer than 10 words and has multiple behavioral outbursts throughout the day.

On the first day, Ms. Gordon realizes that in order to provide for Bruce, she is going to need the knowledge and skills of other professionals. However, before going to others she needs to find out where Bruce is functioning both academically and socially. She starts this process by going to his Individualized Education Plan (IEP) to become familiar with what services have been given

TABLE 8.2

THE SEVEN AREAS OF HUMAN FUNCTIONING AND ASSISTIVE TECHNOLOGIES TO SUPPORT THEM

Area of Human Functioning	Definition	Assistive Technology Examples
Existence	The difficulties in maintaining the functions needed to sustain life	Adapted eating utensils and various dressing aids
Communication	The functions needed to understand and convey information	Magnifiers, closed captioning, and adapted keyboards
Body support and alignment	The difficulties with standing, sitting, or positioning the body	Adapted furniture, head gear, and slings
Travel and mobility	The difficulties in walking, climbing stairs, and generally navigating one's environment	Walkers, canes, and wheelchairs
Environmental interaction	The problems related to activities across environments	Automatic door openers, various switch options, and remote-controlled devices
Education and transition	The functions needed to succeed in school settings	Educational software and computer adaptations
Sports, fitness, and recreation	The problems in participating in fitness-related and other recreational activities	Modified sports equipment and switch-activated scissors

Note. Adapted from Bausch et al., 2006.

to Bruce. She discovers that he is receiving the following services from related services professionals:

- speech,
- occupational therapy, and
- assistive technology.

Ms. Gordon notes that Bruce's paperwork does not mention any contact with his parents other than the annual IEP meetings. Also, there is no record that the related services professionals are following a structured, consistent behavioral plan. Ms. Gordon remembers from her class on autism that it is very important to communicate and collaborate with all stakeholders. Communication and collaboration includes everyone using the same behavioral plan and everyone being kept up-to-date on how Bruce is progressing. Ms. Gordon knows that if the data cannot show behavioral improvements, it will be necessary to redesign the plan and that this redesign must be based on data.

Ms. Gordon realizes that for Bruce to make progress toward his goals of decreasing his behavioral outbursts and adding words to his repertoire she must communicate and collaborate with Bruce's parents and related service professionals. She decides that because the related service professionals work for the school district the best way to communicate with them is via e-mail. Ms. Gordon finds everyone's e-mail on the district's listserv and sends out an e-mail introducing herself, introducing how the e-mail collaboration is going to work, and asking for input from everyone. She also makes sure to tell everyone to use the "reply to all" option when returning an e-mail to ensure everyone is kept in the loop. Ms. Gordon also suggests that e-mail communication and collaboration occur on at least a weekly basis and that everyone meet face-to-face once every 3 weeks.

Ms. Gordon finds out from Bruce's previous teacher that his parents do not have access to the Internet so she will not be able to communicate with them by e-mail. Ms. Gordon decides she can send a note home every day that tells Bruce's parents how his day went and what they need to work on that night. This allows Bruce to have homework like all of the students in the general education setting. Ms. Gordon makes sure to leave space for Bruce's parents to write back to her. Before sending the first note home, she calls Bruce's parents and tells them what she is planning. Ms. Gordon also asks that one of them sign the note every night and put it in Bruce's backpack. This will allow Ms. Gordon to know that Bruce got home with the note and his parents read it. She also suggests that she and Bruce's parents try to schedule regular meetings throughout the school year. These meetings will allow Ms. Gordon and Bruce's parents to discus any concerns and address them as part of the team.

CONCLUSION

We truly believe that an effective program for a child with autism requires not only the specific expertise of a team of professionals that includes the parent; it also requires the team to work together in a partnership. There are three basic outcomes of collaboration: (a) improvement, (b) deterioration, or (c) no change. Measuring the progress of the child in specific targeted areas will help determine the overall effectiveness of the collaboration.

How many times have you heard that a lack of communication is the cause of a particular problem? Professionals must learn to communicate effectively and efficiently; communication is key to any collaboration. "The old wisdom of two heads being better than one is truer than ever before as our schools provide a wider array of services and become more diverse" (Kluth, 2004, p. 242). Thus, communication and collaboration are essential to effectively supporting the educational needs of children with autism.

REFERENCES

Alberto, P. A., & Troutman, A. C. (2005). *Applied behavior analysis for teachers.* Upper Saddle River, NJ: Prentice Hall.

American Association of School Administrators. (2008). *About AASA.* Retrieved from http://www.aasa.org/about/index.cfm

American Speech-Language Hearing Association. (n.d.). *Assistive technology.* Retrieved November 1, 2008, from http://www.asha.org/public/hearing/treatment/assist_tech.htm

Assistive Technology Act of 1998, 29 U. S. C. §3001 et seq. Retrieved January 26, 2009, from http://www.section508.gov/docs/AT1998.html

Bausch, M. E., Ault, M. J., & Hasselbring, T. S. (2006). *Assistive technology planner: From IEP consideration to classroom implementation.* Lexington, KY: National Assistive Technology Institute.

Blackhurst, A. E., & Lahm, E. A. (2000). Foundations of technology and exceptionality. In J. Lindsey (Ed.), *Technology and exceptional individuals* (3rd ed., pp. 3–45). Austin, TX: Pro-Ed.

Brownell, M., & Walther-Thomas, C. (2002). An interview with Dr. Marilyn Friend. *Intervention in School and Clinic, 37*, 223–228.

Brownell, M. T., Yeager, E., Rennells, M. S., & Riley, T. (1997). Teachers working together: What teacher educators and researchers should know. *Teacher Education and Special Education, 20*, 340–359.

Burggraf, K., & Sotomayor, A. (2005). *Best practices in education: Fundamentals of co-teaching.* Charlotte Hall, MD: Day One Publishing.

Burns, R. (1785). *To a mouse.* Retrieved October 4, 2008, from http://www.electricscotland.com/burns/mouse.html

Butler, T., & Coleman, D. (2003). *Models of collaboration: Collaborative strategies: Strategies for electronic collaboration and knowledge management.* Retrieved from http://www.collaborate.com/publication/newsletter/publications_newsletter_september03.html

CAST. (n.d.). *Universal design for learning.* Retrieved May 18, 2008, from http://www.cast.org

Center for Advanced Study in Education. (1990). *Basic strategies for clear communication between teachers and paraeducators: A training program for paraprofessionals working in special education and related services.* New York: City University of New York.

Council for Exceptional Children. (2004). *Parability: The CEC paraeducator standards workbook.* Arlington, VA: Author.

Fussell, P. (1992). *Class: A guide through the American status system.* New York: Touchstone.

Heacox, D. (2002). *Differentiating instruction in the regular classroom: How to reach and teach all learners, grades 3–12.* Minneapolis, MN: Free Spirit.

How Stuff Works. (2008). *What is white noise?* Retrieved from http://www.howstuffworks.com/question47.htm

Individuals with Disabilities Education Improvement Act, PL 108-446, 118 Stat. 2647 (2004).

Karten, T. J. (2005). *Inclusion strategies that work! Research-based methods for the classroom.* Thousand Oaks, CA: Corwin Press.

Kluth, P. (2004). *"You're going to love this kid!": Teaching students with autism in the inclusive classroom.* Baltimore: Paul H. Brookes.

Marcus, L. M., & Schopler, E. (1987). Working with families: A developmental perspective. In D. J. Cohen & A. M. Donnellan (Eds.), *Handbook of autism and pervasive developmental disorders* (pp. 499–512). Silver Spring, MD: V. H. Winston.

Moll, A. M. (2005). *Differentiated instruction guide for inclusive teaching.* Port Chester, NY: Dude Publishing.

National Assistive Technology Research Institute. (n.d.). *Assistive technology planner.* Retrieved October 3, 2008, from http://natri.uky.edu/atPlannermenu.html

National Resource Center for Paraprofessionals. (n.d.). *Appendix 2.* Retrieved October 4, 2008, from http://www.nrcpara.org/report/appendix2

O'Conner, P. T., & Kellerman, S. (2002). *You send me.* New York: Harcourt.

Prizant, B. M., Wetherby, A. M., Rubin, E., Laurent, A. C., & Rydell, P. J. (2006). *The SCERTS model: A comprehensive educational approach for children with autism spectrum disorders.* Baltimore: Paul H. Brookes.

Shannon, C. E., & Weaver, W. (1998). *The mathematical theory of communication.* Urbana: University of Illinois Press.

Smith, D. D. (2007). *Introduction to special education: Making a difference* (6th ed.). Boston: Pearson.

Snell, M. E., Janney, R., Elliot, J., Burton, C. C., Colley, K. N., Raynes, M., et al. (2000). *Collaborative learning: Teacher's guide to inclusive practices.* Baltimore: Paul H. Brookes.

Tomlinson, C. A., & Allan, S. D. (2000). *Leadership for differentiating schools & classrooms.* Retrieved from http://www.ascd.org/portal/site/ascd/index.jsp

Tomlinson, J. (1997). Inclusive learning: The report of the Committee of Enquiry into post-school education of those with learning difficulties and disabilities in England 1996. *European Journal of Special Needs Education, 12,* 184–186.

Bringing It Together:

Notes From the Editors

THE motivation behind this book was driven by a number of factors that currently are impacting the field of autism. First of all, the increasing number of students being identified with autism and the wide range of academic abilities they present has challenged the educational system to examine how to best meet the educational needs for the students who are being served in the general education classroom. In addition, the general education teachers have expressed concern about the lack of resources that have been developed specifically for them and their role as a general educator whose class now includes students with autism. It is for those reasons we developed a book in which the information in one chapter provides a framework for information in the following chapters.

It is common practice that most preservice education programs typically provide an overview of disability areas, but usually do not go beyond that level in preparing teachers to teach students with an identified disability such as autism. School administrators have relayed to us that they often have teachers question them regarding why a student with autism was placed in their class. We have found that teachers are willing to work with the students who make up their class, but understanding the characteristics of the disability and how autism is diagnosed helps the teacher to have a better understanding of how programming decisions are made. Thus, this information provides a framework for the way a classroom will need to be organized including the physical environment, routines, and procedures. Furthermore, this information will assist the teacher in choosing the methods of academic instruction that will be the most effective for students with autism, also realizing that the teacher may have an additional 20 or 25 students in his or her classroom.

As all teachers will agree, their main focus should be on teaching. However, teaching is only a part of what happens in the classroom. The days of students coming into a classroom, sitting in desks lined up in rows while everyone completes his or her work in isolation is almost nonexistent. Classrooms have become a social environment that requires the use of numerous social skills and appropriate behavioral expectations to accompany those skills that may be difficult for some students in the classroom and especially those students with autism. Teachers have expressed that they often feel that they have to be "all things to all students." For that reason alone, we knew the importance of providing information to assist them in dealing with social issues as well as behavioral problems that can be characteristic of students with autism.

The last academic support for the classroom that was included in this book was the chapter on instructional technology. Because the use of assistive technology to address the academic and/or communication needs of students with autism continues to expand, and as noted earlier, teachers are typically only given minimal training in this area, we wanted to provide some very practical ways these tools could be used in the general education classroom. Most students enjoy using technology, while at the same time it allows some students with autism to gain more independence both academically and socially. Using assistive technology also may increase the amount of instructional time that the teacher can provide for the entire classroom.

Last of all, making educational decisions for a child with autism is a team decision, and a critical part of that team is the parents. Thus, the final two chapters move beyond the classroom to provide support for the parents who have a child with autism and also address the numerous levels of collaboration that are involved in providing the best educational plan available. Over the course of a child's educational career, parents will collaborate with many professionals who will be able to provide valuable information that addresses concerns that impact both home and school.

As the editors of this book, we are pleased that we were able to include the knowledge of so many authors who have learned their area of expertise from the years of experience they have spent working with children with autism. Moreover, it is the intent of each of these authors that teachers can take this information and use it as a tool in working more effectively with students with autism in the general education classroom.

ABOUT THE EDITORS

Vicky Spencer has served in the field of special education for more than 20 years as a special education teacher, educational consultant/diagnostician, and assistant professor. She also has worked for the Virginia Department of Education Training and Technical Assistance Center, providing teacher training throughout the state focusing on a variety of academic areas dealing with students with special needs. Dr. Spencer continues to remain actively involved in the field as she collaborates with special education teachers to implement cognitive strategies within the inclusive classroom setting. Her current research interests include cognitive-strategy instruction for students with mild to moderate disabilities, autism, and transition planning. She has presented findings from her research at state, national, and international conferences and published numerous articles that disseminate those findings. Dr. Spencer currently is an assistant professor and the assistant director of operations at the Kellar Institute for Human disAbilities at George Mason University.

Cynthia Simpson has more than 16 years of experience in the public and private sector as a preschool teacher, special education teacher, elementary teacher, educational diagnostician, associate professor of education, and administrator. She maintains an active role in the lives of children and young adults with exceptionalities as an educational consultant in the areas of assessment, inclusive practices, and transition planning. Her professional responsibilities include serving on the National Council for Accreditation of Teacher Education/National Association of Young Children Review Panel, as well as serving as a state advisor to the Texas Educational Diagnostician Association. Dr. Simpson has many publications to her credit (books and articles) and is a featured speaker at the international, national, and state level. She currently is an associate professor and program coordinator for special education in the College of Education at Sam Houston State University. Dr. Simpson has won several awards and received numerous recognitions for her work with individuals with disabilities, as well as her contributions to the field of special education.

ABOUT THE
CONTRIBUTORS

Jeffrey P. Bakken is professor and chair of the Department of Special Education at Illinois State University. His specific areas of interest include transition, teacher effectiveness, assessment, learning strategies, autism, and technology. He has written more than 80 academic publications, including a book, journal articles, chapters, monographs, reports, and proceedings; and he has made more than 190 presentations at local, state, regional, national, and international levels. Additionally, he is on the editorial boards of many scholarly publications, including *Multicultural Learning and Teaching* and *Remedial and Special Education*. Through his work, he has committed himself toward improving teachers' knowledge and techniques, as well as services for students with exceptionalities and their families. Bakken received his doctoral degree from Purdue University.

John T. Blackledge received his doctoral degree in clinical psychology from the University of Nevada, Reno in 2004, after studying under Dr. Steven Hayes, Acceptance and Commitment Therapy's primary developer. He has published more than a dozen journal articles and book chapters on ACT and Relational Frame Theory, has just released an edited book entitled *Acceptance & Commitment Therapy: Theory & Practice*, and has conducted ACT training workshops in the U.S., Australia, and

Ireland. He currently is an assistant professor in the Department of Psychology at Morehead State University.

Stacey Jones Bock is an associate professor in the Department of Special Education at Illinois State University. She has been in the field of autism as a teacher and teacher educator for approximately 16 years. She coauthored the Asperger Syndrome Diagnostic Scale (ASDS), has published numerous professional articles, and made many professional presentations in the area of autism spectrum disorders. Bock also has coordinated a technical assistance project in Kansas and in Illinois, and currently is the director of the Autism Spectrum Institute at Illinois State University. She received her doctoral degree from the University of Kansas.

Thane Dykstra is the director of Behavioral Health Services for Trinity Services, Inc., where he supervises several programs based on clinical behavior analysis interventions, such as Acceptance and Commitment Therapy and Functional Analytic Psychotherapy. Dykstra received his doctoral degree in clinical psychology from the University of Nevada, Reno in 1997.

Cheryl Fielding began her career in public schools as a teacher of children with autism and other developmental disabilities. She later went on to work as an educational diagnostician and behavior specialist. She earned her doctoral degree in special education from Texas Woman's University. Fielding currently is an associate professor in the Educational Psychology Department at the University of Texas-Pan American where she regularly teaches courses in the areas of educational evaluation and behavior. She also is a Board Certified Behavior Analyst who regularly works with children and adults who display challenging behaviors.

Kim Floyd has taught in an inclusive preschool for North Carolina public school system for 7 years, and directed the preschool for 6 years. She has taught at East Carolina University since 1990. Floyd is currently certified in K–12 Special Education, Preschool Handicapped, and Birth–Kindergarten. Her recent publications in the area of technology and instructional programming can be found in *Assistive Technology Outcomes & Benefits, International Journal of Special Education, Early Childhood Education Journal,* and *Teaching & Teacher Education.* Her research interests include integration of assistive technology in PreK–12 settings, effective programming for persons with autism, and technology supports for post-secondary students with learning disabilities. Floyd will complete her Ph.D. in special education in May 2009 from Old Dominion University.

Chris Frawley is a program specialist in curriculum and instruction for the Virginia Department of Education's Training and Technical Assistance Center at Virginia

Commonwealth University. She holds a master's degree in education. She has more than 27 years of experience as a general educator. During her years as an elementary teacher, Ms. Frawley taught many students with disabilities, including students with autism. As a program specialist, she uses her previous teaching experience as a foundation for supporting general and special education teachers in areas such as inclusive practice, effective instruction, and collaborative teaming.

Janet E. Graetz is an assistant professor at Oakland University (Rochester, MI) in human development and child studies. For the past 30 years, her life has revolved around individuals with developmental disabilities. She began classroom teaching in 1970 and taught in various schools and institutional settings until 2001. During the last 15 years, her classroom teaching focused on children with autism spectrum disorders. She attended George Mason University in Virginia and completed her Ph.D. in special education and instructional technology in 2003. That same year, she joined the faculty at Oakland University in special education. Her current research studies include the topic of college students with Asperger's syndrome, spirituality and Asperger's syndrome, and the use of Video Eyewear for adolescents with autism.

Marci Kinas Jerome is an assistant professor at George Mason University (GMU) specializing in the areas of severe disabilities (SD) and assistive technology. Together with her responsibilities as the project coordinator for a statewide collaborative SD training grant, she serves as an instructor in both the assistive technology certificate/master's program and the special education licensure/master's program in the Graduate School of Education at GMU. Her current research interests include the effectiveness of assistive technology on student learning, distance education, and teacher training in severe disabilities.

Nichelle Kempel-Michalak is the Central Regional Consultant for the Illinois Autism Training and Technical Assistance Project in conjunction with Illinois State University. She began working with individuals with developmental disabilities and autism in group home settings during her undergraduate program. Her graduate studies focused on behavioral psychology while working as a clinician in Illinois State University's (ISU) Autism Clinic. She has been an integral part of writing and producing ISU's online autism course.

Carey Lowdermilk is a certified special education teacher who has worked with students with disabilities for more than 6 years. She has experience at both the middle and high school levels. Lowdermilk has had the opportunity to work with children with autism in the general education setting and she also has served as a teacher of children with autism in a pull-out program. Lowdermilk presently is working at a high school where she teaches students with severe levels of disabilities in a life-skills classroom. She has a graduate degree from the University of North Texas in Denton, TX, and presently is pursuing principal certification at the University of Texas Pan American in Edinburg, TX.

John Lloyd Lowdermilk III, has more than 10 years experience working with children and adults in the areas of assistive technology and behavior. He earned a Ph.D. from the University of North Texas (UNT) in special education with an emphasis in emotional and behavioral disorders. While at UNT, he worked with Dr. Lyndal M. Bullock in the Institute for Learning and Behavioral Differences as a multimedia developer of distance education courses. Lowdermilk completed postdoctoral studies at the National Assistive Technology Research Institute (NATRI) in the Department of Special Education and Rehabilitation Counseling at the University of Kentucky. He presently is an assistant professor of special education at the University of Texas Pan-American in Edinburg, TX.

Sharon Lynch is professor of special education at Sam Houston State University. Her areas of interest and research include assessment and evaluation, behavior intervention, and learners with significant needs. She has experience as a speech-language pathologist, special education teacher, educational diagnostician, educational consultant, and university instructor. Lynch is the author of three books for teachers of young children with disabilities and a number of publications in journals, including *Journal of Special Education, Education and Training in Developmental Disabilities, Behavior Disorders, Research and Practice for Persons with Severe Disabilities*, and *Assessment for Effective Intervention*.

Daniel J. Moran received his Ph.D. in clinical/school psychology from Hofstra University in 1998. He is the director of the Family Counseling Center, a division of Trinity Services in Joliet, IL. He recently coauthored *ACT in Practice: Case Conceptualization in Acceptance and Commitment Therapy* (2008) for New Harbinger Press.

Susan M. Palko is a program specialist for the Virginia Department of Education's Training and Technical Assistance Center (T/TAC) located at Virginia Commonwealth University (VCU). Her focus is on autism spectrum disorders, positive behavior supports, early childhood special education, and inclusion. Prior to providing training and technical assistance, she was a classroom teacher for 12 years. Palko completed her master's degree at Virginia Commonwealth University (VCU) in early childhood special education and currently is working on her Ph.D. in special education and disability policy also at VCU.

Lora Lee Smith-Canter received her Ph.D. from the University of South Carolina and currently is a faculty member at East Carolina University teaching special education graduate and undergraduate classes. Dr. Smith-Canter's research interests range across the field of special education, focusing primarily upon social interaction interventions for young children with developmental delays or identified disabilities, multicultural issues in special education, and the role of technology in special education. These interests have resulted in focused academic endeavors, such as published articles and presentations in these areas at state and national conferences. In addition to Dr. Smith-Canter's interest and work in special education research, she views teaching and working with individuals with special needs and educators as her most important and most rewarding role.

Marsha Craft Tripp is an assistant professor of special education at East Carolina University located in Greenville, NC. She was a former Director of Exceptional Children's Services for 25 years in a local school district and taught students with learning disabilities and students with moderate disabilities during the span of her teaching career. She received the Distinguished Service Award in Special Education in 2008 for the state of North Carolina. Her research interests are in the field of autism spectrum disorders and the education of students with moderate disabilities. Craft Tripp's most recent book was *Standards-Based Learning for Students With Disabilities*, which she authored with Dr. Allan Glatthorn.

Kathi Wilhite is an assistant professor at East Carolina University. Wilhite has been a special educator for more than 30 years. Her experiences include public school teaching, special education administration, and state department consultation (Indiana and North Carolina). In addition to her work at East Carolina, she has taught at Indiana University–Purdue University Indianapolis and Ball State University. She is the author of multiple articles and has presented at conferences across the U.S. Wilhite currently leads the Autism Certificate and New Exceptional Children Director programs at East Carolina and teaches a variety of special education courses. Her research interests include autism spectrum disorders, school-based applications of the Behavioral Objective Sequence, and state department of education policy issues.